The publisher and the University of California Press
Foundation gratefully acknowledge the generous
support of the Joan Palevsky Endowment Fund in
Literature in Translation

Gregory of Nazianzus's
Letter Collection

CHRISTIANITY IN LATE ANTIQUITY
THE OFFICIAL BOOK SERIES OF THE NORTH
AMERICAN PATRISTICS SOCIETY

Editor: Christopher A. Beeley, Duke University

Associate Editors: David Brakke, Ohio State University
Robin Darling Young, The Catholic University of America

International Advisory Board:

Lewis Ayres, Durham University • John Behr, St Vladimir's Orthodox Theological Seminary, New York • Brouria Bitton-Ashkelony, Hebrew University of Jerusalem • Marie-Odile Boulnois, École Pratique des Hautes Études, Paris • Kimberly D. Bowes, University of Pennsylvania and the American Academy in Rome • Virginia Burrus, Syracuse University • Stephen Davis, Yale University • Elizabeth DePalma Digeser, University of California Santa Barbara • Mark Edwards, University of Oxford • Susanna Elm, University of California Berkeley • Thomas Graumann, Cambridge University • Sidney H. Griffith, Catholic University of America • David G. Hunter, University of Kentucky • Andrew S. Jacobs, Scripps College • Robin M. Jensen, University of Notre Dame • AnneMarie Luijendijk, Princeton University • Christoph Markschies, Humboldt-Universität zu Berlin • Andrew B. McGowan, Berkeley Divinity School at Yale • Claudia Rapp, Universität Wien • Samuel Rubenson, Lunds Universitet • Rita Lizzi Testa, Università degli Studi di Perugia

1. *Incorruptible Bodies: Christology, Society, and Authority in Late Antiquity*, by Yonatan Moss

2. *Epiphanius of Cyprus: A Cultural Biography of Late Antiquity*, by Andrew S. Jacobs

3. *Melania: Early Christianity through the Life of One Family*, edited by Catherine M. Chin and Caroline T. Schroeder

4. *The Body and Desire: Gregory of Nyssa's Ascetical Theology*, by Raphael A. Cadenhead

5. *Bible and Poetry in Late Antique Mesopotamia: Ephrem's Hymns on Faith*, by Jeffrey Wickes

6. *Self-Portrait in Three Colors: Gregory of Nazianzus's Epistolary Autobiography*, by Bradley K. Storin

7. *Gregory of Nazianzus's Letter Collection: The Complete Translation*, translated by Bradley K. Storin

8. *Jephthah's Daughter, Sarah's Son: The Death of Children in Late Antiquity*, by Maria Doerfler

Gregory of Nazianzus's Letter Collection

The Complete Translation

Translated by

Bradley K. Storin

UNIVERSITY OF CALIFORNIA PRESS

University of California Press
Oakland, California

© 2019 by Bradley K. Storin

Library of Congress Cataloging-in-Publication Data

Gregory, of Nazianzus, Saint, author. | Storin, Bradley K., translator.
Title: Gregory of Nazianzus's letter collection : the complete translation /
   Gregory of Nazianzus; translated by Bradley K. Storin.
Other titles: Correspondence. English | Christianity in late antiquity
   (North American Patristics Society) ; 7.
Description: Oakland, California : University of California Press, [2019] |
   Series: Christianity in late antiquity ; 7 | Includes bibliographical
   references and index.
Identifiers: LCCN 2019020527 (print) | ISBN 9780520304109 (cloth : alk.
   paper) | ISBN 9780520304123 (pbk. : alk. paper) | 9780520972933 (ebook)
Subjects: LCSH: Gregory, of Nazianzus, Saint—Correspondence. | Gregory,
   of Nazianzus, Saint—Criticism and interpretation. | Church history—
   Primitive and early church, ca. 30-600—Sources.
Classification: LCC PA3998.G73 A267 2019 (print) | LCC PA3998.G73 (ebook) |
   DDC 886/.01—dc23
LC record available at https://lccn.loc.gov/2019020527
LC ebook record available at https://lccn.loc.gov/2019981539

26 25 24 23 22 21 20 19
10 9 8 7 6 5 4 3 2 1

CONTENTS

List of Abbreviations   vii

Introduction   1
Prosopography of Gregory of Nazianzus's Letter Collection   17

Arrangement of the Collection   43
Storin Order   43
Maurist Order   49
Translation of Gregory of Nazianzus's Letter Collection   55

Notes   203
Works Cited   223
Index of Biblical, Apocryphal, and Pseudepigraphical Writings   229
Index of Classical Writings   233

ABBREVIATIONS

BIBLICAL, APOCRYPHAL, AND PSEUDEPIGRAPHICAL WRITINGS

Acts	Acts of the Apostles
Col	Colossians
1 Cor	1 Corinthians
2 Cor	2 Corinthians
Deut	Deuteronomy
Eccl	Ecclesiastes
Eph	Ephesians
1 Esd	1 Esdras
Exod	Exodus
Gal	Galatians
Gen	Genesis
Hab	Habakkuk
Heb	Hebrews
Hos	Hosea
Isa	Isaiah
Jas	James
Jer	Jeremiah
Job	Job
John	Gospel of John
Jonah	Jonah
Jude	Jude
1 Kgs	1 Kings

2 Kgs	2 Kings
Luke	Gospel of Luke
4 Macc	4 Maccabees
Mark	Gospel of Mark
Matt	Gospel of Matthew
Num	Numbers
Phil	Philippians
Prov	Proverbs
Ps	Psalms (when different, Septuagint citation followed by Masoretic)
Rom	Romans
1 Sam	1 Samuel
2 Sam	2 Samuel
Sir	Sirach
Song	Song of Songs
1 Thess	1 Thessalonians
1 Tim	1 Timothy
2 Tim	2 Timothy
Titus	Titus

ANCIENT AND LATE ANTIQUE WRITERS AND WORKS

A. Aeschylus
- *A.* *Agamemnon*
- *Eu.* *Eumenides*

Aeschin. Aeschines
- *Ctes.* *In Ctesiphontem*

Aesop
- *Prov.* *Proverbia*

Ambr. Ambrose of Milan
- *Ep.* *Epistula*

Anth. Gr. *Anthologia Graeca*

LIST OF ABBREVIATIONS ix

Apollod.	Apollodorus	
	Bib.	*Bibliotheca*
Ar.	Aristophanes	
	Ach.	*Acharnenses*
	Eq.	*Equites*
	Nu.	*Nubes*
Arist.	Aristotle	
	E.N.	*Ethica Nicomachea*
Bas.	Basil of Caesarea	
	Ep.	*Epistula*
	Spir.	*De spiritu sancto*
C. Th.	*Codex Theodosianus*	
Cl. Alex.	Clement of Alexandria	
	Prot.	*Protrepticus*
	Str.	*Stromateis*
D.	Demosthenes	
	Or.	*Oratio*
Dam.	Damasus of Rome	
	Ep.	*Epistula*
D.H.	Dionysius of Halicarnassus	
	Lys.	*De Lysia*
Diogenian.	Diogenianus	
	Paroe.	*Paroemiographus*
E.	Euripides	
	Med.	*Medea*
	Or.	*Orestes*
	Ph.	*Phoenissae*
	frag.	*fragmentum*

Gr. Naz.	Gregory of Nazianzus	
	Carm.	*Carmen*
	Ep.	*Epistulae*
	Epig.	*Epigramma*
	Epit.	*Epitaphium*
	Or.	*Oratio*
	Test.	*Testamentum*
Gr. Nyss.	Gregory of Nyssa	
	Ep.	*Epistula*
	V. Macr.	*Vita sanctae Macrinae*
Hdt.	Herodotus	
	Hist.	*Historiae*
Hes.	Hesiod	
	Op.	*Opera et dies*
	Th.	*Theogonia*
Hier.	Jerome of Stridon	
	Ep.	*Epistula*
	Vir. ill.	*De viris illustribus*
Il.	*Ilias*	
Iamb.	Iamblichus	
	V.P.	*Vita Pythagorica*
Isoc.	Isocrates	
	Dem.	*Ad Demonicum*
J.	Josephus	
	B.J.	*Bellum Judaicum*
Jul.	Julian	
	Ep.	*Epistula*

Lib.	Libanius of Antioch	
	Ep.	*Epistula*
	Or.	*Oratio*
Luc.	Lucian of Samosata	
	Rh. pr.	*Rhetorum praeceptor*
Mantiss. prov.	*Mantissa proverbiorum*	
Od.	*Odyssea*	
Paus.	Pausanias	
	Gr. desc.	*Graecae descriptio*
Philostr. Jun.	Philostratus the Younger	
	Im.	*Imagines*
Pi.	Pindar	
	Nem.	*Nemea*
	Olymp.	*Olympia*
	P.	*Pythia*
Pl.	Plato	
	Chrm.	*Charmides*
	Cra.	*Cratylus*
	Ep.	*Epistula*
	Grg.	*Gorgias*
	Phd.	*Phaedo*
	Phdr.	*Phaedrus*
	Resp.	*Respublica*
	Tht.	*Theatetus*
Plb.	Polybius	
	Hist.	*Historiae*
Plu.	Plutarch	
	Alex.	*Alexandros*

	Reg. et imp. apophth.	*Regum et imperatorum apophthegmata*
Pythag.	Pythagoras	
	Ep.	*Epistula*
S.	Sophocles	
	Aj.	*Ajax*
S.E.	Sextus Empiricus	
	M.	*Adversus mathematicos*
Simon.	Simonides	
	Epig.	*Epigramma*
Sol.	Solon	
Sophr.	Sophron	
Soz.	Sozomen	
	H.e.	*Historia ecclesiastica*
Str.	Strabo	
	Geogr.	*Geographica*
Th.	Thucydides	
	Hist.	*Historiae*
Thdt.	Theodoret of Cyrrhus	
	H.e.	*Historia ecclesiastica*
Them.	Themistius of Constantinople	
	Or.	*Oratio*
Theoc.	Theocritus	
	Id.	*Idylls*

Thgn.	Theognis	
	El.	*Elegiae*
X.	Xenophon	
	H.G.	*Historia Graeca*
Zos.	Zosimus	

Introduction

GREGORY'S CAREER

Gregory of Nazianzus was born in 329 or 330 CE in southern Cappadocia to wealthy parents who were pro-Nicene Christians. His father (also named Gregory) was the bishop of Nazianzus (ca. 325–74) and had financed the construction of the city's church on the family's property. The younger Gregory and his brother Caesarius enjoyed the fruits of their family's wealth: both spent their adolescence studying, among other subjects, literature, rhetoric, philosophy, and theology (Caesarius eventually specialized in medicine) in cities all across the eastern Mediterranean. For his part, Gregory settled in Athens from the late 340s to the late 350s, where he trained under the famous sophists Prohaeresius and Himerius.[1] He eventually returned to his hometown and in 362 underwent ordination into the priesthood at the hands of his father-bishop.[2] There he became involved in local affairs, advocated for his father, preached sermons, undertook ascetic retreats, and enrolled a small coterie of students into his eclectic curriculum of rhetoric, classical literature, philosophical/theological thought, ascetic contemplation, and scriptural exegesis.[3] In short, he lived the life of a Christian provincial elite.

Gregory's career took a turn as a result of his friend Basil's consecration to the Caesarean episcopate in 370. The two had known each other since their days in Athens, although just how intimate they were is unclear.[4] Whatever the depth of their relationship, it was enough for them to exchange letters; Basil even occasionally hosted Gregory at his ascetic community on his family's property in Pontus. Like Gregory, Basil had been ordained into the priesthood in the early 360s; unlike Gregory, he did not enjoy a stable and good-natured relationship with their bishop, Eusebius of Caesarea. Indeed, Gregory even intervened on Basil's behalf during a dispute between the two.[5] However, all that became moot when Eusebius died in 370. An election to fill the vacancy followed, and after a contentious campaign, Basil emerged victorious.[6] In the wake of his elevation, Basil proved smug toward his flock, dismissive of criticism, eager to keep company with quick-tempered partisans, and concerned to maintain his power against provincial contenders.[7] His new position had profound and material effects on Gregory's position. In 372, Emperor Valens ordered a provincial split: Cappadocia Prima would keep Caesarea as its metropolitan city (with Basil as its bishop), and the new, and more powerful, Cappadocia Secunda would have Tyana as its metropolitan city (with Anthimus as its bishop).[8] Basil protested the split but ultimately resigned himself to securing as much authority as he could muster by establishing new episcopacies that would report to his metropolitanate. His own brother Gregory would become the bishop of Nyssa; a certain Eulalius would become the bishop of Doara; and Gregory—much to his surprise and chagrin—would be appointed the bishop of Sasima. His surreptitious assignment to this unimportant town infuriated Gregory, who rejected it before agreeing to a substitute position as coadjutor to his ailing father-bishop in Nazianzus.[9] Some eighteen months later his father died, and then his mother not long after that, leaving Gregory as the last remaining member of his immediate family (his brother Caesarius had died in 368, and his sister Gorgonia in 369 or 370).[10] He left Nazianzus, moved to Seleucia (modern Silifke, Turkey), and lived for the next several years in the ascetic community devoted to the veneration of Saint Thecla.[11]

Gregory's career took another turn in the months after Basil's death. Valens had been killed in battle in 378, after which Theodosius I ascended to the purple. Theodosius had a pro-Nicene background, and despite ignorance about what shape his theology would take at the level of imperial policy, pro-Nicene bishops from the eastern Mediterranean convened at Antioch in August 379 to strategize the elevation of their own party over the heretofore ascendant Homoians.[12] In addition to agreeing on a Homoousian creedal statement, they decided to dispatch a representative to Constantinople to establish a pro-Nicene presence there in anticipation of the new emperor's arrival. That person was Gregory, who probably attended the council of Antioch and swiftly moved from there to the imperial capital.[13] By October 379, he had set up shop on his cousin Theodosia's estate, where he formed the Anastasia church and served it in the progressively important positions of informal pro-Nicene leader, imperial preacher, bishop of Constantinople, and president of the Council of Constantinople 381.[14] Gregory's presence inspired opposition from those loyal to Demophilus, the city's longtime and well-liked Homoian bishop,[15] which manifested in a raid against the Anastasia on Easter Sunday 380. This attack seems to have caused physical injury and was followed by lawsuits against Gregory.[16] Even among his pro-Nicene friends and allies, intrigue and conflict abounded. The summer of 380 saw the arrival in Constantinople of Maximus, an Egyptian philosopher secretly working on behalf of Peter of Alexandria.[17] Maximus arranged for his own elevation to the episcopacy of Constantinople (a harebrained scheme that offended Gregory but proved meaningless since Demophilus still occupied the recognized episcopal seat) but eventually fled the city after a resounding resistance coalesced.[18] With the arrival of Theodosius in November and the subsequent deposition of Demophilus, Gregory finally gained some degree of security in his position (although local resistance to his presence continued) for the next several months.[19]

The summer of 381 brought a new level of turmoil. A council was scheduled for May and June that would reenact the council of Antioch in 379 on a grander scale, and in the weeks leading up to it, clergy from all over the east began to trickle into Constantinople. Meletius of Antioch was slated for the new council's presidency, but he died in its early sessions and the bishops gathered there made the unorthodox decision to pick his episcopal successor rather than leave the matter to Antiochene locals. The issue was particularly fraught because a candidate back in Antioch already possessed a legitimate claim to the seat: Paulinus, whom western and Egyptian pro-Nicenes supported and whose elevation upon Meletius's death Meletius had agreed to.[20] The eastern bishops gathered in Constantinople, however, supported Flavian, one of Meletius's priests. For his part, Gregory backed Paulinus and thereby alienated his allies from the east. Perhaps he felt that he could rely on the support of Timothy of Alexandria, Dorotheus of Oxyrhynchus, and Acholius of Thessalonica (Paulinus's most important backers), but they regarded Gregory as a provincial outsider who had risen through the ecclesiastical ranks only as a puppet of the now-deceased Meletius. They waved a letter from Bishop Damasus of Rome that advised against transferring bishops from one see to another on the grounds that it violated the fifteenth canon of the Council of Nicaea[21] and then challenged the legitimacy of Gregory's appointment to Constantinople, noting that Basil had consecrated him the bishop of Sasima nine years earlier. Lacking the support of both Flavian's backers and Paulinus's backers, Gregory found himself in an inescapable knot.[22] In the midst of the council's proceedings, he tendered his resignation to Emperor Theodosius and returned to Cappadocia.

His extant texts from the post-Constantinople period provide no evidence that he ever left Cappadocia again, yet he remained active in the church and provincial society. Much of his literary production now took on an autobiographical shine and focused on rehabilitating his standing within his social networks and attacking his adversaries in Constantinople.[23] He even returned to ecclesiastical office as the bishop of Nazianzus from the spring of 382 until the autumn of 383,[24] when his trusted cousin Eulalius took over the position. During his final years of retirement, he remained literarily and perhaps pedagogically active, but our knowledge of the time leading up to his death circa 390 is spotty.[25] However, it is clear that his efforts to remove the stain of controversy resulting from his time in Constantinople and to brand himself as a devoted servant of the church and the truth seem to have been successful: no external criticism of Gregory survives, and his condemnation of the Council of Constantinople has, ironically, become the chief source of modern knowledge of the event.[26]

THE COLLECTION'S PROVENANCE, STRUCTURE, AND THEMATIC COHERENCE

Gregory's letter collection was published sometime between late 383 and early 384 and is thus a product of the final phase of his career.[27] It corresponds both chronologically and thematically to his other post-Constantinopolitan literary output. The notion of compiling the collection originated with his great-nephew Nicobulus, who had recently begun his rhetorical education in Caesarea. Part of the studies included epistolography, so he asked Gregory for models to guide his letter writing, a request to which Gregory responded by sending the collection.[28] Specific ideas governed its content and design, which he announced to Nicobulus in two letters in the collection (Gr. Naz., *Ep.* 52–53). It should provide the young student with "something expedient for eloquence," something that exhibited Gregory's "signature style" of interlacing his letters with instructive maxims and precepts (*Ep.* 52.1, 3). Moreover, another letter offers an overview of the epistolary style—"since you request this too" (*Ep.* 51.1)—that Nicobulus would find modeled in the collection's individual letters. Should he appropriate all this stylistic advice for his own letter writing, Nicobulus stood to gain an inheritance of sorts: "A father in eloquence always appears in a legitimate child no less than parents do in most of his bodily characteristics. Well, such are my features" (*Ep.* 52.3). Indeed, Gregory was offering his literary legacy to the young Nicobulus. *Epistula* 53, however, pushes the collection in an explicitly self-presentational direction, announcing that Gregory included some of Basil's letters in his collection, placed in front of his own, because "I also desire that [Basil and I] be linked with each other in every way while simultaneously providing a model of measure and moderation to others" (*Ep.* 53.2). Like several of his other post-Constantinople writings,[29] the collection romanticizes and publicizes Gregory's friendship with Basil.

While we might be tempted to see Nicobulus as the collection's primary reader, *Epistulae* 52 and 53 subtly indicate that Gregory assumed it would be passed on to Nicobulus's educators in Caesarea, whom, thanks to letters in the collection, we know to be Bishop Helladius (Basil's successor), Stagirius, Eustochius, and Eudoxius. *Epistula* 52 proclaims, as noted above, that a student bears a teacher's characteristics as a child does the parents': this announcement as much holds out a legacy to Nicobulus as it solicits learned readers to investigate *Gregory's* epistolary style so as to discern *his* educational ancestry. Youth, inexperience, and perhaps even lackadaisical effort (Gr. Naz., *Ep.* 175.1) would have prevented Nicobulus from following the trail, but not the four men charged with his education.[30] For its part, *Epistula* 53's claim that Gregory and Basil shared an intimate relationship would have intrigued Nicobulus's four Caesarean educators, all of whom knew—or at least knew of—Basil. Helladius was Basil's successor and probably the former tax assessor for whom Basil wrote his *Epistula* 281. Eustochius received epistolary assistance from Basil in negotiating a conflict with a certain Callisthenes (Bas., *Ep.* 72–73). Gregory of Nyssa, Basil's brother, wrote two friendly letters to Stagirius (Gr. Nyss., *Ep.* 9, 27), and indeed Stagirius's only extant text is included in Gregory of Nyssa's collection (Gr. Nyss., *Ep.* 26). Eudoxius likely knew of Basil, if not personally then at least through Eustochius, Gregory of Nazianzus, or local lore. Beyond them, though, there were probably more readers. Late antique textual publication occurred in the venue of epistolary exchange,[31] and we should expect that Gregory's sending the collection to Nicobulus—and thence to Helladius, Stagirius, Eustochius, and Eudoxius—constituted his tacit permission for its further circulation among those clergy members, imperial and provincial officials, local notables, teachers of rhetoric, students, friends, and even family members throughout Cappadocia and Constantinople who had engaged with his other post-Constantinopolitan writings. Indeed, he likely imagined that many addressees of individual letters would also read the published collection (and see his letters to them therein).

Which letters did Gregory include in the published collection, and in what order? His sole comment on its organization and content comes in *Epistula* 53, which, as noted above, mentions that Basil's letters (which ones?) preceded his own. Otherwise, he nowhere provides a list of addressees, a running total of the letters, or a table of contents. Moreover, the collection as presented in Paul Gallay's two critical editions does not reflect Gregory's original arrangement: Gallay's enumeration and arrangement follow those of the collection's sixteenth- and seventeenth-century Benedictine editors of the Congregation of Saint Maur (*Ep.* 1–244), who arranged them according to supposed chronology, plus five post-Maurist additions (*Ep.* 245–49).[32] Remarkably, the Maurists' (and consequently Gallay's) arrangement turns out to be a reorganization of the letters as transmitted by the six main manuscript families: the u-, v-, d-, f-, g-, and h-families.[33] To varying degrees, each of these organizes the collection into dossiers of letters united by their addressee; the most consistent are the u-, v-, and d-families. For instance, the letters to Nicobulus (*Ep.* 51–54) constitute one dossier, the letters to Basil (*Ep.* 1–2, 4–6, 8, 19, 40, 45–50, 58–60, 245–246, 248) another, the letters to Nectarius of Constantinople (*Ep.* 91, 151, 185–86) another, and the letters to the governor Nemesius (*Ep.* 198–201) yet another. Additionally, the manuscript families sometimes use a particular episode as a thematic core. For example, the following letters constitute a discrete dossier written during Gregory's Lenten silence in 382: *Epistulae* 107–9, to Cledonius; 110 and 119, to Palladius; 111 and 118, to Eugenius; 112–14, to Celeusius; and 116–17, to Eulalius. The manuscript families, for the most part, keep these twelve letters together, despite their multiple addressees. It is also possible for a letter to belong to both an episodic dossier and a prosopographical one: for instance, Gregory wrote not only two silence letters to Palladius (*Ep.* 110, 119) but also *Epistulae* 103 and 170. Further connections become apparent too. Sometimes an addressee of one dossier features in another prosopographical dossier as a courier: for example, Nicobulus's teacher Eudoxius has his own dossier in the collection (*Ep.* 174–80, 187) and features in the dossiers of Sophronius (*Ep.* 37), to whom *Epistulae* 21–22, 29, 39, 93, and 135 are also addressed; Themistius (*Ep.* 38), to whom *Epistula* 24 is also addressed; and Saturninus (*Ep.* 181), to whom *Epistula* 132 is also addressed. What the manuscripts reveal, then, is not a chronological arrangement, as the Maurists had it, but a predominantly prosopographical one. And because they so consistently have the same content (228 letters appear in four or more manuscript families, while only 13 appear in three or fewer) and structure (addressee- or episode-based dossiers), we might posit that, by and large, they reflect an approximate version of Gregory's original.

To give a sense of how extensive, and deliberately implemented, the collection's prosopographical structure is, consider the shape of its two most important epistolary clusters: the letters that connect to Basil, and those that connect to Nicobulus. The cluster of letters centering on Basil naturally features the Basil dossier, but also those of Eusebius of Caesarea (Gr. Naz., *Ep.* 16–18), to whom Gregory wrote on Basil's behalf; Eusebius of Samosata (*Ep.* 42, 44, 64–66), to whom Gregory reached out during Basil's episcopal election; Gregory of Nyssa (*Ep.* 11, 72–74, 76, 81, 182, 197), Basil's brother, to whom Gregory wrote a consoling letter after the latter's death; Amphilochius of Iconium (*Ep.* 9, 13, 25–28, 62, 171, 184), to whom Gregory wrote when Basil was planning a visit; Philagrius (*Ep.* 30–36, 80, 87, 92), to whom Gregory also wrote after Basil's death; and Theodore of Tyana (*Ep.* 77, 115, 121–24, 139, 152, 157, 159–63, 183), with whom Gregory shared the *Philocalia* that he and Basil had edited. It also includes two letters written in the name of Gregory's father-bishop, to "The Church of Caesarea" and to

"The Bishops" (*Ep.* 41 and 43, respectively), during Basil's episcopal election. Other dossiers should also be regarded as part of the Basil cluster because they were written to addressees who can be found among those in Basil's collection, and therefore their presence in Gregory's collection further buttresses his claim in *Epistula* 53 of intimacy with Basil. These addressees are Bosporius (Gr. Naz., *Ep.* 89, 138, 153; Bas., *Ep.* 51), Gregory's brother Caesarius (Gr. Naz., *Ep.* 7, 20; Bas., *Ep.* 26), Candidianus (Gr. Naz., *Ep.* 10; Bas., *Ep.* 3), Cyriacus (Gr. Naz., *Ep.* 211; Bas., *Ep.* 114), perhaps Epiphanius (Gr. Naz., *Ep.* 239; Bas., *Ep.* 258?), perhaps Julian (Gr. Naz., *Ep.* 67–69; Bas., *Ep.* 293?), Leontius (Gr. Naz., *Ep.* 95; Bas., *Ep.* 20, 21?), Meletius (Gr. Naz., *Ep.* 240; Bas., *Ep.* 193), Nectarius (Gr. Naz., *Ep.* 91, 151, 185–86; Bas., *Ep.* 4, 290?), Olympius (Gr. Naz., *Ep.* 104–6, 125–26, 131, 140–44, 146, 154; Bas., *Ep.* 4, 12–13, 131, 211?), perhaps Palladius (Gr. Naz., *Ep.* 103, 110, 119, 170; Bas., *Ep.* 292?), Simplicia (Gr. Naz., *Ep.* 79; Bas., *Ep.* 115), Sophronius (Gr. Naz., *Ep.* 21–22, 29, 37, 39, 93, 135; Bas., *Ep.* 32, 76, 96, 177, 180, 192, 272), Timothy (Gr. Naz., *Ep.* 164; Bas., *Ep.* 291), and Victor (Gr. Naz., *Ep.* 133–34; Bas., *Ep.* 152–53).

For its part, the Nicobulus cluster naturally centers on the young student and accordingly includes his dossier (Gr. Naz., *Ep.* 51–54) and that belonging to his father (*Ep.* 12, 55). However, both men feature as couriers in a number of other dossiers. The addressees are the young student's Caesarean educators—Eudoxius (*Ep.* 174–80, 187), Eustochius (*Ep.* 189–91), Helladius (*Ep.* 120, 127, 167, 172, 219–20), and Stagirius (*Ep.* 165–66, 188, 192)—as well as Africanus (*Ep.* 224), Amphilochius (*Ep.* 9, 13, 25–28, 62, 171, 184), Asterius (*Ep.* 147–48, 150, 155–56), Gregory the Governor (*Ep.* 195), Hecebolius (*Ep.* 196), Julian (*Ep.* 67–69), Olympius (*Ep.* 104–6, 125–26, 131, 140–44, 146, 154), and Sophronius (*Ep.* 21–22, 29, 37, 39, 93, 135). This cluster goes further, though, in that Gregory recommended some of the abovementioned addressees to other individuals, thereby forming additional connections between dossiers. Eudoxius features in the dossiers of Saturninus (*Ep.* 132, 181), Sophronius (*Ep.* 21–22, 29, 37, 39, 93, 135), and Themistius (*Ep.* 24, 38); Amphilochius features in the dossiers of a man or men named Caesarius (*Ep.* 14, 23), Sophronius, and Themistius. Some couriers of Gregory's letters on behalf of Nicobulus and his father appear in other dossiers. Sacerdos features in the Helladius dossier (*Ep.* 120, 127, 167, 219–20), has his own dossier (*Ep.* 99, 212–15), and appears as a courier in the dossiers of Castor (*Ep.* 209–10), Cyriacus (*Ep.* 211), Eudocius (*Ep.* 216–18), Homophronius (*Ep.* 221), Palladius (*Ep.* 103, 110, 119, 170), Photius (*Ep.* 168), Strategius (*Ep.* 169), and Thecla (*Ep.* 56–57, 222–23). Similarly, George (*Ep.* 149) features as a courier not only in the dossier of Asterius (*Ep.* 147–48, 150, 155–56), to whom Gregory recommended Nicobulus's father, but also in those of Nectarius (*Ep.* 91, 151, 185–86) and Theodore of Tyana (*Ep.* 77, 115, 121–24, 139, 152, 157, 159–63, 183). Amazonius (*Ep.* 94) features as a courier in the dossier of Sophronius (*Ep.* 21–22, 29, 37, 39, 93, 135), to whom Gregory also recommended Nicobulus's father. Finally, we should note that in addition to the unitive threads running through it, the Nicobulus cluster bears several prosopographical connections to the Basil cluster (Amphilochius, Sophronius, Olympius, Palladius, Cyriacus, Nectarius, Theodore of Tyana, and even obliquely Gregory of Nyssa, through Stagirius) and thereby gives the collection an even firmer structure.

Alongside the collection's prosopographical threads, thematic ones hold the text together too.[34] Although the letters at times mention Gregory's position as a member of the clergy, those of the appeal, request, intercession, friendship, consolation, and other epistolary types more frequently invoke his possession of intangible qualities, such as his eloquence, philosophical authority, and status as sole heir of Basil's spiritual legacy. The letters collectively bear witness to an author who sees his cultural and social prominence as stemming not from bureaucratic position but from personal, self-crafted eminence. In fact, nearly every reference to a synod or church council in the collection is accompanied by Gregory's rejection of an invitation to it. In that light, perhaps it is not surprising that the collection features just two letters dating to his time in Constantinople, each of which reveals its author's philosophical willingness to endure mistreatment at the hands of malignant forces and makes no mention of his role as the leader of the pro-Nicene movement in the capital.[35]

The collection's thematic motifs, as well as its dossier-based arrangement, should push readers to engage with it in new ways. The individual letters are no doubt valuable for social historians of late antiquity and particularly for Gregory's biographers, but readers of the entire collection, in an order that approximates his autograph version, should not sidestep questions pertaining to authorial voice, apologetic intent, structural design, and publication context. As a whole, the collection stands as a remarkable literary artifact. Not only is it the earliest author-designed letter collection in Greek—a fact that may owe more to historical happenstance than to Gregory's literary innovation—but it also functions in striking ways. What readers encounter here is an autobiographical text whose authorship resides as much in the editorial act of compilation as in the individual acts of epistolographical composition.

ON THE TRANSLATION

The translation in this book, a complete revision of the one made in my doctoral dissertation,[36] is based on Gallay's second critical edition: *Gregor von Nazianz: Briefe,* Die griechischen christlichen Schriftsteller der ersten Jahrhunderte 53 (Berlin: Akademie-Verlag, 1969). The notes indicate where this GCS text varies from that of Gallay's first critical edition, *Grégoire de Nazianze, Lettres,* Collection des Universités de France, publiée sous le patronage de l'Association Guillaume Budé, 2 vols. (Paris: Société d'Édition "Les Belles Lettres," 1964, 1967). For the sake of convenience and clarity, I have retained the Benedictine numeration, the conventional and expected method of identification.

My translation presents Gregory's letter collection in an arrangement that I believe hews closer to the original version than the Maurist and subsequent editions do. Since no autograph copy of the collection survives, I have chosen to follow the structure of the u-family, which has the twin virtues of coherent organization into addressee-based dossiers and near-comprehensive inclusion of the extant letters. However, I have also made several changes. I have plugged into their respective dossiers five of the letters that the u-family does not include (*Ep.* 28, 171, to Amphilochius; 42, to Eusebius of Samosata; 57, to Thecla; 212, to Sacerdos). I have positioned the sixth letter not included in the u-family (*Ep.* 244, to Basilissa) at the end, with no obvious alternative in sight. I have moved *Epistula* 114, to Celeusius, into its addressee-based dossier, since the u-family misidentified the addressee as Basil. I have moved *Epistulae* 16–18, to Eusebius of Caesarea, into the Basil dossier before *Epistula* 19, to Basil, because all four of these letters clearly form an epistolary unit. I have placed *Epistulae* 246, to Basil (= Bas., *Ep.* 169), 247, to Glycerius (= Bas., *Ep.* 170), and 248, to Basil

(= Bas., *Ep.* 171), at the end of the Basil dossier. I have moved *Epistula* 158, to Eulalius, into its addressee-based dossier, since the u-family misidentified the addressee as Helladius. I have moved *Epistula* 74, to Gregory of Nyssa, and *Epistula* 66, to Eusebius of Samosata, into their respective appropriate dossiers. I have moved *Epistula* 145, to Verianus, into the Olympius dossier, since it is clearly the epistolary partner of *Epistula* 144, to Olympius.

My translation omits seven letters from Gallay's editions: *Epistulae* 101, 102, and 202, the "theological letters," which were transmitted among the manuscripts of Gregory's *Orationes,* not his letters (these can easily be found in print and online), and *Epistulae* 88, 241, 243, and 249, which are not authentic to Gregory (the postscript to this introduction presents a fuller discussion of the issues).

By his own admission, Gregory's original collection included letters written by Basil, but because the manuscript families show no consensus as to which of Basil's letters these were, I have chosen to omit them altogether.

I have tried to maintain consistency vis-à-vis two translational conventions: (1) I have used English contractions throughout as a way to preserve Gregory's acknowledged emphasis on his natural, conversational style (see Gr. Naz., *Ep.* 51.4, 51.7); and (2) I have translated the first-person plural as the first-person singular whenever I am certain that Gregory is talking about himself alone.

For the addressees, couriers, and other individuals mentioned in the letters, I have compiled a prosopography that summarizes what is known about each person and lists the references of where they appear in Gregory's letter collection and other writings. This resource frees the translation from the need for excessive annotation.

With respect to the location of places mentioned in the letters, I have provided basic information to the extent that it is known. For further details, I encourage readers to follow up with several atlases and historical geographies that I have used: Tim Cornell and John Matthews, *Atlas of the Roman World* (New York: Checkmark Books, 1982); Angelo di Berardino and Gianluca Pilara, eds., *Historical Atlas of Ancient Christianity,* Institutum Patristicum Augustinianum (St. Davids, PA: ICCS Press, 2013); William M. Ramsay, *The Historical Geography of Asia Minor,* Royal Geographical Society's Supplementary Papers 4 (London: John Murray, 1890; repr., London: Elibron

Classics, Adamant Media, 2005); and F. van der Meer and Christine Mohrmann, *Atlas of the Early Christian World,* edited and translated by Mary F. Hedlund and H. H. Rowley (New York: Nelson, 1958).

The notes aim at laconism rather than prolixity. On a few occasions, events referred to are known from other works, which I indicate, but much of the collection pertains to people, events, and localities that are simply otherwise unknown. In such cases, I have opted to keep silent rather than offer any speculation. Citations for the referenced scriptural and classical works are embedded within the translation itself rather than given in the notes. By and large, Gregory's addressees would have been able to recognize his allusions, paraphrases, and quotations by virtue of their participation in elite literary culture. I have therefore tried to allow the reader as much access to Gregory's discourse as both his addressees and the collection's earliest readers would have had.

Finally, I must alert readers that this translation is something of a companion piece to my monograph on Gregory's collection, also published by University of California Press in the Christianity in Late Antiquity series. There I make a robust argument for the unity and coherence of the collection and for reading it as a single autobiographical text. This introduction, its notes, and the bibliography have been kept to a minimum in the hopes that readers will engage with my exegesis and argumentation there.

POSTSCRIPT ON THE AUTHENTICITY OF *EPISTULAE* 88, 241, 243, AND 249

Epistula 88

Two anomalies cast doubt on the attribution of *Epistula* 88 to Gregory. First, it is the only one of "his" letters to be excluded from all six main manuscript families, a fact that led Gallay to question its Gregorian attribution.[37] This letter appears only in three composite manuscripts, and within these it enjoys no stability of location—that is, it has a different place in each and syntactically shows itself to have been added by a later scribe. For instance, in the fourteenth-century Parisinus gr. 902, *Epistula* 88 appears between *Epistulae* 209 and 210. The opening addresses are as follows:

Ep. 209: To Castor (Κάστορι)

Ep. 88: To Nectarius of Constantinople, the one appointed after his [i.e., Gregory's] retirement (Πρὸς Νεκτάριον Κωνσταντινουπόλεως χειροτονηθέντα μετὰ τὴν αὐτοῦ ὑποχώρησιν)

Ep. 210: To the same (Τῷ αὐτῷ [i.e., Κάστορι])

There are two peculiarities here. First, the syntax varies among the opening addresses: *Epistulae* 209 and 210 use a dative construction, whereas *Epistula* 88 uses a prepositional phrase. Both are acceptable for epistolary headings, but the difference suggests that a later scribe inserted *Epistula* 88 between *Epistulae* 209 and 210 while making a copy. Second, proper identification of *Epistula* 210's addressee relies on *Epistula* 209 directly preceding it in the manuscript, again suggesting that *Epistula* 88 was inserted into the manuscript by a later editor and was not among the letters in the original Parisinus gr. 902.

The second anomaly that invites suspicion is that *Epistula* 88 appears as *Epistula* 63 in the collection of John Mauropus, the eleventh-century metropolitan bishop of Euchaita. In other words, the latter collection attributes the letter to John.

Gallay cautiously attributes the letter to Gregory. In response to the first anomaly, he suggests that the letter perhaps belonged to a seventh manuscript family, one that has since disappeared from the tradition. His response to the second anomaly is that John himself may have copied the letter, only to have it end up in his own collection rather than that of Gregory. Gallay admits that he is inclined toward Gregorian authorship because the letter's content can reasonably be understood in the context of Gregory's life. Its upbeat and friendly tone may not reflect the hostility that Gregory's contemporaneous autobiographical poems display toward Nectarius, but, Gallay claims, "he could not have [written] it differently,"[38] given Nectarius's appointment and his own disgrace. Despite this inclination, though, Gallay admits that "in the end, doubt on the authenticity of letter 88 remains."[39] Indeed, his reconstruction of how the letter came to enter the Gregorian corpus (the first anomaly) and later to leave it (the second anomaly) is as speculative as it is unlikely. John McGuckin has marked the letter as "mis-ascribed," an opinion with which I agree. In his argument against Gregorian authorship, he cites the two anomalies discussed above and notes that the letter's content does not correspond with what we know of Gregory's post-Constantinople writings. First, the letter praises its addressee as an oratorical ornament to Constantinople, but oratory "was a skill which Nektarios simply did not possess," and Gregory does not bestow this kind of compliment lightly. Second, the letter's high hopes for the future of the friendship with Nectarius do not align with the cold tone of all of Gregory's letters to him: *Epistulae* 91, 151, 185, 186, and 202 (also not included in this collection). Indeed, the incongruity of *Epistula* 88's warmth when compared with the functional tone of the other letters, along with the manuscript evidence, pushes against Gregorian authorship.[40]

Epistula 241

Basil of Caesarea is the author of *Epistula* 241. It was transmitted among the manuscripts of his epistolary collection and appears only in the f-family of Gregory's collection (after four other letters of Basil's) and among four composite manuscripts. It seems that this letter was accidentally pulled out of Basil's collection and moved into Gregory's.[41]

Epistula 243

None of the manuscripts of Gregory's letter collection include *Epistula* 243. Indeed, the Maurists did not even provide its text, instead noting its title and address before referring readers to the works of Gregory of Nyssa, whom they believed wrote it.

Epistula 249

For centuries, *Epistula* 249 was attributed to Gregory of Nazianzus: it appears in the u- and v-families. An eleventh- or twelfth-century Byzantine copyist first doubted this attribution, noting in a marginal comment that "this letter belongs to Gregory of Nyssa, not to the Theologian."[42] Only in the twentieth century did the author's identity become a subject of lively debate. Giorgio Pasquali followed Fronton du Duc's 1615 editio princeps of Gregory of Nyssa's letters in ascribing it to him,[43] but that identification was called into question by Ernst Honigmann, Paul Devos, and Gallay.[44] The arguments in favor of Gregory of Nazianzus rest largely on stylistic, historical, and biographical grounds. The main issues have been the identity of the addressee (who is not, according to Honigmann, Devos, and Gallay, Flavian of Antioch, Meletius's successor, but rather some other Flavian), the tension between the author and Helladius (better understood within Gregory of Nazianzus's life than Gregory of Nyssa's), and Greek turns of phrase or words that appear to be more characteristic of Gregory of Nazianzus than Gregory of Nyssa. The sole voice of protest to this attribution raised during the 1960s was that of Jean Daniélou, who countered Honigmann's and Devos's arguments with alternative historical and biographical ones.[45] Gallay's second critical edition responded to Daniélou with additional stylistic and biographical arguments in favor of authorship by Gregory of Nazianzus.[46]

Daniélou notwithstanding, scholarly consensus accepted Honigmann, Devos, and Gallay's attribution. However, three articles published in 1984 by Christoph Klock, Berhard Wyss, and Pierre Maravel, respectively, weakened the security of that identification. Following on the declaration of Reinhart Staats that "Devos's linguistic arguments are indeed entirely deficient,"[47] Klock's short piece rejected Devos's and Gallay's stylistic arguments, noting that all supposed instances of Gregory of Nazianzus's unique style also appeared in Gregory of Nyssa's writings.[48] Klock also compared *Epistula* 249's narrative of the confrontation between the author and Helladius with other confrontation narratives in the writings of both Gregorys and concluded that it corresponded to the style in Gregory of Nyssa's *Epistulae* 6 and 11 but not to that of any writing by Gregory of Nazianzus. Maravel and Wyss likewise demonstrated that any stylistic or lexical feature identified by Devos or Gallay as indicative of Gregory of Nazianzus can also be amply found in Gregory of Nyssa's writings.[49] Moreover, Wyss compiled a daunting list of fifteen literary particularities in *Epistula* 249 that have multiple parallels in the latter's corpus but none in the former's, casting substantial suspicion on any claim of authorship by Gregory of Nazianzus. Maravel, however, delivered the coup de grâce, persuasively countering all of Devos's stylistic arguments and making new points in favor of attribution to Gregory of Nyssa based on the author's syntax, standard epistolary length, and method of biblical citation, as well as historical considerations. As Anna Silvas notes, the now resolved problem of authorship was raised by the external evidence of the letter's placement in Gregory of Nazianzus's collection.[50] In other words, it is hard to imagine that, had the letter been originally transmitted in Gregory of Nyssa's collection, anyone would have made an argument in favor of Gregory of Nazianzus's authorship.

PROSOPOGRAPHY OF GREGORY OF NAZIANZUS'S LETTER COLLECTION

Much prosopographical information is already widely available; for this reason, here I provide only basic information to orient readers to Gregory's relationships with his couriers and addressees. Some are quite well known, in which cases I offer suggestions for further reading and encourage perusal of the primary sources listed therein (I have listed primary sources that help to contextualize the individuals within Gregory's social network, but these lists are not intended to be exhaustive). Others are quite obscure, and readers will no doubt find our ignorance about them as frustrating as I have. For the sake of brevity, I use these abbreviations to refer to the following works:

G Paul Gallay, ed. and trans., *Grégoire de Nazianze: Lettres,* Collection des Universités de France, publiée sous le patronage de l'Association Guillaume Budé, 2 vols. (Paris: Société d'Édition "Les Belles Lettres", 1964, 1967).

H-M Marie-Madeleine Hauser-Meury, *Prosopographie zu den Schriften Gregors von Nazianz* (Bonn: Hanstein, 1960).

L Louis-Sébastien Le Nain de Tillemont, *Mémoires pour servir à l'histoire*

	ecclésiastique des six premiers siècles: Volume 9, Les vies de Saint Basile, de Saint Grégoire de Nazianze, de Saint Grégoire de Nysse, et de Saint Amphiloque (Paris: Charles Robustel, 1703).
PLRE	A. H. M. Jones, J. R. Martindale, and J. Morris, eds., *The Prosopography of the Later Roman Empire: Volume 1*, ad 260–395 (Cambridge: Cambridge University Press, 1971).
S	Otto Seeck, *Die Briefe des Libanius zeitlich geordnet* (Leipzig: J. C. Hinrich'sche Buchhandlung, 1906).
V	Raymond Van Dam, "Governors of Cappadocia during the Fourth Century," *Medieval Prosopography* 17 (1996): 7–94.

. . .

ABLABIUS	Addressee of Gr. Naz., *Ep.* 233. Also known from Gr. Nyss., *Ep.* 21; Lib., *Ep.* 921, 1015. Teacher of rhetoric from Galatia who might be identical to Novatianist bishop of Nicaea in the 410s. See also H-M 22 ("Ablabius"); *PLRE* 2 ("Ablabius 2"); S 35 ("Ablabius I").
ADAMANTIUS	Addressee of Gr. Naz., *Ep.* 235. Perhaps a teacher of rhetoric. See also H-M 22 ("Adamantius"); *PLRE* 12 ("Adamantius 2"); S 48 ("Adamantius III").
ADELPHIUS	Addressee of Gr. Naz., *Ep.* 204–6. Also known from Gr. Nyss., *Ep.* 20; perhaps Lib., *Ep.* 1049.

	Young elite in Navila with position in local church. 392: *consularis Galatiae*. Addressee of Gr. Naz., *Ep.* 204 may be different from addressee of *Ep.* 205–6. See also H-M 22–23 ("Adelphius I–II"); *PLRE* 13 ("Adelphius 2"); S 48–49 ("Adelphius").
AERIUS	Co-addressee of Gr. Naz., *Ep.* 61. Brother of ALYPIUS. See also H-M 23 ("Aerius").
AFRICANUS	Addressee of Gr. Naz., *Ep.* 224, on behalf of NICOBULUS (1). Perhaps also known from Lib., *Ep.* 49. Cappadocian government official with authority over Nazianzus. 395: *praefectus urbis Constantinopolitanae*? See also H-M 24–25 ("Africanus"); *PLRE* 27 ("Africanus 4"); S 49–50 ("Africanus"); V 22–23 ("Africanus").
ALYPIANE (1)	Mentioned at Gr. Naz., *Ep.* 12.1, to NICOBULUS (1), 195.5, to GREGORY (3), 196.4, to HECEBOLIUS. Also known from Gr. Naz., *Test.* Gregory's niece; wife of NICOBULUS (1); mother of NICOBULUS (2). See also H-M 25–26 ("Alypiana I"); *PLRE* 46 ("Alypiana").
ALYPIANE (2)	Mentioned at Gr. Naz., *Ep.* 158.1, to EULALIUS. Virgin known to EULALIUS. See also H-M 26 ("Alypiana II").
ALYPIUS	Addressee of Gr. Naz., *Ep.* 61, 82–83, on behalf of EUPHEMIUS, 84, on behalf of FORTUNATUS, 85, on behalf of LUCIANUS, 86;

mentioned at *Ep.* 207.2, to JACOB, 208.2, to JACOB.

Also known from Gr. Naz., *Epig.* 103.

Cappadocian magistrate, brother of AERIUS. Not to be identified with Gregory's brother-in-law mentioned at Gr. Naz., *Or.* 8.20.

See also G 1:104 n. 3, 105 n. 3, 2:100 n. 2; H-M 26–28 ("Alypius I," "Alypius II," "Alypius III," "Alypius IV"); L 456–57; *PLRE* 47 ("Alypius 5," "Alypius 6"); V 24–27 ("Alypius").

AMAZONIA
Mentioned at Gr. Naz., *Ep.* 159.1, to THEODORE (1).

Virgin who perhaps had familial connection to Gregory.

See also H-M 28–29 ("Amazonia").

AMAZONIUS
Addressee of Gr. Naz., *Ep.* 94; mentioned at *Ep.* 39.2, to SOPHRONIUS.

Constantinopolitan friend of Gregory.

See also H-M 29 ("Amazonius I," "Amazonius II").

AMPHILOCHIUS (1)
Addressee of Gr. Naz., *Ep.* 63.

Also known from Gr. Naz., *Carm.* 2.2.6.102; *Epig.* 126, 131–38; *Epit.* 103–9; Bas., *Ep.* 150; Lib., *Ep.* 634, 670–71, 1140.

Uncle of Gregory, father of AMPHILOCHIUS (2). Pre-361: lawyer; post-361: teacher of rhetoric.

See also H-M 29–30 ("Amphilochius I"); *PLRE* 57 ("Amphilochius 2"); S 59 ("Amphilochius II").

AMPHILOCHIUS (2)
Addressee of Gr. Naz., *Ep.* 9, on behalf of EUTHALIUS, 13, on behalf of NICOBULUS (1), 25, 26, 27, 28, on behalf of GLAUCUS, 62, 171,

184; mentioned at *Ep.* 22.2, to SOPHRONIUS, 23.3, to CAESARIUS (2), 24.1, to THEMISTIUS, 63, to AMPHILOCHIUS (1).

Also known from Gr. Naz., *Epig.* 118–21; *Epit.* 118–21; *Test.*; Bas., *Ep.* 150, 161, 163.1, 176, 188, 190–91, 199–202, 217–18, 231–236, 248; *Spir.* 1.1; Lib., *Ep.* 634, 670–71; *C. Th.* 16.1.3; his own extant corpus.

Cousin of Gregory; son of AMPHILOCHIUS (1). 362–65: lawyer; 373–94: bishop of Iconium; 381: designated "standard-bearer of orthodoxy."

See also H-M 30–32 ("Amphilochius II"); *PLRE* 58 ("Amphilochius 4"); S 59 ("Amphilochius III").

ANTHIMUS (1)   Mentioned at Gr. Naz., *Ep.* 48.6, 50.3, 50.7, to BASIL.

Also known from Gr. Naz., *Or.* 13.3, 43.58; Bas., *Ep.* 92.1, 120.1, 121.1, 122.1, 210.5.

Bishop of Tyana during provincial split of Cappadocia in early 372.

See also H-M 32–33 ("Anthimus I").

ANTHIMUS (2)   Mentioned at Gr. Naz., *Ep.* 128.2, to PROCOPIUS.

Soldier or military officer.

See also H-M 33 ("Anthimus II"); *PLRE* 70 ("Anthimus").

ANYSIUS   Addressee of Gr. Naz., *Ep.* 90, 226; mentioned at *Ep.* 227.1, to URSUS.

Constantinopolitan friend of Gregory.

See also H-M 34 ("Anysius I," "Anysius II").

ASTERIUS   Addressee of Gr. Naz., *Ep.* 147–48, on behalf of NICOBULUS (1), 150, on behalf of GEORGE, 155–56.

> Probably *assessor* to OLYMPIUS. Perhaps governor of Cappadocia after provincial split of 382.
>
> See also G 2:39 n. 1; H-M 34–35 ("Asterius I"); L 528; *PLRE* 119 ("Asterius 4"); V 41–42 ("Asterius").

AURELIUS   Mentioned at Gr. Naz., *Ep.* 140.3, to OLYMPIUS.

Soldier who deserted retinue of OLYMPIUS.

See also H-M 37 ("Aurelius"); *PLRE* 131 ("Aurelius 5").

BASIL   Addressee of Gr. Naz., *Ep.* 1–2, 4–6, 8, 19, 40, 45–50, 58–60, 245–46, 248; mentioned at *Ep.* 16.4, to EUSEBIUS (2), 25.2, to AMPHILOCHIUS (2), 41.8, to "The Church of Caesarea," 42.5, to EUSEBIUS (1), 43.3, to "The Bishops," 53.1, to NICOBULUS (2), 76.1, to GREGORY (2), 80.1, to PHILAGRIUS, 115.3, to THEODORE (1).

Also known from Gr. Naz., *Epig.* 2–11, 79; *Epit.* 119; *Or.* 5.39, 9.4–6, 10.3–4, 11.1–3, 12.4, 13.1–2, 13.4, 18.1–4, 18.35–37, 18.41, 30.16, 43; his own extant corpus.

Brother of GREGORY (2). 357: established monastic community at Annesi; 360: appointed lector; 362: ordained priest; 370–79: bishop of Caesarea. Leader in pro-Nicene movement.

See also Paul Jonathan Fedwick, ed., *Basil of Caesarea: Christian, Humanist, Ascetic. A Sixteen-hundredth Anniversary Symposium*, 2 vols. (Toronto: Pontifical Institute of Medieval Studies, 1981); Philip Rousseau, *Basil of Caesarea*, Transformation of the Classical Heritage 20 (Berkeley: University of California Press, 1994).

Basilissa	Addressee of Gr. Naz., *Ep.* 244. Also known from Gr. Naz., *Epig.* 150, 154. Sister of George. Probably leader of ascetic community. See also G 2:132 n. 3; H-M 38 ("Basilissa I").
Bosporius	Addressee of Gr. Naz., *Ep.* 89, 138, 153; mentioned at *Ep.* 183.9, perhaps to Theodore (1), 184.2–3, to Amphilochius (2), 185.2, 185.5, to Nectarius. Also known from Gr. Naz., *Carm.* 2.2.3.242; Bas., *Ep.* 51, 141.2. 356–ca. 405: bishop of Colonia. See also G 2:26 n. 1, 161 ("page 74") n. 3; H-M 45–47 ("Bosporius").
Caesarius (1)	Addressee of Gr. Naz., *Ep.* 7, 20; mentioned at *Ep.* 29.4, 29.8, 29.9, to Sophronius, 30.1, to Philagrius, 80.1, to Philagrius. Also known from Gr. Naz., *Carm.* 2.1.1.165–229, 2.1.90.1, 2.1.91.4; *Epig.* 77–78, 85–86, 88–100; *Or.* 7, 8.23; *Test.*; Bas., *Ep.* 32.1. Brother of Gregory. Physician to Emperor Julian; member of Constantinopolitan Senate; *comes thesaurorum* in Bythinia. 368: died of infection after earthquake at Nicaea. See also H-M 48–50 ("Caesarius I"); *PLRE* 169–70 ("Caesarius 2").
Caesarius (2)	Addressee of Gr. Naz., *Ep.* 23, on behalf of Amphilochius (2). Perhaps also known from Lib., *Ep.* 764, 1113–14, 1147, 1199, 1227, 1308, 1383–84, 1399, 1435, 1441, 1443–44, 1447, 1449, 1451–52, 1456, 1459, 1468; Them., *Or.* 71.91b.

Perhaps brother of ALYPIUS. If identical with figure in abovementioned citations, then 362–63: *vicarius Asiae;* 363–64: *comes rei privatae;* 365: *praefectus urbis Constantinopolitanae.*

See also H-M 51 ("Caesarius II"); *PLRE* 168–69 ("Caesarius 1").

CAESARIUS (3) Addressee of Gr. Naz., *Ep.* 14, on behalf of EULALIUS and HELLADIUS (2).
Identical to CAESARIUS (2)?
See also H-M 51 ("Caesarius III"); *PLRE* 170 ("Caesarius 3").

CANDIDIANUS Addressee of Gr. Naz., *Ep.* 10.
Also known from Bas., *Ep.* 3.
Governor of Cappadocia, Ibora, or Pontus Polemoniacus.
See also G 1:13 n. 1; H-M 51 ("Candidianus"); *PLRE* 178–79 ("Candidianus 2"); V 43–45 ("Candidianus").

CASTOR Addressee of Gr. Naz., *Ep.* 209, on behalf of SACERDOS, 210, on behalf of SACERDOTIS; mentioned at *Ep.* 211, to CYRIACUS.
Made a donation to monastery of Sacerdos.
See also H-M 52 ("Castor").

CELEUSIUS (1) Addressee of Gr. Naz., *Ep.* 112–14.
Cappadocian magistrate?
See also H-M 52–53 ("Celeusius I"); L 520–22; *PLRE* 190 ("Celeusius"); V 45–47 ("Celeusius").

CELEUSIUS (2) Mentioned at Gr. Naz., *Ep.* 152.5, to THEODORE (1).
Priest at Nazianzus.
See also H-M 53 ("Celeusius II").

CLEDONIUS	Addressee of Gr. Naz., *Ep.* 107–9 (+ *Ep.* 101–2).
	Perhaps also known from Gr. Naz., *Carm.* 2.2.1.121; *Test.*
	379–82?: Priest at Nazianzus who led church while Gregory was in Constantinople.
	See also H-M 53–54 ("Cledonius I," "Cledonius II," "Cledonius III," "Cledonius IV").
CYRIACUS	Addressee of Gr. Naz., *Ep.* 211, on behalf of SACERDOS.
	Magistrate in Cappadocia Prima.
	See also G 2:103; H-M 58 ("Cyriacus"); L 549; V 47–49 ("Cyriacus").
DIOCLES	Addressee of Gr. Naz., *Ep.* 232.
	Cappadocian notable.
	See also H-M 62 ("Diocles").
EPIPHANIUS	Addressee of Gr. Naz., *Ep.* 239.
	Also known from his own extant corpus; perhaps Bas., *Ep.* 258.
	Perhaps the famous bishop of Salamis. If not, otherwise unknown.
	See also H-M 64 ("Epiphanius").
EUDOCIUS	Addressee of Gr. Naz., *Ep.* 216, on behalf of SACERDOS, 217, 218, on behalf of SACERDOS.
	Cappadocian monk; adversary-turned-ally of SACERDOS.
	See also H-M 66 ("Eudocius").
EUDOXIUS	Addressee of Gr. Naz., *Ep.* 174, on behalf of NICOBULUS (2), 175, on behalf of NICOBULUS (2), 176, 177, on behalf of NICOBULUS (2), 178–80, 187; mentioned at *Ep.* 37.2, to SOPHRONIUS, 38.3, to THEMISTIUS, 181.2, to SATURNINUS.

	Rhetor in school of EUSTOCHIUS, where he instructed NICOBULUS (2). See also H-M 66–67 ("Eudoxius I," "Eudoxius II"); S 132 ("Eudoxius II," "Eudoxius III").
EUGENIA	Mentioned at Gr. Naz., *Ep.* 160.1, to THEODORE (1). Perhaps also known from Gr. Naz., *Test.* Perhaps Gregory's niece. See also H-M 69 ("Eugenia I," "Eugenia II").
EUGENIUS	Addressee of Gr. Naz., *Ep.* 111, 118; mentioned at *Ep.* 129.2, to PROCOPIUS. Cappadocian deacon and monk. See also G 2:150 ("page 6") n. 5; H-M 69 ("Eugenius").
EULALIUS	Addressee of Gr. Naz., *Ep.* 116–17, 158, on behalf of ALYPIANE (2); mentioned at *Ep.* 14.3, to CAESARIUS (3), 15.4, to LOLLIANUS, 152.5, to THEODORE (1), 182.4, to GREGORY (2), 183.5, perhaps to THEODORE (1). Also known from Gr. Naz., *Carm.* 2.2.1.130–38; *Epig.* 151; *Or.* 13. Cousin of Gregory; brother of HELLADIUS (2). 383–?: bishop of Nazianzus. See also H-M 70 ("Eulalius").
EUPHEMIUS	Mentioned at Gr. Naz., *Ep.* 83.3, to ALYPIUS, 103.3, to PALLADIUS (1), 230.4, to THEODOSIUS. Relative of Gregory. References in letters may be to the same person or to three different people. See also H-M 72 ("Euphemius II-IV").
EUPRAXIUS	Mentioned at Gr. Naz., *Ep.* 65.1, to EUSEBIUS (1). Otherwise unknown.

PROSOPOGRAPHY 27

EUSEBIUS (1) — Addressee of Gr. Naz., *Ep.* 42, on behalf of BASIL and EUSTATHIUS, 44, 64–66.
Also known from Gr. Naz., *Or.* 33.5, 43.37; Bas., *Ep.* 27, 30, 48, 85, 98, 100, 127, 136, 138, 141, 145, 162, 166–67, 198, 237, 241, 268, 271.
Crucial supporter of BASIL before his episcopal election. Ca. 360–78: bishop of Samosata; 374: exiled to Thrace.
See also H-M 73–74 ("Eusebius von Samosata"); Rousseau, *Basil of Caesarea*, 254–58.

EUSEBIUS (2) — Addressee of Gr. Naz., *Ep.* 16, on behalf of BASIL, 17–18; mentioned at *Ep.* 19.2, to BASIL, 42.2, to EUSEBIUS (1).
Also known from Gr. Naz., *Or.* 18.33–35, 43.28, 43.31, 43.33, 43.37.
362–70: bishop of Caesarea.
See also H-M 75–77 ("Eusebius III"); Rousseau, *Basil of Caesarea*, 254–58.

EUSEBIUS (3) — Addressee of Gr. Naz., *Ep.* 231.
Cappadocian notable.

EUSTATHIUS — Mentioned at Gr. Naz., *Ep.* 42.4, to EUSEBIUS (1).
Deacon at Nazianzus.

EUSTOCHIUS — Addressee of Gr. Naz., *Ep.* 189–91.
Perhaps also known from Jul., *Ep.* 41.
Athens-trained sophist; teacher of NICOBULUS (2); rival of STAGIRIUS; employer of EUDOXIUS.
See also H-M 78–79 ("Eustochius"); *PLRE* 313 ("Eustochius 5").

EUSTRATIUS — Mentioned at Gr. Naz., *Ep.* 106.1, to OLYMPIUS.
Relative of Gregory at Nazianzus.

EUTHALIUS   Mentioned at Gr. Naz., *Ep.* 9.3, to
             AMPHILOCHIUS (2), 149.1, to GEORGE.
             Deacon at Nazianzus.

EUTROPIUS   Addressee of Gr. Naz., *Ep.* 70–71.
             Also known from Lib., *Ep.* 979; *Or.* 1.159.
             360s: *magister epistularum;* ca. 369: *magister
                 memoriae;* 371/72: *proconsul Asiae;* 380–81:
                 praefectus praetorio Orientis; 387: *consul
                 posterior.*
             See also H-M 80–81 ("Eutropius"); *PLRE* 317
                 ("Eutropius 2").

EVAGRIUS (1) Addressee of Gr. Naz., *Ep.* 3, on behalf of
                 EVAGRIUS (2).
             Father of EVAGRIUS (2). 362: perhaps *comes
                 rerum privatarum.*
             See also H-M 64 ("Euagrius I"); S 128 ("Eva-
                 grius").

EVAGRIUS (2) Mentioned at Gr. Naz., *Ep.* 3.1, to
                 EVAGRIUS (1).
             Student of Gregory. Perhaps to be identified
                 with Evagrius of Pontus.
             See also G 1:120 ("page 2") n. 4; H-M 64
                 ("Euagrius II"); John McGuckin, *St Gregory
                 of Nazianzus: An Intellectual Biography*
                 (Crestwood, NY: St. Vladimir's Seminary
                 Press, 2001), 86.

EVAGRIUS (3) Mentioned at Gr. Naz., *Ep.* 228.2, to
                 PANSOPHIUS.
             Also known from Gr. Naz., *Test.*
             Deacon at Nazianzus. Perhaps to be identified
                 with EVAGRIUS (2).
             See also G 2:168 ("page 120") n. 6; H-M 64–65
                 ("Euagrius III"); L 430.

EVOPION	Mentioned at Gr. Naz., *Ep.* 231.1, to EUSEBIUS (3). Daughter of EUSEBIUS (3).
FORTUNATUS	Mentioned at Gr. Naz., *Ep.* 84.1, to ALYPIUS. Deacon at Nazianzus.
GEORGE	Addressee of Gr. Naz., *Ep.* 149, on behalf of PHILADELPHIUS; mentioned at *Ep.* 150.3, to ASTERIUS, 151.2, to NECTARIUS, 163.2, 163.6, to THEODORE (1). Also known from Gr. Naz., *Epig.* 154. Brother of BASILISSA. Deacon, then priest, at Nazianzus. See also H-M 83–84 ("Georgius II–V").
GIGANTIUS	Addressee of Gr. Naz., *Ep.* 100. Also known from Gr. Naz., *Epig.* 1–2. Monk at Constantinople. True name is likely Sigantius. See also G 1:131 ("page 117") n. 4; H-M 85–86 ("Gigantius I–II"); L 513.
GLAUCUS	Mentioned at Gr. Naz., *Ep.* 28.1, 28.2, to AMPHILOCHIUS (2). Otherwise unknown. Glaucus is likely a nickname. See also H-M 86 ("Glaucus").
GLYCERIUS	Addressee of Gr. Naz., *Ep.* 247; mentioned at *Ep.* 246.1–2, to BASIL, 248.1, to BASIL. Deacon in Cappadocia.
GREGORY (1)	Mentioned at Gr. Naz., *Ep.* 7.4, 7.6, to CAESARIUS (1), 44.6, to EUSEBIUS (1), 46.3, to BASIL, 63.2, to AMPHILOCHIUS (1), 79.1, to SIMPLICIA; *Ep.* 41, 43 are written in his name.

Also known from Gr. Naz., *Epig.* 12–23; *Epit.* 55–65; *Or.* 6.11, 8.4, 18.
Father of Gregory and CAESARIUS (1); husband of NONNA. 329–74: bishop of Nazianzus.
See also H-M 88–90 ("Gregor der Ältere").

GREGORY (2) Addressee of Gr. Naz., *Ep.* 11, 72–74, 76, 81, 182, on behalf of EULALIUS, 197.
Also known from Bas., *Ep.* 38, 58; *C. Th.* 16.1.3.
Brother of BASIL; husband of THEOSEBIA. 371/72–94: bishop of Nyssa; 381: designated "standard-bearer of orthodoxy."
See also H-M 91–92 ("Gregor von Nyssa"); Anna Silvas, *Gregory of Nyssa: The Letters—Introduction, Translation, and Commentary,* Supplements to Vigiliae Christianae 83 (Leiden: Brill, 2007), 1–57.

GREGORY (3) Addressee of Gr. Naz., *Ep.* 195, on behalf of NICOBULUS (2).
Cappadocian official.
See also H-M 92–93 ("Gregorius IV"); L 545; *PLRE* 403 ("Gregorius 6"); S 166 ("Gregorius III"); V 51–52 ("Gregorius").

HECEBOLIUS Addressee of Gr. Naz., *Ep.* 196, on behalf of NICOBULUS (2).
Governor of Cappadocia.
See also G 2:87–88 n. 1; H-M 94 ("Hecebolius"); L 545; *PLRE* 409 ("Hecebolius 3"); V 52–53 ("Hecebolius").

HELLADIUS (1) Addressee of Gr. Naz., *Ep.* 120, 127, on behalf of NICOBULUS (1), 167, on behalf of NICOBULUS (2), 172, 219, on behalf of SACERDOS, 220, on behalf of SACERDOS; mentioned at

Ep. 183.5, perhaps to THEODORE (1), 216.5, to EUDOCIUS, 221.4, to HOMOPHRONIUS.
Also known from *C. Th.* 16.1.3.
379–ca. 394: bishop of Caesarea (immediate successor to BASIL); 381: designated "standard-bearer of orthodoxy"; mid-382: helped NICOBULUS (2) find sophists in Caesarea; late 382: engaged in jurisdictional conflict with THEODORE (1) after provincial split in 382.
See also H-M 94–95 ("Helladius I").

HELLADIUS (2)

Mentioned at Gr. Naz., *Ep.* 14.3, to CAESARIUS (3), 15.4, to LOLLIANUS.
Also known from Gr. Naz., *Carm.* 2.2.1.131–34; *Epig.* 151–53.
Cousin of Gregory; brother of EULALIUS. Died young.
See also H-M 96 ("Helladius II").

HELLEBICHUS

Addressee of Gr. Naz., *Ep.* 225, on behalf of MAMAS.
Also known from Lib., *Ep.* 868, 884, 898, 925; *Or.* 1.232, 20.6, 21.5, 21.7, 22.12, 22.42, 23.26.
383–88: *magister militum per Orientem*.
See also *PLRE* 277–78 ("Ellebichus").

HERACLIANUS

Addressee of Gr. Naz., *Ep.* 97.
Constantinopolitan friend of Gregory.

HOMOPHRONIUS

Addressee of Gr. Naz., *Ep.* 221, on behalf of SACERDOS.
Monk in ascetic community of SACERDOS. Perhaps clergy member.

HYPERECHIUS

Mentioned at Gr. Naz., *Ep.* 134.2, to VICTOR.
Otherwise unknown.

JACOB	Addressee of Gr. Naz., *Ep.* 207, on behalf of SIMPLICIA, 208, on behalf of SIMPLICIA. Provincial official in Cappadocia. See also G 2:99 n. 1; H-M 100 ("Iacobus"); L 726; *PLRE* 450 ("Iacobus 3"); V 57–58 ("Iacobus").
JULIAN	Addressee of Gr. Naz., *Ep.* 67, on behalf of NICOBULUS (1), 68–69. Also known from Gr. Naz., *Or.* 19; perhaps Bas., *Ep.* 293. Longtime friend of Gregory in Cappadocia. 374/75: *peraequator*. See also H-M 110–11 ("Iulianus III"); *PLRE* 472 ("Iulianus 17"); S 191 ("Iulianus VIII").
LEONTIUS (1)	Addressee of Gr. Naz., *Ep.* 95. Perhaps also known from Bas., *Ep.* 20–21. Constantinopolitan friend of Gregory. See also H-M 112 ("Leontius II").
LEONTIUS (2)	Mentioned at Gr. Naz., *Ep.* 143.3, to OLYMPIUS. Priest at Nazianzus. See also H-M 112 ("Leontius III").
LEUCADIUS	Mentioned at Gr. Naz., *Ep.* 238.prol., to "The Brotherhood at Sannabodae." Abbot of double monastery in Cappadocia.
LIBANIUS	Addressee of Gr. Naz., *Ep.* 236. Also known from his own extant corpus. Famous sophist at Antioch. See also *PLRE* 505–7 ("Libanius 1"); Lieve Van Hoof, "Libanius' *Life* and Life," in *Libanius: A Critical Introduction,* ed. Van Hoof (Cambridge: Cambridge University Press, 2014), 7–38.

LOLLIANUS	Addressee of Gr. Naz., *Ep.* 15, on behalf of EULALIUS and HELLADIUS (2). Cappadocian notable. See also H-M 114 ("Lollianus").
LUCIANUS	Mentioned at Gr. Naz., *Ep.* 85.1, to ALYPIUS. Priest at Nazianzus. Otherwise unknown.
MACEDONIUS	Addressee of Gr. Naz., *Ep.* 237. Cappadocian clergy member.
MAMAS	Mentioned at Gr. Naz., *Ep.* 225.3, to HELLEBICHUS. Son of a soldier. Lector. See also H-M 116 ("Mamas").
MELETIUS	Addressee of Gr. Naz., *Ep.* 240. Otherwise unknown.
MODARIUS	Addressee of Gr. Naz., *Ep.* 136, 137, on behalf of THEODORE (2). 380–82: *magister militum* in Thrace. See also *PLRE* 605 ("Modares").
NECTARIUS	Addressee of Gr. Naz., *Ep.* 91, on behalf of PANCRATIUS, 151, on behalf of GEORGE, 185, on behalf of BOSPORIUS, 186, on behalf of "Gregory's cousin" (+ *Ep.* 202). Also known from Bas., *Ep.* 4, perhaps 290. Member of Constantinopolitan Senate. *Praetor urbanus.* 381–97: bishop of Constantinople (immediately after Gregory's departure). See also H-M 126–28 ("Nectarius"); *PLRE* 621 ("Nectarius 2").
NEMESIUS	Addressee of Gr. Naz., *Ep.* 198, on behalf of VALENTINIANUS, 199, on behalf of THEODOSIUS, 200–201.

Also known from Gr. Naz., *Carm.* 2.2.7.
Provincial official in Cappadocia.
See also G 2:90 n. 1; H-M 128 ("Nemesius"); L 540–41; *PLRE* 622 ("Nemesius 2"); V 61–62 ("Nemesius").

NICOBULUS (1) Addressee of Gr. Naz., *Ep.* 12, 55; mentioned at *Ep.* 13.3, to AMPHILOCHIUS (2), 21.3, to SOPHRONIUS, 67.1, to JULIAN, 126.3, to OLYMPIUS, 127.2, to HELLADIUS (1), 146.4, 146.6, to OLYMPIUS, 147.2, to ASTERIUS, 148.3, to ASTERIUS, 224.5, to AFRICANUS.
Also known from Gr. Naz., *Carm.* 2.2.5.
Nephew-in-law of Gregory; husband of ALYPIANE (1). Soldier; *praefectus mansionis;* perhaps provincial official.
See also G 1:19 n. 1; H-M 128–31 ("Nicobulus I"); *PLRE* 629 ("Nicobulus 1").

NICOBULUS (2) Addressee of Gr. Naz., *Ep.* 51–54; mentioned at *Ep.* 157.2, to THEODORE (1), 167.1, to HELLADIUS (1), 174.4, to EUDOXIUS, 175.1, to EUDOXIUS, 176.5, to EUDOXIUS, 177.3, to EUDOXIUS, 187.3, to EUDOXIUS, 188.2, to STAGIRIUS, 190.3, to EUSTOCHIUS, 192.5, to STAGIRIUS, 195.5, to GREGORY (3), 196.4, to HECEBOLIUS.
Son of NICOBULUS (1) and ALYPIANE (1). Student under STAGIRIUS, EUSTOCHIUS, and EUDOXIUS.
See also G 1:126–27 ("page 66") n. 2; H-M 132 ("Nicobulus II").

NONNA Mentioned at Gr. Naz., *Ep.* 7.7, to CAESARIUS (1), 60.2, to BASIL.
Also known from Gr. Naz., *Carm.* 2.1.1.117–39, 2.1.11.57–76, 2.1.92; *Epig.* 24–74; *Epit.* 66–100; *Or.* 7.4, 7.8, 8.4–5, 18.30, 18.42.

	Mother of Gregory and CAESARIUS (1); wife of GREGORY (1). See also H-M 134–35 ("Nonna I").
OLYMPIANUS	Addressee of Gr. Naz., *Ep.* 234. Perhaps provincial official in Cappadocia. See also G 2:125 n. 1; H-M 136 ("Olympianus"); *PLRE* 642 ("Olympianus"); V 63–64 ("Olympianus").
OLYMPIAS	Mentioned at Gr. Naz., *Ep.* 193.1, to VITALIANUS. Also known from Gr. Naz., *Carm.* 2.2.6. Daughter of VITALIANUS. Provincial noblewoman, not to be identified with famous patron of John Chrysostom. See also Neil McLynn, "The Other Olympias: Gregory Nazianzen and the Family of Vitalianus," *Zeitschrift für antikes Christentum* 2 (1998): 227–48.
OLYMPIUS	Addressee of Gr. Naz., *Ep.* 104, on behalf of PHILUMENA, 105, on behalf of PAUL (2), 106, on behalf of EUSTRATIUS, 125, 126, on behalf of NICOBULUS (1), 131, 140, on behalf of AURELIUS, 141–42, 143, on behalf of LEONTIUS (2), 144, 146, on behalf of NICOBULUS (1), 154; mentioned at *Ep.* 145.3, to VERIANUS, 147.3, to ASTERIUS. 382: governor of Cappadocia. See also G 2:149, 155; H-M 137–39 ("Olympius"); L 382, 525–27; *PLRE* 646 ("Olympius 10"); S 225 ("Olympius XI"); V 64–66 ("Olympius").
PALLADIUS (1)	Addressee of Gr. Naz., *Ep.* 103, on behalf of EUPHEMIUS, 110, 119, 170, on behalf of SACERDOS.

Sophist. 381: *comes sacrarum largitionum*; 382–84: *magister officiorum*. Possible that addressee of Gr. Naz., *Ep.* 103, 170 should be distinguished from addressee of *Ep.* 110, 119.
See also H-M 140–41 ("Palladius I–III"); *PLRE* 660 ("Palladius 12").

Palladius (2) — Mentioned at Gr. Naz., *Ep.* 82.1, to Alypius.
Otherwise unknown.

Pancratius — Mentioned at Gr. Naz., *Ep.* 91.4, to Nectarius.
Otherwise unknown.

Pansophius — Addressee of Gr. Naz., *Ep.* 228, on behalf of Evagrius (3), 229.
Clergy member in Caucasian Iberia.

Paul (1) — Mentioned at Gr. Naz., *Ep.* 77.16, to Theotecnus.
Implied to be leader of the Pascal attack on the Anastasia in 380.

Paul (2) — Mentioned at Gr. Naz., *Ep.* 105.2, to Olympius.
Otherwise unknown.

Peter — Addressee of Gr. Naz., *Ep.* 242.
Bishop. Otherwise unknown.

Philadelphius — Mentioned at Gr. Naz., *Ep.* 149.1, to George.
Otherwise unknown.

Philagrius — Addressee of Gr. Naz., *Ep.* 30–36, 80, 87, 92.
Also known from Gr. Naz., *Epig.* 100; Bas., *Ep.* 323.
Athenian classmate and friend of Gregory.
See also H-M 145 ("Philagrius II").

PHILUMENA	Mentioned at Gr. Naz., *Ep.* 104.2, to OLYMPIUS. Widow with children.
PHOTIUS	Addressee of Gr. Naz., *Ep.* 168, on behalf of SACERDOS. Otherwise unknown. See also H-M 147 ("Photius").
POSTUMIANUS	Addressee of Gr. Naz., *Ep.* 173. 383: *praefectus praetorio Orientis*. See also H-M 148 ("Postumianus"); *PLRE* 718 ("Postumianus 2").
PROCOPIUS	Addressee of Gr. Naz., *Ep.* 128, on behalf of ANTHIMUS (2), 129, on behalf of EUGENIUS, 130. Perhaps also known from Lib., *Ep.* 929. Government official at Constantinople and perhaps Cappadocia. See also G 2:18 n. 1; H-M 149–50 ("Procopius I–II"); *PLRE* 743 ("Procopius 5–8"); S 247 ("Procopius I–III"); V 66–67 ("Procopius").
PRONOIUS	Mentioned at Gr. Naz., *Ep.* 189.2, to EUSTOCHIUS. Student recommended to Eustochius.
REGIANUS	Mentioned at Gr. Naz., *Ep.* 129.3, to PROCOPIUS. Otherwise unknown.
SACERDOS	Addressee of Gr. Naz., *Ep.* 99, 212–15; mentioned at *Ep.* 168.2, to PHOTIUS, 169.2, to STRATEGIUS, 170.2, to PALLADIUS (1), 209.1, to CASTOR, 211.1, to CYRIACUS, 216.4, to EUDOCIUS, 218.1, to EUDOCIUS, 219.2, to HELLADIUS (1), 220.2, to HELLADIUS (1), 221.3, to HOMOPHRONIUS, 222.3, to THECLA; alluded to in *Ep.* 217, to Eudocius.

Brother of THECLA. Priest and monk. Protégé of Gregory.
See also H-M 152 ("Sacerdos").

SACERDOTIS   Mentioned at Gr. Naz., *Ep.* 210.3, to CASTOR.
"Sacerdotis" may be a nickname for THECLA, sister of SACERDOS.

SATURNINUS   Addressee of Gr. Naz., *Ep.* 132, 181, on behalf of EUDOXIUS.
Also known from Bas., *Ep.* 132; Lib., *Ep.* 857, 897; Them., *Or.* 16.206a–b.
Pre-361: *cura palatii*; 373: *comes rei militaris*; 377–78: *magister equitum*; 382–83: *magister militum*; 383: *consul posterior*. Still influential in 388.
See also *PLRE* 807–8 ("Flavius Saturninus 10").

SIMPLICIA   Addressee of Gr. Naz., *Ep.* 79; mentioned at *Ep.* 207.2, to JACOB, 208.3, to JACOB.
Also known from Bas., *Ep.* 115.
Cappadocian notable.
See also H-M 154–56 ("Simplicia I–II").

SOPHRONIUS   Addressee of Gr. Naz., *Ep.* 21, on behalf of NICOBULUS (1), 22, on behalf of AMPHILOCHIUS (2), 29, on behalf of CAESARIUS (1), 37, on behalf of EUDOXIUS, 39, on behalf of AMAZONIUS, 93, 135.
Also known from Bas., *Ep.* 32, 76, 96, 177, 180, 192, 272; Lib., *Ep.* 883, 924.
Athenian classmate of Gregory; friend of CAESARIUS (1). 365: *notarius*; 370s: *magister officiorum*; 382?: *praefectus urbis Constantinopolitanae*. Retired in Caesarea by 390.
See also H-M 156 ("Sophronius"); *PLRE* 847–48 ("Sophronius 3").

STAGIRIUS	Addressee of Gr. Naz., *Ep.* 165–66, 188, on behalf of NICOBULUS (2), 192, on behalf of NICOBULUS (2); mentioned at *Ep.* 190.2, to EUSTOCHIUS. Also known from Gr. Nyss., *Ep.* 9, 26 (= Stagirius's sole surviving letter), 27. Athens-trained sophist in Caesarea; teacher of NICOBULUS (2); rival of EUSTOCHIUS. See also H-M 157–58 ("Stagirius"); *PLRE* 851 ("Stagirius").
STRATEGIUS	Addressee of Gr. Naz., *Ep.* 169, on behalf of SACERDOS. Classmate and friend of Gregory in Athens; sophist in Caesarea. See also H-M 158 ("Strategius"); *PLRE* 858 ("Strategius 3").
THECLA	Addressee of Gr. Naz., *Ep.* 56–57, 222–23. Sister of SACERDOS. See also H-M 158–60 ("Thecla I," "Thecla II," "Thecla III," "Thecla IV").
THEMISTIUS	Addressee of Gr. Naz., *Ep.* 24, on behalf of AMPHILOCHIUS (2), 38, on behalf of EUDOXIUS. Also known from his own extant corpus. Philosopher. Member of Constantinopolitan Senate. Proconsul of Constantinople. 384: *praefectus urbis Constantinopolitanae*. See also H-M 160 ("Themistius I"); *PLRE* 889–94 ("Themistius 1"); Peter Heather and David Moncur, trans., *Politics, Philosophy, and Empire in the Fourth Century: Select Orations of Themistius,* Translated Texts for Historians 36 (Liverpool: Liverpool University Press, 2001), 43–68, 137–48, 199–217, 285–97; Robert J. Penella, trans., *The Private*

Orations of Themistius, Transformation of the Classical Heritage 29 (Berkeley: University of California Press, 2000), 1–45.

THEODORE (1) — Addressee of Gr. Naz., *Ep.* 77, 115, 121–24, 139, 152, on behalf of EULALIUS and CELEUSIUS (2), 157, on behalf of NICOBULUS (2), 159, on behalf of AMAZONIA, 160, on behalf of EUGENIA, 161–62, 163, on behalf of GEORGE, perhaps 183, on behalf of BOSPORIUS.
Early 380s: bishop of Tyana.
See also H-M 161–67 ("Theodorus I–VIII," "Theodorus X," "Theodorus XI"); *PLRE* 898 ("Theodorus 14"); V 69–73 ("Theodorus").

THEODORE (2) — Mentioned at Gr. Naz., *Ep.* 137.2, to MODARIUS.
Otherwise unknown.
See H-M 167 ("Theodorus XII").

THEODOSIUS — Addressee of Gr. Naz., *Ep.* 230, on behalf of EUPHEMIUS; mentioned at *Ep.* 199.4, to NEMESIUS.
Perhaps also known from Gr. Naz., *Test.*
Perhaps Cappadocian *notarius*.
See also H-M 169–70 ("Theodosius II–III?").

THEOSEBIA — Mentioned at Gr. Naz., *Ep.* 197.5–6, to GREGORY (2).
Also known from Gr. Naz., *Epig.* 164; *Epit.* 123.
Wife of GREGORY (2).
See also G 2:164 ("page 89") n. 3; H-M 171–72 ("Theosebia I–II").

THEOTECNUS — Addressee of Gr. Naz., *Ep.* 78; perhaps mentioned at *Ep.* 98.1, to "The Decurions."
Deacon at Nazianzus.
See also H-M 171–72 ("Theotecnus I–II").

TIMOTHY	Addressee of Gr. Naz., *Ep.* 164. Also known from Bas., *Ep.* 291. Constantinopolitan friend of Gregory. Perhaps a priest. See also H-M 174 ("Timotheus"); L 514.
URSUS	Addressee of Gr. Naz., *Ep.* 227, on behalf of ANYSIUS. Otherwise unknown. See also H-M 174–75 ("Ursus").
VICTOR	Addressee of Gr. Naz., *Ep.* 133, 134, on behalf of HYPERECHIUS. Also known from Bas., *Ep.* 152–53; perhaps Lib., *Ep.* 1525; *Or.* 2.9, 57.50; Them., *Or.* 8.116d, 9.120c–121a, 11.149c. 362–63: perhaps *comes rei militaris*; post-363–ca. 379: *magister equitum*; post-369: *consul posterior*. See also *PLRE* 957–59 ("Victor 4").
VALENTINIANUS	Addressee of Gr. Naz., *Ep.* 203; mentioned at *Ep.* 198.2, to NEMESIUS. Relative of Gregory in Cappadocia. See also G 2:93 n. 3; H-M 177–78 ("Valentinianus II").
VALENTINUS	Mentioned at Gr. Naz., *Ep.* 176.3, to EUDOXIUS. Perhaps rhetor or sophist in Caesarea. See also H-M 178 ("Valentinus").
VERIANUS	Addressee of Gr. Naz., *Ep.* 145; mentioned at *Ep.* 144.1, 144.4 to OLYMPIUS. Cappadocian notable. See also H-M 178 ("Verianus").

VITALIANUS   Addressee of Gr. Naz., *Ep.* 75, 193–94.
Also known from Gr. Naz., *Carm.* 2.2.3, 2.2.6.
Cappadocian notable.
See also H-M 179–80 ("Vitalianus I–II"); Neil
   McLynn, "The Other Olympias."

ARRANGEMENT OF THE COLLECTION

Storin Order	Maurist Number	Addressee	Page
1	52	Nicobulus	55
2	53	Nicobulus	56
3	51	Nicobulus	56
4	54	Nicobulus	57
5	60	Basil	57
6	1	Basil	58
7	2	Basil	58
8	4	Basil	58
9	5	Basil	60
10	6	Basil	61
11	46	Basil	62
12	8	Basil	62
13	16	Eusebius (of Caesarea)	63
14	17	Eusebius (of Caesarea)	63
15	18	Eusebius (of Caesarea)	64
16	19	Basil	65
17	58	Basil	65
18	59	Basil	68
19	48	Basil	68
20	49	Basil	70
21	50	Basil	70
22	45	Basil	71
23	47	Basil	72
24	40	Basil	72
25	245	Basil	73
26	41	"The Church of Caesarea"	73

27	43	"The Bishops"	75
28	246	Basil	75
29	247	Glycerius	77
30	248	Basil	77
31	103	Palladius	77
32	170	Palladius	78
33	119	Palladius	78
34	110	Palladius	79
35	211	Cyriacus	79
36	91	Nectarius	79
37	186	Nectarius	80
38	185	Nectarius	80
39	151	Nectarius	80
40	219	Helladius	82
41	220	Helladius	83
42	127	Helladius	83
43	167	Helladius	83
44	172	Helladius	84
45	120	Helladius	84
46	216	Eudocius	85
47	217	Eudocius	85
48	218	Eudocius	86
49	221	Homophronius	87
50	215	Sacerdos	87
51	213	Sacerdos	88
52	99	Sacerdos	88
53	214	Sacerdos	88
54	212	Sacerdos	89
55	183	Theodore (of Tyana)	89
56	163	Theodore (of Tyana)	90
57	121	Theodore (of Tyana)	91
58	123	Theodore (of Tyana)	92
59	139	Theodore (of Tyana)	92
60	77	Theodore (of Tyana)	93
61	159	Theodore (of Tyana)	95
62	157	Theodore (of Tyana)	95
63	124	Theodore (of Tyana)	96
64	160	Theodore (of Tyana)	96
65	161	Theodore (of Tyana)	96
66	115	Theodore (of Tyana)	97
67	152	Theodore (of Tyana)	97
68	162	Theodore (of Tyana)	98
69	122	Theodore (of Tyana)	98
70	168	Photius	99
71	169	Strategius	99

ARRANGEMENT OF THE COLLECTION 45

72	209	Castor	99
73	210	Castor	100
74	81	Gregory of Nyssa	100
75	72	Gregory of Nyssa	100
76	73	Gregory of Nyssa	101
77	74	Gregory of Nyssa	101
78	76	Gregory of Nyssa	101
79	197	Gregory (of Nyssa)	102
80	182	Gregory (of Nyssa)	103
81	11	Gregory (of Nyssa)	104
82	195	Gregory the Governor	105
83	107	Cledonius	106
84	109	Cledonius	106
85	108	Cledonius	106
86	116	Eulalius	107
87	117	Eulalius	107
88	158	Eulalius	107
89	118	Eugenius	108
90	111	Eugenius	108
91	95	Leontius	108
92	239	Epiphanius	108
93	20	Caesarius	109
94	7	Caesarius	109
95	14	Caesarius	111
96	23	Caesarius	112
97	21	Sophronius	112
98	93	Sophronius	113
99	135	Sophronius	113
100	37	Sophronius	114
101	29	Sophronius	114
102	39	Sophronius	114
103	22	Sophronius	116
104	189	Eustochius	116
105	190	Eustochius	117
106	191	Eustochius	118
107	100	Gigantius	119
108	228	Pansophius	120
109	229	Pansophius	120
110	230	Theodosius	120
111	174	Eudoxius	121
112	175	Eudoxius	122
113	176	Eudoxius	122
114	187	Eudoxius	122
115	177	Eudoxius	122
116	178	Eudoxius	122

117	179	Eudoxius	125
118	180	Eudoxius	126
119	32	Philagrius	126
120	87	Philagrius	128
121	92	Philagrius	128
122	33	Philagrius	129
123	34	Philagrius	129
124	35	Philagrius	129
125	36	Philagrius	131
126	31	Philagrius	131
127	30	Philagrius	132
128	80	Philagrius	132
129	224	Africanus	133
130	227	Ursus	133
131	225	Hellebichus	134
132	237	Macedonius	134
133	155	Asterius	134
134	147	Asterius	135
135	148	Asterius	136
136	150	Asterius	136
137	156	Asterius	137
138	204	Adelphius	137
139	205	Adelphius	139
140	206	Adelphius	139
141	233	Ablabius	140
142	173	Postumianus	141
143	132	Saturninus	142
144	181	Saturninus	142
145	133	Victor	143
146	134	Victor	143
147	136	Modarius	143
148	137	Modarius	144
149	70	Eutropius	144
150	71	Eutropius	145
151	94	Amazonius	145
152	38	Themistius	146
153	24	Themistius	146
154	112	Celeusius	147
155	113	Celeusius	147
156	114	Celeusius	148
157	138	Bosporius	149
158	153	Bosporius	149
159	89	Bosporius	150
160	240	Meletius	150
161	226	Anysius	150

162	90	Anysius	151
163	193	Vitalianus	151
164	194	Vitalianus	152
165	75	Vitalianus	152
166	207	Jacob	152
167	208	Jacob	153
168	82	Alypius	153
169	83	Alypius	154
170	86	Alypius	154
171	84	Alypius	155
172	85	Alypius	155
173	61	Aerius and Alypius	155
174	3	Evagrius	157
175	55	Nicobulus (the Elder)	157
176	12	Nicobulus (the Elder)	157
177	97	Heraclianus	158
178	128	Procopius	158
179	129	Procopius	159
180	130	Procopius	159
181	9	Amphilochius	160
182	13	Amphilochius	160
183	63	Amphilochius (the Elder)	161
184	25	Amphilochius	162
185	62	Amphilochius	162
186	26	Amphilochius	163
187	27	Amphilochius	163
188	184	Amphilochius	163
189	28	Amphilochius	164
190	171	Amphilochius	164
191	234	Olympianus	165
192	67	Julian	165
193	69	Julian	166
194	68	Julian	166
195	64	Eusebius of Samosata	166
196	44	Eusebius of Samosata	167
197	65	Eusebius of Samosata	168
198	231	Eusebius	169
199	42	Eusebius of Samosata	170
200	66	Eusebius of Samosata	170
201	141	Olympius	171
202	142	Olympius	173
203	105	Olympius	173
204	104	Olympius	173
205	143	Olympius	174
206	144	Olympius	174

207	145	Verianus	175
208	131	Olympius	176
209	125	Olympius	176
210	140	Olympius	177
211	106	Olympius	178
212	126	Olympius	178
213	146	Olympius	179
214	154	Olympius	180
215	196	Hecebolius	181
216	238	"The Brotherhood at Sannabodae"	181
217	149	George	182
218	199	Nemesius	183
219	198	Nemesius	183
220	200	Nemesius	184
221	201	Nemesius	185
222	242	Peter	185
223	164	Timothy	185
224	188	Stagirius	186
225	165	Stagirius	186
226	166	Stagirius	187
227	192	Stagirius	188
228	96	Hypatius	189
229	232	Diocles	189
230	10	Candidianus	189
231	15	Lollianus	192
232	203	Valentinianus	192
233	98	"The Decurions"	193
234	78	Theotecnus	194
235	235	Adamantius	195
236	56	Thecla	196
237	57	Thecla	196
238	223	Thecla	196
239	222	Thecla	198
240	79	Simplicia	199
241	236	Libanius the Sophist	201
242	244	Basilissa	201
—	88	(Nectarius)	**
—	101	(Cledonius)	**
—	102	(Cledonius)	**
—	202	(Nectarius)	**
—	241	(Aburgius)	**
—	243	(Evagrius)	**
—	249	(Flavian)	**

ARRANGEMENT OF THE COLLECTION 49

Maurist Number	Storin Order	Addressee	Page
1	6	Basil	58
2	7	Basil	58
3	174	Evagrius	157
4	8	Basil	58
5	9	Basil	60
6	10	Basil	61
7	94	Caesarius	109
8	12	Basil	62
9	181	Amphilochius	160
10	230	Candidianus	189
11	81	Gregory (of Nyssa)	104
12	176	Nicobulus (the Elder)	157
13	182	Amphilochius	160
14	95	Caesarius	111
15	231	Lollianus	192
16	13	Eusebius (of Caesarea)	63
17	14	Eusebius (of Caesarea)	63
18	15	Eusebius (of Caesarea)	64
19	16	Basil	65
20	93	Caesarius	109
21	97	Sophronius	112
22	103	Sophronius	116
23	96	Caesarius	112
24	153	Themistius	146
25	184	Amphilochius	162
26	186	Amphilochius	163
27	187	Amphilochius	163
28	189	Amphilochius	164
29	101	Sophronius	114
30	127	Philagrius	132
31	126	Philagrius	131
32	119	Philagrius	126
33	122	Philagrius	129
34	123	Philagrius	129
35	124	Philagrius	129
36	125	Philagrius	131
37	100	Sophronius	114
38	152	Themistius	146
39	102	Sophronius	114
40	24	Basil	72
41	26	"The Church of Caesarea"	73
42	199	Eusebius of Samosata	170
43	27	"The Bishops"	75

44	196	Eusebius of Samosata	167
45	22	Basil	71
46	11	Basil	62
47	23	Basil	72
48	19	Basil	68
49	20	Basil	70
50	21	Basil	70
51	3	Nicobulus	56
52	1	Nicobulus	55
53	2	Nicobulus	56
54	4	Nicobulus	57
55	175	Nicobulus (the Elder)	157
56	236	Thecla	196
57	237	Thecla	196
58	17	Basil	65
59	18	Basil	68
60	5	Basil	57
61	173	Aerius and Alypius	155
62	185	Amphilochius	162
63	183	Amphilochius (the Elder)	161
64	195	Eusebius of Samosata	166
65	197	Eusebius of Samosata	168
66	200	Eusebius of Samosata	170
67	192	Julian	165
68	194	Julian	166
69	193	Julian	166
70	149	Eutropius	144
71	150	Eutropius	145
72	75	Gregory of Nyssa	100
73	76	Gregory of Nyssa	101
74	77	Gregory of Nyssa	101
75	165	Vitalianus	152
76	78	Gregory of Nyssa	101
77	60	Theodore (of Tyana)	93
78	234	Theotecnus	194
79	240	Simplicia	199
80	128	Philagrius	132
81	74	Gregory of Nyssa	100
82	168	Alypius	153
83	169	Alypius	154
84	171	Alypius	155
85	172	Alypius	155
86	170	Alypius	154
87	120	Philagrius	128
88	—	(Nectarius)	**

89	159	Bosporius	150
90	162	Anysius	151
91	36	Nectarius	79
92	121	Philagrius	128
93	98	Sophronius	113
94	151	Amazonius	145
95	91	Leontius	108
96	228	Hypatius	189
97	177	Heraclianus	158
98	233	"The Decurions"	193
99	52	Sacerdos	88
100	107	Gigantius	119
101	—	(Cledonius)	**
102	—	(Cledonius)	**
103	31	Palladius	77
104	204	Olympius	173
105	203	Olympius	173
106	211	Olympius	178
107	83	Cledonius	106
108	85	Cledonius	106
109	84	Cledonius	106
110	34	Palladius	79
111	90	Eugenius	108
112	154	Celeusius	147
113	155	Celeusius	147
114	156	Celeusius	148
115	66	Theodore (of Tyana)	97
116	86	Eulalius	107
117	87	Eulalius	107
118	89	Eugenius	108
119	33	Palladius	78
120	45	Helladius	84
121	57	Theodore (of Tyana)	91
122	69	Theodore (of Tyana)	98
123	58	Theodore (of Tyana)	92
124	63	Theodore (of Tyana)	96
125	209	Olympius	176
126	212	Olympius	178
127	42	Helladius	83
128	178	Procopius	158
129	179	Procopius	159
130	180	Procopius	159
131	208	Olympius	176
132	143	Saturninus	142
133	145	Victor	143

134	146	Victor	143
135	99	Sophronius	113
136	147	Modarius	143
137	148	Modarius	144
138	157	Bosporius	149
139	59	Theodore (of Tyana)	92
140	210	Olympius	177
141	201	Olympius	171
142	202	Olympius	173
143	205	Olympius	174
144	206	Olympius	174
145	207	Verianus	175
146	213	Olympius	179
147	134	Asterius	135
148	135	Asterius	136
149	217	George	182
150	136	Asterius	136
151	39	Nectarius	80
152	67	Theodore (of Tyana)	97
153	158	Bosporius	149
154	214	Olympius	180
155	133	Asterius	134
156	137	Asterius	137
157	62	Theodore (of Tyana)	95
158	88	Eulalius	107
159	61	Theodore (of Tyana)	95
160	64	Theodore (of Tyana)	96
161	65	Theodore (of Tyana)	96
162	68	Theodore (of Tyana)	98
163	56	Theodore (of Tyana)	90
164	223	Timothy	185
165	225	Stagirius	186
166	226	Stagirius	187
167	43	Helladius	83
168	70	Photius	99
169	71	Strategius	99
170	32	Palladius	78
171	190	Amphilochius	164
172	44	Helladius	84
173	142	Postumianus	141
174	111	Eudoxius	121
175	112	Eudoxius	122
176	113	Eudoxius	122
177	115	Eudoxius	122
178	116	Eudoxius	122

ARRANGEMENT OF THE COLLECTION 53

179	117	Eudoxius	125
180	118	Eudoxius	126
181	144	Saturninus	142
182	80	Gregory (of Nyssa)	103
183	55	Theodore (of Tyana)	89
184	188	Amphilochius	163
185	38	Nectarius	80
186	37	Nectarius	80
187	114	Eudoxius	122
188	224	Stagirius	186
189	104	Eustochius	116
190	105	Eustochius	117
191	106	Eustochius	118
192	227	Stagirius	188
193	163	Vitalianus	151
194	164	Vitalianus	152
195	82	Gregory the Governor	105
196	215	Hecebolius	181
197	79	Gregory (of Nyssa)	102
198	219	Nemesius	183
199	218	Nemesius	183
200	220	Nemesius	184
201	221	Nemesius	185
202	—	(Nectarius)	**
203	232	Valentinianus	192
204	138	Adelphius	137
205	139	Adelphius	139
206	140	Adelphius	139
207	166	Jacob	152
208	167	Jacob	153
209	72	Castor	99
210	73	Castor	100
211	35	Cyriacus	79
212	54	Sacerdos	89
213	51	Sacerdos	88
214	53	Sacerdos	88
215	50	Sacerdos	87
216	46	Eudocius	85
217	47	Eudocius	85
218	48	Eudocius	86
219	40	Helladius	82
220	41	Helladius	83
221	49	Homophronius	87
222	239	Thecla	198
223	238	Thecla	196

224	129	Africanus	133
225	131	Hellebichus	134
226	161	Anysius	150
227	130	Ursus	133
228	108	Pansophius	120
229	109	Pansophius	120
230	110	Theodosius	120
231	198	Eusebius	169
232	229	Diocles	189
233	141	Ablabius	140
234	191	Olympianus	165
235	235	Adamantius	195
236	241	Libanius the Sophist	201
237	132	Macedonius	134
238	216	"The Brotherhood at Sannabodae"	181
239	92	Epiphanius	108
240	160	Meletius	150
241	—	(Aburgius)	**
242	222	Peter	185
243	—	(Evagrius)	**
244	242	Basilissa	201
245	25	Basil	73
246	28	Basil	75
247	29	Glycerius	77
248	30	Basil	77
249	—	(Flavian)	**

Translation of Gregory of Nazianzus's Letter Collection

Gr. Naz., *Ep.* 52
Late 383–early 384

To Nicobulus,

1. You're requesting flowers from the meadow in late autumn and arming the aged Nestor with your current demand for something expedient for eloquence from me, who long ago abandoned the delight of all discourse and society. 2. Yet you're not imposing upon me a struggle of Eurystheian[1] or Herculean proportions, but one quite gentle and suited to me, collecting for you as many of my epistles as I can. Now here it is! Put this sash[2] [*Il.* 14.219] around your books; it's designed not for love but for eloquence, not for display but for utility even in our own courtyard. 3. Each writer, more or less, has a signature style: my words are instructive in maxims and precepts whenever permissible. A father in eloquence always appears in a legitimate child no less than parents do in most of his bodily characteristics. Well, such are my features. 4. For your part, please give me back the very act of writing as well as the profit that you glean from what I write here. I could neither request nor demand any better reward, or anything more advantageous to the requester or more fitting to the giver, than this.

Gr. Naz., *Ep.* 53
Late 383–early 384

To Nicobulus,

1. Since I've always preferred the great Basil to myself, even if the opposite would have seemed true to him, still now I prefer him because of the truth no less than because of our friendship. I therefore offer my epistles with his set down first. 2. For I also desire that we be linked with each other in every way while simultaneously providing a model of measure and moderation to others.

Gr. Naz., *Ep.* 51
Late 383–early 384

To Nicobulus,

1. Of those who write epistles (since you request this too), some write ones longer than they should be, while others write ones that are too inadequate; both miss the right measure just as some people, when shooting at targets, come up too short and others overshoot. The failure is equal, even though it came about in opposite ways. 2. Necessity is the appropriate measure of epistles. One ought write neither too much when there are not many subjects nor too little when there are many. 3. Why? Should wisdom be measured by either the Persian rope [cf. Call., *Aet.,* frag. 1] or the infant-cubits[3] [cf. Philostr. Jun., *Im.* 1.5.1; Luc., *Rh. pr.* 6], and should we write so imperfectly that it is not actually writing, but rather an imitation of noonday shadows or lines that meet before your eyes, whose lengths diminish and are vaguely glimpsed rather than plainly seen, recognized by certain parts of their extremities, and are copies of copies, to speak in a fashionable way? We ought to hit the right measure squarely, fleeing immoderation on both sides. 4. Indeed, that's what I know about concision. As to clarity, here's the notable point: one ought to avoid highly stylized language as much as possible, and instead incline toward the conversational. And, to speak concisely, the very best epistle and the one that has the best qualities is the one that persuades both the commoner and the educated—the former being as though down among the masses, the latter as though above the masses—and is recognizable at once. Similarly, it would be tacky for a riddle to be understood and a letter to require interpretation. 5. The third feature of epistles is grace. This we should preserve if we're not to write letters utterly dry and devoid of

beauty, adornment, and polish, as they say—for instance, without practical maxims, proverbs, and sayings, or even jokes and riddles, things that make language sweet—but we ought not appear to be overly indulgent in them. For the former is boorish, the latter pretentious. 6. They should be used like purple dye in woven robes. We should admit figures of speech, but just a few and not shameless ones. We should toss away antitheses, parallels, and equal sentences to the sophists, and if we do employ them anywhere, we ought to do so in a mocking, not serious, way. 7. Here's the conclusion to my discourse, which I heard a refined man say about an eagle: when the birds were deciding the question of kingship, and each approached the others in their finest appearance, the eagle's most beautiful feature was that he did not think himself to be beautiful. It's most important that we keep unconcerned with beauty in our epistles and be as close as we can to naturalness. 8. My thoughts on epistles are such that I send them to you through an epistle. Perhaps you shouldn't hold me to them [in my own practice], since I'm busy with more important matters. As to anything else, you'll pour your own effort into it, being a good student, and refined men will teach you.

Gr. Naz., *Ep.* 54
Late 383–early 384?

To Nicobulus,

To laconicize is to compose not the fewest syllables, as you suppose, but the fewest about the most. Thus, I would even say that Homer is breviloquent and Antimachus prolix. How so? I judge length by subjects, not by letters.

Gr. Naz., *Ep.* 60
373–74

To Basil,

1. One part of executing your command is within my control, but the other part—and the greater part, I believe—is within Your Reverence's control. The part within my control pertains to effort and willingness. For at no time back then was I fleeing from your company; rather,[4] I always pursue it, and now I'm really yearning for it. 2. But the part within Your Holiness's control is the straightening out of our affairs. Indeed, I'm tending to my lady mother, as she has been worn down by illness for a while now. And if I wouldn't leave

her in an uncertain state, know well that I wouldn't be deprived of your presence. Only, help her with your prayers, one on behalf of her health and another on behalf of me for my journey.

Gr. Naz., *Ep.* 1
360–62

To Basil,

1. I confess that I lied when, because of our friendship and union while we were still in Athens, I made a promise to join you and practice philosophy with you. I have nothing better to say than that. 2. But I didn't lie willingly; rather, one law trumped another—the one mandating care for parents[5] over the one pertaining to friendship and intimacy.[6] 3. By no means would I continue to lie should you accept the following proposition: sometimes I'll join you, but occasionally you should be willing to join me so that all our affairs may be shared in friendship's equality of honor. In this way, I can still have your company without upsetting my parents.

Gr. Naz., *Ep.* 2[7]
360–62

To Basil,

1. Under your cross-examination, [I'll admit that] I can't stand the Tiberina,[8] with its mud and bad weather! You mudless tiptoer, you! You plains tramper! Soaring, aloft, borne about by the arrow of Abaris,[9] so that you escape Cappadocia despite being Cappadocian![10] 2.. Or do I have it wrong? Is it that you're pallid and cramped and take the sunshine as your only reward, while I'm the one who's getting fat, I'm the one who has a full belly, I'm the one who has no constraints placed upon him? 3. But those things don't apply to you: you live amid luxury and wealth while lounging about in the agora. I don't praise this. So quit slinging my mud at me—you didn't make your city, nor I my bad weather—or, in return for the mud, I'll chuck back at you hucksters and any other lousy thing that the cities offer.

Gr. Naz., *Ep.* 4
360–62 (after Gr. Naz., *Ep.* 2)

To Basil,

1. Go ahead, mock and disparage my region. Whether you're playing around or being serious doesn't matter. Simply let yourself

smile, take advantage of our education, and enjoy our friendship. Everything that comes from you pleases me—whatever it may be, however it may be. 2. It seems to me that you're scoffing at these regions not merely to scoff, but, if I catch your drift, to draw me to yourself, like those who dam up streams to draw them in a different direction. Your words[11] are always like this to me. 3. For my part, I'll admire your Pontus and Pontic burrow[12] as an abode fit for exile, what with the ridges that loom overhead; the beasts that put to the test your trust in the location; the isolated spot that lies down below, even if it is a mousehole with the august appellations of thinkery [Ar., *Nu*. 91–104], monastery, and school; the thickets of wild flora and the wreath of rugged mountains that puts shackles on you, not a crown; 4. the mediocre climate and the longed-for sun, which you can make out only as if through smoke, O Pontic and Sunless Cimmerians [*Od*. 11.13–19], sentenced not only to a six-month-long night (which, in fact, people say is the case) but also to not having even one unshaded part of being alive, the whole of life being one long night and truly the shadow of death [Ps 22(23):4], to use a phrase from scripture. 5. Shall I praise the road, both narrow and treacherous [cf. Matt 7:14]? Whether it leads to the Kingdom or to Hell, I don't know; for your sake, may it lead to the Kingdom! As to the region in between, what do you want? Should I falsely call it an Eden and the fount that was divided into the four sources from which the whole world takes drink [Gen 2:10–14], or a dry and waterless desert that some Moses will make habitable once he uses his staff to make a stone gush forth [Exod 17:1–6]? 6. For whatever escaped the rocks became dried-up gullies, and whatever escaped the gullies became thornbushes, and what loomed over the thornbushes became a cliff. The road on top is also steep and dangerous on either side; it focuses the mind of travelers and trains them for safety. 7. The river rages down below; to you, O Grandiloquent One and Maker of New Names, it must seem like the tranquil Strymon of Amphipolis,[13] but it is no richer in fish than in stones, and it feeds into no lake but rushes down into the deep. 8. For it is great and fearful, and it drowns out the psalmodies of those who stand over it. Compared to this, the cataracts and the catadupes are nothing![14] That's how loudly it inveighs against you day and night. 9. Rugged and impassible, muddy and undrinkable—its only beneficial aspect is that it doesn't sweep away your abode when the torrents and storms drive you crazy. 10. That's what I think about those Islands of the Blessed, if you are in fact blessed. 11. Go ahead, admire the crescent-shaped bends that choke off, rather than fortify, access to your foothills, the ridges that hang overhead—making for you a life like Tantalus's [cf. *Od.* 11.582–92]—and the drafts of cold air and the earth's ventholes that refresh you when you're worn out, 12. and the songbirds that do indeed sing, but about hunger, and do indeed fly, but over the desert. You say that no one comes for a visit except to go hunting, but you should also add, except to gaze upon you dead folk. 13. Maybe these words are too long for an epistle and too short for a comedy, but if you'll put up with my game in due measure,[15] you'll act rightly. If not, I'll add even more.

Gr. Naz., *Ep.* 5
360–62 (after Gr. Naz., *Ep.* 4)

To Basil,

1. Since you are putting up with my game in a measured way,[16] I'll also add the following. Here's my prelude, taken from Homer: "Go, change it up, and sing of the decoration inside" [cf. *Od.* 8.492].[17] A shelter without roof or door! A hearth without fire or smoke! Walls dried by fire lest we—Tantaluses and sentenced to thirst while standing in water—be bombarded by globules of mud! 2. That pitiful and foodless banquet to which, as though to the table of Alcinous,[18] not to the poverty of the lotus-eaters [cf. *Od.* 8.83–84, 91–97], I—young, shipwrecked, and suffering—was summoned from Cappadocia. 3. For I remember those so-called loaves and soups, but I shall also remember slipping my teeth on the morsels of food and then getting them mired down in the food and having to drag them out as if from a swamp. 4. You'll make a sanctimonious tragedy of these conditions, since it was out of your own bad experiences that you came to possess your grandiloquence. If the mighty woman (I mean your mother)—truly a caretaker of the poor!—had not rescued me right away by appearing in the nick of time like a harbor to those caught in a storm, I would have been long dead, pitied instead of praised for my Pontic trust. 5. How could I pass by those vegetableless gardens that don't deserve the name? And the pile of Augean manure [cf. Apollod., *Bib.* 2.5.5] that we cleared out of the house and

used to fill the gardens after I, a vintner, and you, a glutton, dragged the dung-bearing[19] wagon with these necks and these hands that still bear the scars of the toils—O Earth, Sun, Air, and Virtue [cf. Aeschin., *Ctes.* 260; D., *Or.* 18.127?]! (for I can write in a tragic style too)—not to bridge the Hellespont [Hdt., *Hist.* 7.33–36] but to flatten out a riverbank? 6. So if you're not upset by my words, neither at all am I. But if you are, how much more am I by what happened there! I'll let the rest slide out of respect for the other people whom I quite enjoyed.

Gr. Naz., *Ep.* 6
360–62 (after Gr. Naz., *Ep.* 5)

To Basil,

1. What I previously wrote about your Pontic lifestyle was just me playing around, not being serious. What I write now, though, is me at my most serious. 2. Who would put me for one month in those former days [cf. Job 29:2] when I lived luxuriously with you in hardship? For our voluntary distress was preferable to involuntary delight. 3. Who would give me those psalmodies, the vigils, the prayerful visitations to God, and the seemingly immaterial and incorporeal life? Who among the brothers divinized and elevated by you would give me intimacy and harmony? 4. Who would give me a craving for and an incitement to virtue, which we safeguarded in written rules and canons? Who would give me diligence for the divine scriptures and the light within them that is discovered only with the guidance of the Spirit? 5. Or—if I may turn to smaller, less important matters—who would give me my daily services and personal labors? Who would give me the wood-gathering and stonecutting? Who would give me the gardening work and ditchdigging? Who would give me the golden plane tree, more valuable even than that of Xerxes [Hdt., *Hist.* 7.31], under which was seated not an enfeebled king but a diligent monk?[20] 6. "It was I who planted it, Apollos who watered it"—that is, Your Dignity—"but God who increased it" [1 Cor 3:6] for our honor, to keep a memento of our diligence at your property, just like Aaron's blossoming rod is said and believed to be in the ark [Num 17:8–10]. 7. It's really quite easy to pray for these things, but not so much to receive them. But come be with me, breathe with me, work with me on virtue, and preserve with

me the profit we used to cull through our prayers, lest we fade little by little like a shadow when the day comes to a close. 8. Oh, may I breathe you in more than the air! I live only when I'm with you either in person or, if I'm absent, in my thoughts.

Gr. Naz., *Ep.* 46
370–74[21]

To Basil,[22]

1. How can your affairs be small grapes to me, my divine and sacred captain? What kind of word escapes the fence of your teeth [*Il.* 4.350]? How have you been so bold as to say this (to be a bit bold myself)? How could your mind come up with the idea, or your ink write it, or your paper accept it? 2. Eloquence! Athens! Virtues! The sweat produced by eloquence! Look, you're even turning me into a member of a tragic chorus by what you write! Are you ignorant of me or yourself—the eye of the world, the great voice and bugle [Isa 27:13; Matt 24:31], the palace[23] of eloquence? 3. Are your concerns trivial to Gregory? By what could anyone upon the earth be awestruck if not Gregory by you? 4. There is among the seasons one springtime, among the stars one sun, around all things one sky, over all things your voice, if I'm sufficient to decide such matters and if you haven't tricked me with a spell (which I don't think happened). 5. If you're going to charge me with not being awestruck in proportion to Your Dignity, charge it against all human beings too! For no one else has been or will be awestruck in a worthy manner except for you and Your Grandiloquence, if one could praise oneself and if the custom of eloquence allowed it. 6. But if I'm charged with casting scorn, why not with insanity first? Or rather, are you irritated that I'm practicing philosophy? Let me say this: it alone is more exalted than Your Eloquence.

Gr. Naz., *Ep.* 8
362

To Basil,

1. I praise the introduction to your epistle—but what of yours isn't praiseworthy? You too were sentenced, just like I had written about myself when I was forced into the priest's rank. 2. Yet this was not our goal: if ever any were, we stand as reliable witnesses to each other of our affection for the ordinary and low-standing philosophy. 3. But

perhaps it's better that this cannot be—I don't know what to say as long as I'm ignorant of the Spirit's plan. 4. Now that it has happened, we must put up with it, as is certainly plain to me, especially because this critical time introduces many heretical tongues against us,[24] and I must not put either my own life or the hopes of those who have trusted me to shame.

Gr. Naz., *Ep.* 16
Mid-360s

To Eusebius,

1. Since I'm crafting my eloquence for a man who feels no affection for falsehood and who is the quickest of all at detecting it in another person, even if tightly interwoven among clever and manifold labyrinths, and moreover, since artifice is no friend of mine (I'll admit it, even if it's a bit vulgar to do so), given that I have been formed and molded by the Word, I therefore write the present words. 2. Accept my frankness, or you'll no doubt do a disservice to the truth by robbing me of my freedom and forcing me to keep the anguish of my distress within myself like a subcutaneous and malignant disease. 3. For my part, I'm glad that you pay honor to me (even if I am just a [regular] human being, as someone said long ago [cf. Acts 14:15?]) and summon me to synods and spiritual assemblies. 4. However, I cannot abide by the insult that Your Reverence issued, and still issues, against my most honorable brother Basil,[25] whom I have taken from the beginning, and still have now, as a partner in life, word, and the most exalted philosophical practice—and I could hardly fault myself for my judgment of him. 5. Thus let me speak in a measured way[26] so that I don't seem to praise myself by showing my admiration for his qualities. 6. By dishonoring him and honoring me, you come off as patting a man on the back with one hand while slapping his face with the other,[27] or removing the foundation of a house while painting its walls in various colors and beautifying its exterior. 7. Well, should you be persuaded by me, here's what you'll do (and I expect to be heeded, for that's the right thing): if you were to treat him in an equitable way, he would give you the same treatment. But like a shadow to the body, I, being of little account and ready for peace, will follow him. 8. I'm not doing so in a pathetic manner with the result that I only occasionally intend to

practice philosophy and belong to the better portion [cf. Luke 10:42] while I neglect the chief point of my account—affection, especially for such an important man and priest, whom I recognize to be the best of everyone I know in life, word, and conduct. For my distress will not overshadow the truth.

Gr. Naz., *Ep.* 17
Mid-360s (after Gr. Naz., *Ep.* 16)

To Eusebius,

1. I didn't write my epistle with a tone more insolent (as you complained) than spiritual or philosophical—and it was reasonable to do so, so long as it didn't also bring distress against "the most eloquent Gregory."[28] 2. For even if you hold a superior rank to me,[29] you should still grant me a modicum of liberty and just frankness. Therefore, be nicer to me! 3. But if you end up deciding that my epistle is that of a household slave and not that of someone obliged to look you in the eye, of course I'll take your punches without shedding a tear. Or will I be held accountable for that too? Everyone but Your Reverence deserves to suffer that. For it belongs to the high-minded man to accept the liberty of friends rather than the flattery of enemies.

Gr. Naz., *Ep.* 18
Mid-360s (after Gr. Naz., *Ep.* 17)

To Eusebius,

1. I have not been mean-spirited toward Your Reverence at all! Don't accuse me of that! But having acted with a small degree of liberty and boldness just to cool and assuage my vexed state, I now admit defeat: I am bowed down, I went and pledged myself to the canon. 2. And why wouldn't I, acquainted as I am with you and the laws of the Spirit? But even if I was far too mean-spirited and ignoble, the current situation does not allow you to keep dwelling on it, what with the beasts running roughshod through the church and your own valiance and manliness so purely and genuinely waging war on behalf of the church.[30] 3. If it seems right, then, I'll come and help you with prayers, join you in the contest, serve you, and anoint you with cries of encouragement like children who are commanded to cheer for the best combatant.

Gr. Naz., *Ep.* 19
Mid-360s (after Gr. Naz., *Ep.* 16–18)

To Basil,

1. It's time for sound judgment and endurance, so that no one appears manlier than us and so that all our sweat and toils don't suddenly amount to nothing. Why do I write these words, and from what position? 2. Our bishop, the most God-beloved Eusebius (from now on, we must think of and write about him like this), has a quite conciliating and friendly attitude toward us, and, like iron in fire, he is softening with time. 3. And I also imagine that a letter of exhortation and invitation is on its way to you, as he indicated to me and as many of those who plainly know his affairs persuaded me. 4. Let's beat him to the punch by either making a personal appearance or writing him a letter, or, better yet, by first sending him a letter and then making a personal appearance lest, when defeated later, we be put to shame since we could have claimed a victory by taking the defeat in a noble and philosophical way, something that many people demand from us. 5. Come on, listen to me for that very reason, and because of the critical time at hand, when a cohort of heretics is ravaging the church, some of whom are already here and stirring up trouble, others of whom will be here shortly, according to a report. 6. I fear they'll drag off the word of truth if the spirit of Bezalel [cf. Exod 31:1–5, 35:30–33],[31] the sage architect of strong arguments and teachings, is not roused as soon as possible. 7. But if you think I should be there too, spending time and making the rounds with you, I'll not run away from this.

Gr. Naz., *Ep.* 58
372–74[32]

To Basil,

1. From the beginning and still now, I have regarded you as my guide in life, my teacher of doctrines, and everything fine that someone might say. Even if someone else is a praiser of your qualities, he is so either wholly alongside me or after me—so inferior am I to Your Reverence and so purely am I yours. And it's no surprise: where intimacy is greater, the experience is greater, and where experience is more abundant, the testimony is more complete. 2. And if being alive offered me any further advantage, it would be your

friendship and intimacy. That's how I feel about these things; I hope it continues to be so! What I write now, though, I write unwillingly, but I write nonetheless. Don't be irritated with me, or it is I who will be irritated if I should not be trusted to say and write these words to you with goodwill.

3. Many of those who rightly think that our interests are united have condemned us for not being more assertive about the faith. Some publicly charge us with impiety, others cowardice. Impiety, from those who believe our views are unsound; cowardice, from those who allege timidity. Why do I even need to mention the concerns of other people? Let me explain to you what recently happened.

4. There was a symposium, and more than a few of our notable friends took part in the symposium; among them was also a man who belonged to those who wear the name and habit of piety.[33] There was no drinking yet, but as usually happens at symposia, there was a discussion about us, who were proposed as the subject [of discussion] in the place of another topic. Since everyone admires your qualities and agrees that we practice philosophy equally and speaks of our friendship, Athens, and our cooperation and concord in all things, the so-called philosopher reckoned the affair a travesty.

5. "What's this, gentlemen?" he said, yelling quite thunderously. "What liars and flatterers you are! If it seems right, let the men be praised for other things; I would have no objection. But I'm not conceding the main point: Basil is praised erroneously for his orthodoxy, and so too is Gregory; the former betrayed the faith in his discourses, and the latter was an accomplice to the betrayal by tolerating it." 6. "How can this be," I said, "you fool, you new Dathan and Abiron [Num 16:1–40] in your madness? Where do you get off coming to me as a dictator of doctrine? How are you making yourself a judge of important matters?" 7. "Just now I have come," he said, "from the commemoration of the martyr Eupsychius"[34]—this is how he was—"and there I heard the great Basil speaking of the Father and Son as God excellently and perfectly, and as no one else could so easily. But he brushed off the Spirit," and he compared you to rivers that run past rocks while scooping up sand.[35] 8. And looking at me, he said, "For your part, admirable man, you already thus speak of the Spirit as God"—and he recalled some phrase of mine that I employed

to speak of God at a crowded synod before applying this famous scriptural passage to the Spirit: "For how long will we hide the lamp under the bushel?" [Matt 5:15]—"but [Basil] makes faint gestures and merely sketches his account, but does not speak the truth with frankness, overwhelming his audience in a more political than pious way and shrouding his duplicity with the force of his discourse."

9. "That's true," I said, "only because I practice my philosophy outside of danger, lying in hiding, remaining unknown to the masses—neither what I say nor that I speak is even approximately known. But [Basil's] discourse is more important, because it is more conspicuous, on account of who he is and his church. 10. Everything he says is public, and the fighting around him is fierce in that heretics strive to lay hold of his literal meaning and even Basil himself, so that what[36] is cast out of the church is, more or less, the sole remaining spark of truth and life-giving power, while everything within his jurisdiction is overtaken and vice takes root in the city and, from the church, as if a base of operations, overruns the entire community. 11. So, while we briefly yield to the season like a passing cloud, it is better to use discretion than to be demolished by the clarity of our proclamation. For no harm comes to us from recognizing the Spirit as God from [Basil's] other phrases that lead to this conclusion (for the truth does not reside in one's vocalization more than in one's thought); however, for the truth to be persecuted because of one man would be a substantial loss to the church."

12. Those who were present didn't accept my discretion, as if it were a stale joke made at their expense. Instead, they railed against me too, that my discretion was more cowardice than strategic choice, that it's much better to use the truth to guard our interests than to handicap them and not add any further adherents through my so-called discretion. 13. The particulars, then, of what I said, what I heard, and how irritated I became at my detractors (nearly beyond the due measure and my usual style) would be too long to describe now and perhaps unnecessary. 14. The end of my story is that I thus sent them away. But you, my divine and sacred captain, must teach me just how far I should advance in speaking of the Spirit as God, what phrases I should employ, and the extent to which I should use discretion, so that I can use them against our opponents. 15. For me,

as the one who knows you and your interests better than everyone else, and who has both given and received assurance on these questions often, to lack instruction on this now would be the silliest and sorriest thing of all.

Gr. Naz., *Ep.* 59
372–74

To Basil,

1. A smarter person would have foreseen this,[37] but I had no fear in writing to you, old-fashioned and foolish as I am. My letter upset you, but, let me say, neither rightly nor fairly but quite unnecessarily. 2. And while you haven't confessed your dismay, you haven't concealed it either; if you did, you did so skillfully, by veiling the appearance of dismay as if with a shameful mask. 3. As for me, if I acted deceptively and maliciously, I would be hurt not so much by your dismay as by the truth, but if simply and with my customary goodwill, I would indict my own sins, not your disposition. However, you would do well to get these things straightened out yourself instead of feeling contempt for your advisers. 4. Then you'll have a good view of your own situation and be able to advise others on such matters. If God grants it, you readily have me, who will be present, and who will fight on your side and contribute whatever I can. For who would be reticent? Who wouldn't be confident to speak and fight for the truth under and alongside you?

Gr. Naz., *Ep.* 48[38]
Easter 372

To Basil,

1. Have you not stopped bad-mouthing me as uneducated, dense, unfriendly, and undeserving of life because I dared to take note of what I've suffered? Even you would have to admit that I'm doing nothing else wrong, nor, as far as I can tell, have I pointed out, to a small or large degree, the vices that have materialized around you—and may I not know of it!—with this sole exception: I knew that I had been tricked—yes, after quite a long time, but I knew it. 2. And I accuse the throne of suddenly making you more exalted than me. I'm also tired of being held accountable for your actions and of having to defend myself to those who plainly know our original and current relationship. Of the things I'm going through,

this is the most ridiculous, or the most pitiable, that the same person should be both injured and held accountable, which is precisely what has happened to me now. 3. Some hold me accountable for one thing and for whatever each wants according to his character or the measure of his anger against me. The most beneficent of them charge me with disdain, contempt, and my being cast aside as need be, like the cheapest and most worthless chattel, or like those scaffolds upon which arches stand but which, after construction, are removed and thrown away. 4. So I'll let them rejoice and say what they may; no one will stifle the autonomy of my tongue. But for my wage, pay me the happy and empty hopes you yourself procured against those who propagate the slander, that it was because of honor that you insulted me, as if I were disposable and available for precisely these things. 5. For my part, I'll make myself as clear as I can; don't be angry with me, for I'll repeat what I also said at the precise moment of the suffering, although not so much that I get too fired up or become so dismayed at what happened that my thoughts are stolen away and I forget what I said: 6. "I'll not acquire weapons or learn tactics that I haven't previously learned, back when the occasion seemed more intense, with everyone armed and running riot (you know the diseases of the weak). Nor will I support the bellicose Anthimus: although he is an untimely warrior, I am unarmed, unwarlike, and quite susceptible to wounds. 7. Rather, take him to battle yourself, if that's what pleases you (for necessity often makes weaklings become warriors), or seek out those who will fight when he grabs your mules while watching the straits, just like Amalek of old, who shut in Israel [Exod 17:8–16]. But before everything, give me some tranquility! 8. Why should I fight for pups and birds that belong to other people as if, in fact, for souls and canons?[39] Why should I defraud the metropolis of the luminous inhabitants of Sasima, or lay bare and reveal the secret of your intention when it ought to be concealed?"[40] 9. But as for you, man up and be powerful! Draw all glory to yourself like rivers do torrents, preferring neither friendship nor intimacy to virtue and piety. As a result, you'll come off not as the sort who worries about the consequences of his actions but as someone who belongs to the one Spirit. 10. As for me, I'll gain this alone from your friendship: distrust of friends and treating nothing as preferable to God.

Gr. Naz., *Ep.* 49
Easter 372

To Basil,

1. You charge me with idleness and lethargy because I haven't taken hold of Sasima, or conducted myself like a bishop, or armed you for battle against each other, as if I were meat thrown to dogs. But to me the greatest activity is inactivity. 2. So that you recognize one of my virtues, [let me say that] I strive so eagerly for the quiet life that I think, in this regard, everyone holds me as a standard of highmindedness! 3. Were everyone to imitate me, the churches would have no trouble and the faith—now a weapon to each of the contenders—would not be brushed aside.

Gr. Naz., *Ep.* 50
Easter 372

To Basil,

1. So hotly and coltlike do you prance about in your letter! And as you are just now getting a taste of glory, it's no surprise that you want to parade for me whatever glory you come across, so that you may thus make yourself even more august, just like painters who paint beautiful things. 2. It seems to me, though, that a detailed description of everything—the concerns of bishops and the parts of my epistle that disgust you (my starting point, my argument, and my conclusion)—is too long for an epistle and a task suited not to a formal defense but rather to a narrative history. 3. To tell you as concisely as possible, the most noble Anthimus came to me along with some bishops, either to pay my father a visit (for this seemed to be the case) or to pursue what he [Anthimus] pursued. 4. He entered into a great trial regarding many subjects—the provinces, Sasima, Limna,[41] my own appointment—while doting, interrogating, threatening, pleading, blaming, lauding, and demarcating his own jurisdiction, as though it were right for us to look only to him and his new metropolis, since it is the greater one. 5. "Why are you including my city within your jurisdiction, since I reckon my church [in Caesarea] as truly and from long ago the mother of the churches?" He finally went away without success, after he huffed and puffed and prosecuted me for being a Basilist, as if it were Philippism [cf. D., *Or.* 18.294].[42] 6. Do I appear to have done you wrong in this regard?

I don't think so. But take a close look at the epistle's content, if it stands against me as an insolent man.[43] They issued me a synodical subpoena, but when I opposed it and declared it an insult, they thought that the next best thing was to summon you through me to deliberate on these matters. 7. Lest their initial plan go into effect,[44] I supported this course of action, deciding that everything should be up to you: if, where, and when exactly you want to meet them. This is the behavior of someone who pays honor, not someone who insults. And since I'm doing nothing wrong in this matter, tell me what remains. If it's necessary that you must learn about it from me, I will read you Anthimus's epistle that he—insulting, chiding, and singing something like a victory ode against us at our defeat—sent to me when he took over Limna as I protested and issued threats. 8. Furthermore, is there any reason for me, on the one hand, to butt heads with him because of you and, on the other, to displease you by gratifying him? If for no other reason than because we are both priests, O Admirable Man, you should have learned of these matters earlier and not have issued insults back then. 9. But if you remain too ostentatious and ambitious, and continue to lecture me from a superior position, as a metropolitan bishop to a micropolitan bishop, or even an apolitan bishop,[45] I too have pride with which to oppose yours. That's altogether the easiest, and perhaps the more sensible, way.

Gr. Naz., Ep. 45
Late 370

To Basil,

1. Once I knew that you had been placed on the exalted throne and that the Spirit had prevailed in displaying the lamp on the lampstand [Matt 5:15]—not that it shone faintly before—I confess that yes, I was pleased. And why wouldn't I be, seeing as I did the community of the church in bad shape and needing real guidance? 2. But I did not run straight [to you], nor will I, not even if you were to make this request yourself—first of all, so that you may preserve your solemnity and not appear to be gathering up your partisans out of some tactlessness and excitement, as your detractors might say, 3. and second, so that I may busy myself with something steady and irreproachable. "When, then, will you come?" you'll probably say, "and for how long will you avoid me?" For as long as God bids, and

until the shadows of the current attackers and bewitchers have passed by. 4. For the lepers, I know plainly, won't keep David shut out of Jerusalem for much longer [2 Kgs 5:6–7].

> Gr. Naz., *Ep.* 47
> 372–74

To Basil,

1. I'm learning that you are disturbed by the recent innovation and that you are taking issue with a certain sophistic officiousness, customary of those in power—and it's no surprise. For I'm not ignorant of their jealousy and that many members of your entourage use you to look to their own interests and kindle the spark of pettiness. 2. Well, when it comes to that, I have no fear that, in these predicaments, you are suffering unphilosophically or in a manner unworthy of yourself and me. However, I also think that now is the time when my Basil will become especially distinguished—when the philosophy that you've collected for yourself at every stage of life will be put on full display—and will rise above the abuses like a high wave and remain unshaken while others quiver. 3. But if it seems right, I'll also be present in person, perhaps to share an opinion (as if the sea needs water and you an adviser!). I will, in any event, profit from it and treat our being insulted together philosophically.

> Gr. Naz., *Ep.* 40[46]
> Summer 370

To Basil,

1. Don't be surprised if I seem to say something strange, something no one has ever told you. By my lights, you seem to have the reputation of a man who is established, steady, and firm in his thinking, yet you deliberate and act with more simplicity than steadiness. 2. For someone free of vice is slower to suspect vice, such as in the current situation. You summoned me to the metropolis[47] for a council that would appoint a bishop. And since it was plausible and persuasive, the pretext was this: you seemed to be ill, breathing your last, yearning to see me and to speak about your funeral arrangements—I didn't know what would happen or what my presence could contribute to the matter. 3. Feeling my heart sink at the prospect, I got a move on. For is there anything more important to me than your life or more distressful to me than your departure?

I let out streams of tears, I moaned, and only then did I first begin to feel myself being unphilosophically disposed—for what part of your funeral speech did I not complete? 4. But when I realized that bishops were gathering in the city, I checked my haste and wondered, first of all, if you had neither observed proper decorum nor leashed the tongues of the masses, which quickly abuse the guileless; second, if you don't think that these things are fitting for you and me, for whom word, life, and all things are shared, being joined together, as we are, by God from the beginning; and third (I must say this too), whether you thought that such appointments belong to the more reverent individuals but not to the more powerful and to those more at home among the crowds. 5. For these reasons, then, I turned around and went back. But if you too think it good, let flight from intervening troubles and wicked suggestions be the decided course of action. I'll see Your Reverence whenever the matters are set in order and the time is right, and I'll rebuke you even more severely.

Gr. Naz., Ep. 245
Date unknown

To Basil,

The mime, as you style him, but a reverent man, as I do, asked me to write to you so that he would be clearly heard.

Gr. Naz., Ep. 41[48]
Summer 370

To the Church of Caesarea,

1. I am but a mere shepherd who has presided over a little flock and who ranks low among servants of the Spirit. Grace, though, is neither confined to nor circumscribed by locations. 2. Therefore, and especially since my discourse pertains to shared and important concerns, let my frankness be delivered both to the little and to those who deliberate with much gray hair, a trait that perhaps betokens greater wisdom than most. 3. You are deliberating not about trifles or happenstances but about things that compel the community to go in one direction or another, depending on whether they go well or badly. For my discourse to you concerns the church, on whose behalf Christ suffered, and the individual who will present it to God [cf. Eph 5:27] and lead it. 4. The eye is the lamp of the body, as we have heard [Matt 6:22]—it not only sees and is seen corporeally but also

contemplates and is contemplated spiritually—but the bishop is the lamp of the church, a point obvious to you even if I hadn't written it. 5. Accordingly, it must be the case that, just as the body is guided well when it's clean but poorly when it's unclean, the same holds true in the case of the church with respect to its presider. It can go in one of two ways: with him it can risk complete ruin or obtain complete salvation. 6. So take heed for the whole church, as the body of Christ [cf. Col 1:24], but especially for your own, which from the beginning was, currently is, and is regarded as the mother of nearly all the churches, and the one to which the community looks, like a ring circumscribing its center point, not only because of the orthodoxy proclaimed by all [its bishops] from long ago but also because of the grace of concord that God has clearly bestowed upon it. 7. So then, after you summoned me to an examination about this matter too, acting correctly and canonically, I was vanquished by old age and illness; it would be best and most pleasant to me in every way if I were present in person, with the Spirit having strengthened me (for nothing is unbelievable to believers), so that I would both help you out in some way and partake of the blessing in person. But if the severity of my infirmity should prevail, I can at least help in absentia.

8. I'm convinced that other candidates among you are worthy of the presidency, owing to the greatness of the city, which has been governed accordingly and by such great men from long ago. But of the honorable among you, I can prefer no one to my most God-beloved son Basil the priest (I speak with God as my witness), a man purified in both life and word, and the only person among everyone—or at least him especially—able in both respects to resist the present age and to check the heretics' garrulousness. 9. I am also writing these words to the priests, monks, dignitaries, city councilors, and all the people. If this, then, seems right and my vote holds sway, since it is so correct and sound, [and] since it is reckoned with God, I am and will be present spiritually, or rather, I have already cast my hand and I remain confident in the Spirit. 10. But if another choice and not this one seems right and these important things are decided against the interest of country and kinship, and the turbulent hand again drags precision away, you would be doing what pleases yourselves, while I, for my part, would draw back into myself.

Gr. Naz., *Ep.* 43[49]
Summer 370

To the Bishops,

1. How sweet you are, benevolent and abounding in love! Seeing that you'll make a resolution regarding the bishop, I imagine, you have summoned me to the metropolis. At least, this is the feeling I'm getting from you in spite of the fact that you have not publicly announced the necessity of my presence, or even the location or time; you just suddenly indicated to me that you had begun, 2. like certain people who don't think to pay honor or who are unenthusiastic about having partners, but who avoid my presence so that they don't run into me, who is unwilling. That's how you are, and I'll put up with the insult. I will, however, offer my support, such as it is—for that's how I am. 3. Obviously, some have nominated certain individuals, each in line with his own temperament and estate, which is bound to happen in important situations. For my part, I can prefer no one, not even someone devout, to my most honorable son Basil the priest. 4. For among those we know, who would we find more tested in life or more powerful in speech, and thoroughly trained on all sides in the beauty of virtue? But if weakness is an allegation, [let me remind you that] you're nominating not an athlete but a teacher, someone who can, to some degree, simultaneously strengthen and prop up the weak, whoever they might be. 5. If you were to receive this vote of mine, I would be present and participate either spiritually or even bodily. But if you're heading toward foregone conclusions, and if alliances shall prevail against justice, I am glad to be overlooked. Let that be your task, but keep ours in your prayers.

Gr. Naz., *Ep.* 246 (= Bas. *Ep.* 169)
After 370

To Basil,

1. You have gracefully undertaken this courteous and compassionate task of rounding up the captives of the despicable Glycerius (for the time being, I must write like this) and by concealing our shared disgrace as much as possible. Nevertheless, now that you've learned of my complaints against him, Your Reverence should thus undo the dishonor. 2. I appointed this Glycerius, someone you currently regard as imposing and august, as deacon of the church at Venasa[50] so that he

would both minister to the priest and manage the work of the church. Even if he is intractable in some respects, at least he's not averse to manual labor. 3. But as soon as he was settled, he neglected the work as if there had never been any to begin with! He rounded up some pitiful virgins under his own authority and sovereign power and tried to lead a company of them, with some joining him willingly (you know the readiness of youths about such things) and others unwillingly. After conferring the name and habit of patriarch upon himself, he suddenly gave himself an air of authority. 4. He came to it not by means of a righteous and pious procedure, but to procure a means of livelihood for himself, as anyone does with one profession or another. Little by little, he made the entire church unstable, by despising his own priest (a man respectable for his conduct and age), despising the rural bishop and me (as if we're worthless), and confusing and disturbing the city and the whole priesthood at all times. 5. And finally, because he was slightly censured by a statement that the rural bishop and I made, that he not hold us in such low regard (for he was also training the young people in the same madness), he contrived quite a daring and savage deed. 6. He became a fugitive by carrying off as many virgins as he could and watching over them during the night. These things will seem especially horrifying to you. Take note of the occasion too: the synod was convened there and a crowd had come together from every side, as usually happens. He marched in his own chorus, dancing around and followed[51] by young men, inspiring great disgust among the reverent and a lot of laughter among the dissolute and those ready with the tongue. 7. And these atrocities didn't satisfy him, even though they were outrageous enough. This admirable young man, along with his band of pirates, has gone so far as to wantonly insult and dishonor the virgins' parents, who, as I'm learning, cannot bear their childlessness, want to recall[52] the dispersion, and fall down at their daughters' feet with the usual lamentations. Don't let these things appear tolerable to Your Reverence, for the ridicule is shared by all of us; make a point of commanding him to return with the virgins. 8. He would get some degree of leniency should he return with your letter. If not, well, send the virgins back to their mother, the church. 9. And if this can't be done, at the very least don't allow those who want to return home to be bullied, but decree that they do return; otherwise, I must testify before God and humanity that they don't possess virtue and that they stand in violation of the church's rules. It would be best for Glycerius to return with a full understanding of his error and an appropriate self-possession. If not, let him be deposed of his ministry.

Gr. Naz., *Ep.* 247 (= Bas. *Ep.* 170)
After 370

To Glycerius,

1. How much longer will you continue in your madness, and resolve on a wicked course for yourself, and provoke me, and shame the common order of monks? Return to me, then, confident in the God whose leniency I imitate. 2. For even if I censure you like a father, I'll also pardon you like a father. You have my word, for there are many others who also supplicate me, and before all of them your priest, whose gray hair and good heart I respect. 3. If you keep your distance from me, you'll have completely fallen from your rank, and you shall fall from God along with your robe and the melodies with which you lead the young women not to God but toward perdition.

Gr. Naz., *Ep.* 248 (= Bas. *Ep.* 171)
After 370 (after Gr. Naz., *Ep.* 246–47)

To Basil,

1. The day before yesterday, I sent you a letter about Glycerius and the virgins.[53] As of today they have not yet returned; I don't know the reason or the circumstances. I don't want to lay this charge against you, that you're doing this to malign me either because you hold a grudge against me or because you're doing a favor for others. 2. Since they have nothing to fear, then, let them come. As for you, be the guarantor of this promise. For I too feel the pain of severed limbs, if they were rightly severed. But should they resist, let them be a burden for others and let my hands be washed of the affair.

Gr. Naz., *Ep.* 103
382

To Palladius,[54]

1. If someone should ask me, "What's the best thing in life?," I would say, "Friends." "Who among them should we honor most?" I would say, "The good ones." "And who do you identify as first among those?" I know that I would put no other before Your Virtue. 2. And

I'm writing these words not to flatter your position of power but, by not omitting anything under your power, to honor your character, whose herald I am, albeit a small one—not only your herald but also your fellow combatant, enhancing your power with my prayers. 3. I intended to stop my epistle right here, but, given that I not only revere the divinity but also ask for acts of beneficence, accept your supplicant Euphemius so long as you're not annoyed by me (for my affairs cause you no annoyance; I can compare this request to previous ones) but induced to remember me. 4. Again I'm introducing him to you, and again I'm beseeching you not only to welcome the young man in a beneficent manner but also to excuse my slowness, since I've been busy about my little house tending urgently to the affairs of orphans, and to guide him onward for my honor and the glory of Your Excellence. 5. For while there are many whom you have treated well, and will treat well, he'll bring you no less distinction, as I would inform you if I were there in person. Even now, I deserve to be trusted, and he deserves pity because of his orphanhood and love because of his character, not to mention because of our blood relation.

Gr. Naz., *Ep.* 170
Summer 381–early 384

To Palladius,

1. It's not because of my audacity that I'm confident in sending you letters frequently, but because of your clemency. Since I cannot be any other way—God has designed me like this!—I take no surfeit from conversing with you by letter. 2. But to my most honorable son and fellow priest Sacerdos (whom I have especially loved and continue to love as a genuine practitioner of philosophy and someone united with God through his way of life), as he, because of you, rushes for the sake of his household to the great city, I don't know what greater gift I could give than making him known to Your Excellence.

Gr. Naz., *Ep.* 119[55]
Easter 382

To Palladius,

When I was fasting, I put my tongue to death with Christ, and I raised it up with his resurrection. To me, this is the mystery of quietude, that I may offer the sacrifice of purified speech in the same way that I offered the sacrifice of an unspeaking mind.

Gr. Naz., *Ep.* 110
Easter 382

To Palladius,

This is a new style of correction: since I didn't restrain my tongue with quietude when I was speaking, I have learned to keep silent, training like with like. This is also Christ's law [cf. Rom 3:20, 28; Gal 2:16]: since he does not purify us by issuing laws, he tames the human being with humanity according to the great beneficence of his ministration for us.

Gr. Naz., *Ep.* 211
Summer 381–early 384

To Cyriacus,

1. I'm certain that you honor reverent people and perform acts of kindness for the poor. Now you have an opportunity to do both. Here's how. My most honorable, God-beloved son and fellow priest Sacerdos is, because of his piety and zeal for the matter, the head of a hospital crowded with those who bear the marks of disease. 2. Thanks to the donation of the most honorable Castor, the hospital serves the Liriand and Caberine properties,[56] which lie adjacent to his estate and help to fund the hospital. 3. By liberating them from every abuse,[57] you'll furnish the poor with no small part of their cure, and you'll furnish yourself with no small part of the recompense owed, as you know, to the pious. 4. It's clear that, having rushed at once toward this act of beneficence, you'll be giving forethought to your future security, because, however Your Sagacity contrives it, whoever intends to be wicked around these regions cannot be.

Gr. Naz., *Ep.* 91
Spring 382

To Nectarius,

1. My situation is as it is. I live quietly without war and politics, cherishing the risk-free prize of verbal stillness[58] before everything. I've gained some profit from tranquility too now that, by the mercy of God, I've sufficiently recovered from my illness. 2. You are prospering, though, and exercising your reign, as the divine David says [Ps 44:5(45:6)]. May God, who honors you with the priesthood, share in it with you and hold it in higher favor than every insult! 3. That we might give each other a demonstration of confidence and not

succumb to any human passion while we stand before God, I'm putting some requests to you and you should eagerly assent to me. 4. For a host of reasons, I'm worried about my son the most genuine Pancratius. Please accept him graciously and recommend him to your keener friends so that he may obtain his goal. 5. His goal is to receive freedom from public service with a military appointment, since no single career path is unmolested by bad people, as you too know.

Gr. Naz., Ep. 186
Spring 382–early 384

To Nectarius,

1. What would you have done had I brought you my problems in person? No doubt you would have wholly exerted yourself to free me from abuse, if I must surmise from past experiences. 2. Now too, do me this favor through my most courteous cousin[59] as she, through me, falls prostrate before you, who respects the supplicant's age; you who respects her disposition and reverent bearing, uncommon among most women; 3. you who respects, in addition to her other qualities, a woman's freedom from social conflict and the fact that she's now having problems with her relatives; you who, before all else, respects my exhortation. 4. What's important in this favor is your haste in delivering the beneficence that I request. For even the unjust judge in the gospel gave the benefaction to the widow, but only after much supplication and assiduity [Luke 18:17]. 5. From you we need speediness so that she doesn't get worn down in a foreign country by anxieties and miseries, although I most plainly know that Your Godliness will make her feel at home in a foreign place.

Gr. Naz., Ep. 185
Mid-383–early 384?[60]

To Nectarius,

1. Whenever someone praises one of your qualities and everyone puts forward your good reputation as if we were out in the agora, I make my contribution in my own way, and no less than them, because you are even deigning to honor me as a beloved child also consoles a father's old age. 2. That's why even now I'm confident in bringing this exhortation to you on behalf of Bosporius, the most respectable and God-beloved bishop. While I'm ashamed that this great man should need my letter, he for whom lifestyle and age

should guarantee respect, I would be no less ashamed to keep silent and craft no argument about him, since I possess a voice, pay honor to faith, and, above all, know the man well. 3. Obviously, it is you, then, who will put an end to the dispute over the dioceses in accordance with the Spirit's grace within you and the canonical procedure. 4. Don't let Your Reverence think it tolerable that our affairs are openly posted in public courts.[61] Even if the judges of these matters are Christian, as they surely are by the beneficence of God, what do the sword and the Spirit have in common? 5. If I were to allow it, how or where would it be right to include an account about the faith amid the other disputes? Is today Bosporius, the God-beloved bishop, a heretic to me? Does his gray hair hang in the balance today, even though he, who is the teacher of us all, guided many out of error and gave an important demonstration of his orthodoxy? 6. No, I exhort you, don't allow room for such frivolous prosecutions. But if possible, reconcile the divisions and let it be added to your commendations. If it's not possible, at least don't let all of us be treated so poorly through such an insult, we with whom he has both lived and grown old, and we whom you know to be a precise herald of the divinity both amid danger and outside it and who subtract nothing from the single inaccessible Godhead. 7. Pray for me too, I exhort you, in my intense bouts with illness. I, and all those with me, send greetings to the brotherhood with you. Be strong, be cheerful! May you, renowned in the Lord, lay a universal foundation for us and the churches!

Gr. Naz., *Ep.* 151
Spring 382–early 384

To Nectarius,

1. Many nobly try to guess what's in your mind, but they can't figure it out at all. Yet they don't disbelieve me when I flaunt the fact that you think I deserve no small amount of respect and honor. One of them is also my most honorable son George: 2. after having fallen into many hardships and having grown sufficiently weary in his troubles, he finds one refuge for salvation, being brought to you through me and obtaining some act of beneficence from the most honorable courtier in your household. 3. If you please, then, grant the favor to him and his need, and, if you please, also to me. I know that you've determined to give me everything, and you're persuading me of it by your actions.

Gr. Naz., *Ep.* 219
Early 383–early 384

To Helladius,

1. The words that I composed for you,[62] I composed with goodwill so that I would get an especially fair hearing for my appeal, or at least so that I would be pardoned for the exhortation. 2. There are many who do not approve of your action toward my most honorable brother and fellow priest Sacerdos, as if it stemmed from animosity toward certain people rather than a process of responsible decision-making; while they may be perhaps ignorant of the sequence of events, they do not praise it, seeing the outcome on its own. 3. Well, you ought to know this for yourself. For it's not my place to meddle in your affairs, and it's you who dictates practical rules to others. For my part, I'm appealing to Your Goodness, first of all, to allow the man to keep every occupation with which he was concerned, as it's not easy for anyone, let alone the most enduring and philosophical person, to practice philosophy so strenuously that he must tolerate being deprived of such toils and such routine. 4. But if you can't, as a second option, please arrange for the care of the poor as you see fit through individuals that you've examined personally, but have regard for his anxiety for the monastery and the brothers in it, and don't upset him with a new situation, and don't further upset those who cling to routine and who, as if they were one body, don't tolerate their limbs being severed. Some of them came to me and indeed made this complaint. 5. If you take the man to have any respectable quality about himself, then, for that very reason, give him the respect that he and his gray hair deserve; he demonstrates to others, whom he supports in a godly fashion, a reverence far more mature than his age with respect to his efforts in feeding the poor and presiding over the brothers. 6. If you think it a minor thing, though, don't entirely disrespect me and my request. Before all else, relax your anger and acrimony toward him! Yes, I appeal to you, reconcile with him like a father with a child! 7. If he has caused you any grief, which I don't think is the case, forgive me for it, and neither say nor write anything about him that is unworthy of him or unworthy of Your Clemency. If it's already been written, throw it away. 8. Don't advertise acrimony that is better concealed than made known to outsiders, so that, among other things, you may teach by example how to bear with him patiently.

Gr. Naz., *Ep.* 220
Early 383–early 384 (after Gr. Naz., *Ep.* 219)

To Helladius,

1. One part of what you wrote[63] is gentle and good-natured, while another part is—I cannot say what, except—upsetting to me, and as I'm persuading myself, quite reasonably so. 2. For even if my brother and fellow priest Sacerdos was justly accused (and I'm not sure about that), it's still upsetting. How could it not be, when such reverence and such toils are instantaneously wiped out? 3. But if these accusations are simply a slander contrived by those who envy him, it would even be grievous that he, whose way of life is joined to yours, would be estranged because of insults. 4. Well, in the present matters, I know the best and most advantageous resolution; adopt it for yourself! I'm sending you the brother in person, but more important, I'm personally escorting him as he sets out to put you at ease and truthfully inform you of everything. 5. He claims that on some points he is ready to defend himself, but he is prepared to show other points as lies. Indeed, he has convinced me of this, that he crafts his words with the fear of God.

Gr. Naz., *Ep.* 127
382

To Helladius,

1. It's generally a pleasant thing to address Your Reverence, but even more so in my current state. For my desperation on a nearly daily basis makes me cling to you all the more, as if I were unfairly gaining some final profits. 2. Since I'm acknowledging profit, I owe compensation to my most venerable son Nicobulus, from whom the profit came. Through you, I'm doing what the poor do when they look to the rich to get some benefits from them, thereby dissolving my debt to the man. 3. For he needs freedom from politics, since he has been accustomed to it for too long a time. To this end, deign to cooperate with him.

Gr. Naz., *Ep.* 167
382

To Helladius,

1. Here's a reminder of my friendship with you: my sweetest son Nicobulus, first of those in my family in whom I take a keen interest.

Do me the favor of introducing him to the keenest of teachers. Do me the further favor of training his character for virtue. 2. This will happen if he is urged to pay you regular visits and, most important, if he knows that he's not being overlooked, since the eye of an educator is itself silent instruction. 3. As one high priest to another, you'll owe me spiritual compensation, if it's not too coarse to say; as an eloquent person to a lover of eloquence, you'll owe me eloquent compensation.

Gr. Naz., *Ep.* 172
Easter 383

To Helladius,

1. I took pleasure in your letter, and why shouldn't I, since you too are remembering the dead? Like the symbols of the festival at hand, my gratitude is even greater. 2. Add what you ask, however, to what you give. If it's expedient, pray for me, that I may be remembered again and that I may remember the festival. If it's not, pray that I'm transported to the place where the habitation of all who are glad resides [Ps 86:7], to either understand or watch the true festival. For I've had my fill of life's twists and turns.

Gr. Naz., *Ep.* 120
Easter 383

To Helladius,

1. Taught to look for the objects of my hope in faraway places [Heb 11:13], to borrow from your opening remarks,[64] I'm already rejoicing in the present affairs. For I know that the holy day of Easter, when we met up, is a mystical initiation into the good things over there,[65] in that the festival is a "passing over" [cf. Exod 12:11]. You did well to remember me with what you sent and what you wrote. 2. For my part, I've already gone through many Easters, and this has been the advantage of living a long life. But now that I'm leaving this heavy and dark Egypt of life and being freed from the brick and mortar [Exod 1:14] in which I've been confined, I desire with purity to migrate to the Promised Land [cf. Num 34:1–15]. 3. Pray these things for me and on my behalf, if my success in what is most important matters to you at all. For your part, though, may you, in the enjoyment of life, be able to celebrate many times with the ecclesiastical community! 4. If you were to let my old age wind down under favorable conditions by giving this church a bishop whom the Holy

Spirit will show forth, you would be doing a good deed—and what is more deserving of paternal blessings than that?

Gr. Naz., *Ep.* 216
Summer 381–early 384

To Eudocius,⁶⁶

1. The agreeable person is also compassionate; the compassionate is also genuine; the genuine is also reliable in counsel. 2. Accordingly, since I am quite seasoned with respect to piety and have had experience with lots of gentlemen and customs (experience, after all, is the mother of intelligence) 3. and you are like a recently bridled colt, just now at the beginning of your godly struggles (the beginner, after all, is more enthusiastic and powerful, empowered by the Spirit's fervor to perform his obligations successfully in some respects, but to make mistakes due to ignorance in other respects), 4. when you are with me, please honor me as an old man, respect me as a father, and use me as a mediator in your disagreement with my most respectable brother and fellow priest Sacerdos, for he is here in person. 5. Consequently, by making amends with each other, you'll help the bishop, you'll bring an end to the offense that you've brought to the masses, and, most important of all, you'll appease God, so that you don't end up instantaneously destroying this great and really glorious business—I mean, your agreement and covenant for the godly life.

Gr. Naz., *Ep.* 217
Summer 381–early 384 (after Gr. Naz., *Ep.* 216)

To Eudocius,⁶⁷

1. After the war, the alliance! And while it's right to offer advice first and then act, I reversed the order: I'm offering advice after the action. 2. Well, if I needed to flatter and take the worse course, I would have found many avenues of flattery, inasmuch as it's an easy thing to do and one that, nowadays, proves successful with the masses. But since causing injury is not in my interest, especially to a soul still newly initiated and just now approaching the good, listen to the truth. 3. Your beginning was unphilosophical; your helpers and those who play their own game using someone else's character gave you love in a wicked way. 4. But now, were you to change direction and cure your sinfulness, perhaps some health will come to you [Jer 40(33):6], even if it hurts. But if you remain with the same people

and take pride in an evil victory, your plague will be painful [Jer 10:19], as divine scripture says—"How shall I be healed?" [Jer 15:18]. Indeed, I'll make your affairs my concern! 5. Even though I'm like this, and even though I'm writing like this, if you yearn for a meeting, I'll not refuse you.

Gr. Naz., Ep. 218
Summer 381–early 384 (after Gr. Naz., Ep. 217)

To Eudocius,[68]

1. I confess: my fellow priest the noble and good Sacerdos is my friend, and may he continue to be, and in this all the more because he's embracing you. 2. For in his accusations he wasn't abandoning his affection; rather, he issued a brotherly censure instead of an acrimonious accusation. 3. Of course, I'm not so irresponsible and rash (lest you suspect it) as to pass judgment before hearing both of you out. In the same epistle that you condemned as an act of boldness,[69] I upbraided not you (unless you read it cursorily) so much as those who hang around you and snatch some special enjoyment from your pettiness. 4. What, then, was I trying to do? You might know it like this: horsebreakers use certain colors and noises, as well as the hillsides and plains of certain regions, to train colts, not to scare them but to teach them not to get scared. With this in mind, I also composed my epistle in a somewhat rougher way. 5. Indeed, there are many training exercises in philosophy, and thanks be to God that I found you to be not unphilosophical and bound to material concerns but sufficiently gentle and belonging to our sheepfold [cf. John 10:16], due to which you write in a mild manner and yearn for a meeting. 6. Were you to do me this favor, you would be doing the better thing and—know it well!—I would regard you with a father's eyes. If a snowstorm blocks your way, though, I would greet you with an exhortation for the time being. 7. Well, let me even now persuade you to prefer nothing to friendship and unanimity with my brother Sacerdos, and don't think that what happened is anything other than a test of the Wicked One, who begrudges your philosophical practice. 8. However, in the first test, fight valiantly and manfully, not so that it leads to a second and a third fight, and even further ones, but so that he goes away, defeated and disgraced. Indeed, I know his fighting style, having spent much time learning it in my many fights with him.

Gr. Naz., *Ep.* 221
Summer 381–early 384

To Homophronius,

1. You summon me to a synod. I prayed that my body would be in good enough shape to be there with you of my own volition, so that I might see your sacred house, Christ's residence, the root of the holy branches, the truly joyous mother of joyous children [cf. Ps 112(113):9]. 2. I'm certain of this; I've been persuaded in the Lord; therefore, I speak with confidence. If anything upsetting comes upon you even now, don't let Israel's lamp be quenched [2 Sam 2:17], even if it's fanned by the breezes of the Wicked One, and don't let God's kindness be concealed further, kindness that he conceals with ineffable words of support among those who fear him; rather, he will be all the more glorified and wondrous through your endurance and the hope that doesn't disappoint [cf. Rom 5:5]. 3. Exhort my most honorable son Sacerdos neither to lose heart nor to suffer anything unworthy of himself, but to exploit the opportunity to take grievances as the raw material of philosophical practice. 4. Let him still serve our most honorable bishop, and let him still strengthen the brothers, especially so that our work is not destroyed, work that is so important and acclaimed, work that we instituted in the Lord. 5. If that's not possible, I'll still show restraint and prevail over Envy, so that I don't give wicked people, who hate me without cause [Ps 34(35):19], any grip on me.

Gr. Naz., *Ep.* 215
Summer 381–early 384

To Sacerdos,

1. What is terrible to us? Nothing except straying from God and divine things. Let the rest be as God designs; he ordains us for righteousness through either favorable weapons on the right or ominous weapons on the left [cf. 2 Cor 6:7]. 2. The one who administers our life knows the reasons for these things. Let us fear only one thing: unphilosophical suffering. 3. We take care of the poor, show brotherly love, and revel in the singing of psalms as much as possible. Say we're not permitted this; let's practice philosophy another way—grace is not impoverished. Let us be alone; let us contemplate; let us purify the mind with divine expositions, some-

thing that's perhaps even more exalted than the aforementioned things. 4. But say we're not like this; should we think that we've fallen short of everything just because we strayed from one thing? Of course not, but let us still keep hold of the favorable hope. Let's see if anything remains for us, and let's not suffer the same way as colts do, who buck their riders when they get spooked by loud noises because they're unaccustomed to frights.

Gr. Naz., Ep. 213
Summer 381–early 384

To Sacerdos,

1. If you didn't expect any difficulty when you began to approach philosophy, your starting point was unphilosophical and I blame those who molded you.[70] 2. But if you did expect difficulty but didn't encounter any, thanks be to God! If you did encounter it, you should suffer it with endurance or know that you're failing in your performance.

Gr. Naz., Ep. 99
Summer 381–early 384

To Sacerdos,

I'm learning that you're taking up a life of withdrawal, and I hope that you become a John the Baptist or even an Elijah of Carmel for us, and our haters can cry foul at this alone: our conference with God and our dedication to higher things while being delivered from public life and troubles. Consequently, they would at least do right by us unwillingly, since they cannot do so willingly.

Gr. Naz., Ep. 214
Summer 381–early 384

To Sacerdos,

1. Nothing exceptional is untested. What has been tormented by public affairs, like gold in a furnace, is more exceptional. 2. If this has been made sufficiently philosophical for you, thanks be to God! But if not quite yet, I offer myself and my experiences to you. I've been insulted, I've been hated. Inasmuch as it was up to those who wanted to do it, what terrible thing have I not suffered? What did I do next? I removed myself from the causes of my distress. 3. Were there any better services than these that I could've provided myself? And so, as

you reflect on these words, take it upon yourself to confess thanks to God for the abuse, even if you don't do so to those who committed it.

Gr. Naz., *Ep.* 212
Summer 381–early 384

To Sacerdos,

1. It is to you—my young hope, mature in your youth!—that I send my greetings. I want and pray for whatever is best for you. 2. Among the good things, though, the first is something that you're not unaware of, which is always possessing God and being God's possession through an affinity with and ascent to him. I'm certain that this is also the advice that you would give, and have given, yourself.

Gr. Naz., *Ep.* 183
383–early 384

To Theodore,[71]

1. Envy, which nothing easily escapes, has got a hold of us too. Look, even we Cappadocians are splitting into factions, so to speak—a vice previously unheard of and unbelieved!—so that "no flesh may boast before God" [1 Cor 1:29] and so that we might realize we're all human and refrain from rashly passing judgment against others. 2. From this unfortunate circumstance, however, I pull some benefit (if I should speak in a counterintuitive way), and really, I'm plucking roses from the thorns, as the saying goes. 3. Anyway, I've neither met with Your Reverence face-to-face nor conversed with you by letter before now, but I've been illuminated only by the report about you, and now it's become necessary for me to contact you by letter, with much gratitude to the one who granted me this opportunity. 4. I will, then, omit writing to the other bishops about whom you sent me an epistle, for it's not yet time for this; at the same time, my illness makes me more hesitant to do so. What I'm writing to you, I'm also writing to them through you. 5. Let my lord and most God-beloved bishop Helladius stop meddling in my affairs. For he is conducting investigations within his orbit not in a spiritual way but in a contentious way and not with the precision of canons but with the satisfaction of his wrath in mind, as is clear from his timing and the group that he has unreasonably mobilized to his side. For I must say it like this and not get worked up. 6. If my body had been in good

enough shape so that I could preside over the church of Nazianzus, to which I was proclaimed at the outset—but not to Sasima, as some are incorrectly persuading you[72]—I wouldn't have been so miserable or so ignorant of the divine rules as to neglect the church or chase after the comforts of life in the place of wages reserved for those who labor for God and those who get the best return on investment from the talent entrusted to them [cf. Matt 25:14–30]. 7. What benefit do I, poorly advised about the most important matters, get from my many labors and high hopes? Since even my body is in bad shape, which is clear to all, and since I fear no pressure as a result of my retirement for the reason that I just mentioned, and since I've seen the church clinging to me but harmed by circumstances and nearly dissolved by my dissolution, I petitioned, both earlier and now, my lords the most God-beloved bishops, specifically those in my homeland, to give a head to this church, which, in concert with God, they have given, someone worthy of both my desire and your prayers.[73] 8. Know that these are the facts, Most Honorable Lord, and instruct the rest of the bishops to accept him and vote for him and to not burden my old age by letting these aspersions convince you.

9. Let me add this to my letter: as to my lord Bosporius, my most God-beloved fellow minister, if your examination discovers anything wicked in his faith—an entirely illegitimate phrase to utter!—judge for yourself (I won't mention his advanced age and my own testimony).[74] 10. But if the provincial clergy's investigation contrives heresy and a new accusation, don't be swept up in the aspersions and don't make them stronger than the truth, I exhort you, lest you discourage many of those who prefer to act well.

11. May we and the church freely give you, our universal pride, good health, good cheer, and progress with God.

Gr. Naz., *Ep.* 163
383–early 384

To Theodore,

1. Let God graciously offer you to the churches for our glory and for the advantage of the masses, since you are so well considered and steadfast in spiritual affairs as to make a real simpleton out of me, who is regarded as superior by virtue of my age. 2. Well then, since you want to take me as a partner in a certain spiritual problem—I'm

referring, of course, to the oath that George, the person from Paspasa,[75] seems to have sworn—I'll tell Your Reverence what comes to my mind. 3. By my reasoning, many people make themselves a laughingstock by thinking of oaths prescribed against curses as oaths but supposing that documents written without the words spoken aloud are merely outward shows that don't constitute an oath. 4. How are we to understand that a record of one's debts obliges someone more than a simple agreement and that a written oath is something different than a spoken oath? I believe, in short, that an oath is a guarantee between one who asks and one who acquiesces. 5. Surely it isn't enough for a dismissal of the charge to claim that he had been forced into making it (what forced him was the law that he feared) or that he later won in court. The very fact that he stood in court violated the oath. 6. In this regard, I've even convinced George not to concoct pretexts for his sins [Ps 140(141):4] or contrive arguments as advocates for his trespass but to realize that the document constitutes an oath and to shed tears privately with God and with Your Reverence regarding his sin, even if I previously deceived myself and thought it something different. 7. Well, I've discussed these matters with the man, and it's clear that once you discuss the details with him you'll make him all the more contrite, and as a great healer of souls and having treated him with the canonical rule for the extent of time you thought right, you'll thus bestow on him an act of beneficence for the time served in penance. The measure of time, after all, is the measure of contrition.

Gr. Naz., *Ep.* 121
383–early 384

To Theodore,

1. I take pleasure in the symbols of love, and especially at such an important time, and from a man at once so newly installed and so mature in youth [Ps 143(144):12] (to greet you with the words from scripture—that's how it calls someone greater in intelligence than he is in years). 2. And so, while the ancient fathers used to pray for their children to have, among other things, heaven's dew and the earth's richness [Gen 27:28]—unless you're fond of understanding these words in a higher sense—I'll repay you with everything in a spiritual way. 3. May the Lord fulfill all your requests [Ps 19:6(20:5)]! May you

become a father to such children (if I should pray for you with concision and affection) as you have shown yourself to be to your fathers whenever we're glorified by you in other respects.

Gr. Naz., *Ep.* 123
383–early 384

To Theodore,

1. I enjoy[76] your presence and I'm fond of your company, even though I otherwise advise myself to stay home and practice philosophy in tranquility. For, out of everything else, this is what I find to do me the most good. 2. But since the air is still turbulent and my illness hasn't gone away, be patient for a bit longer—I exhort you—and pray for my health. When the opportunity arises, I'll give my attention to your wishes.

Gr. Naz., *Ep.* 139
Late 383

To Theodore,

1. The one who raised up his slave David from the task of shepherding to a royal office [cf. Ps 77(78):70] and Your Reverence from the flock to the task of shepherding—the one who, by his own will, administers our affairs and those of all who pin their hopes on him—he makes Your Perfection come to know even now the dishonor to which I've been subjected by the lordly bishops in the matter of their votes, some consenting to my situation, others rejecting me. 2. Certainly, I wouldn't implicate Your Reverence, who only recently came to know the problems and didn't know, so it seems, most the details of my story. 3. These words, then, will suffice, for I don't want to annoy you any further, lest I come off as burdensome just when I've initiated our friendship. I'll explain what I can as someone who deliberates with God. 4. I retired from the church at Nazianzus, not to despise God or to disregard my little flock—may no philosophical soul suffer that feeling!—but, first of all, to avoid being controlled by such an important mandate and, second, because I had been afflicted with illness and thought that I wouldn't be up to such important concerns. 5. Since even you were putting pressure on me by reproaching my withdrawal, and since I couldn't put up with the complaints that came at me from all sides, and since that period was difficult in that an assault from my enemies loomed over me to

the detriment of the whole universal church, I was finally laid low by a defeat painful to the body, but not as bad as one to the soul. 6. I'm surrendering this lowly body to the church as much as I can, thinking it more desirable to suffer anything in a bodily way than be stricken in a spiritual way, and to strike the masses that already suspect the worst about me based on their past experience. 7. Now that you know about these things, join me in prayer and accept my decision. Perhaps it wouldn't be bad to also say: imprint reverence upon yourself.

Gr. Naz., *Ep.* 77[77]
Mid-380

To Theodore,

1. I'm learning that you've become resentful of the outrages committed against us by the monks and beggars. And it's unsurprising that you, still unharmed and without firsthand experience of our calamities, are growing impatient at such events. 2. Given that I've been tested by even greater calamities and taken my share of violence, please let me be thought fairly reliable when advising Your Reverence what gray hair teaches and reason shows us. 3. What happened was terrible, even beyond terrible—who would argue with that? The altars were violated and sacramental objects demolished; we stood between the initiates[78] and the stone throwers; we even offered petitions as a remedy against the stonings; they forgot the modesty of virgins, the decency of monks, the misery of beggars—they did damage to their own pitifulness by their harshness.

4. However, perhaps it's better to be patient and, from our experience, to give an example of patience to the masses. For a rational argument does not persuade most people in the same way as practice, the silent exhortation. 5. I think that it's a great thing to exact justice from those who acted unjustly. I say a great thing (for it's even beneficial for the correction of others), but much better than this, and more godlike, is the endurance of sufferings. For while the former curbs vice, the latter persuades people to be kind, which is far better and more wholesome than simply not being vicious. 6. Let's think that a great act of beneficence lies before us, and let's forgive anything done against us, so that we too may obtain forgiveness and pay kindness in advance for kindness.

7. Phineas was called a zealot because he ran a spear through the Midianite woman along with the adulterer and removed the reproach from the sons of Israel [Num 25:6–11], but he was praised even more for praying for an errant people. Well then, let us too stand up and make atonement, and let the plague abate and let it be reckoned to us for righteousness, as it is written [Ps 105(106):30–31]. 8. Moses too was praised for killing the Egyptian who subjected the Israelite to horrible treatment [Exod 2:11–12], but he was admired more for curing through prayer his sister Mariam, made leprous because of her grumbling [Num 12:1–16]. 9. Consider the following examples too. The Ninevites were threatened with catastrophe, but they paid off their sin with tears [Jonah 3:1–10]. Manasseh was the most transgressive among the kings but the most renowned among the saved because of his lament [2 Chron 33:1–20]. 10. "What shall I do with you, Ephraim?" God says [Hos 6:4]. The story contains terrible wrath, yet protection is supplied too [Hos 11:8–9]. Is anything swifter than beneficence? The disciples begged for Sodomic fire [Gen 19:24; Luke 17:29] against those who led Jesus out, but he disdained vengeance [Luke 9:54–56].[79] Peter cut off the ear of Malchus, one of the attackers, but Jesus restored it [John 18:10]. 11. What about the person who asked if we should forgive a brother who erred seven times? Isn't he accused of being too stingy? For to the "seven times" is added "seventy-seven times" [Matt 18:21–22].[80] What about the debtor in the gospels, the one who wouldn't forgive the very things for which he was forgiven [Matt 18:24–34]? Didn't he pay for it bitterly? What about the example set by the [Lord's] Prayer [Matt 6:12; Luke 11:4]? Doesn't it want us to exchange one act of forgiveness for another?

12. Now that we've got so many examples, let's imitate God's beneficence and not want to learn for ourselves just how wicked retribution for sin is. Do you see the progression of kindness? First it legislates, then it commands, promises, threatens, reproaches, brandishes, restrains, and threatens again. Only when it's constrained does it strike a blow, and this just slightly, leaving open some room for making amends. 13. Accordingly, let's not suddenly lash out—that wouldn't be safe—but let's chasten them with fear and then conquer them with beneficence, and let's make them debtors of our reverence, tormented more by their conscience than by our wrath. Let's not

cause a fig tree that can still produce fruit to wither up; let's not condemn its soil as useless and infertile, soil that the gardener's protection and care might perhaps cure [Luke 13:6–9]. 14. Let's not destroy an important and renowned deed on account of, perhaps, the Wicked One's insult and envy, but rather let's want to come off as beneficent instead of perfect, as lovers of the poor instead of lovers of the court. Let's not put up with those who would secretly enkindle[81] us to this more than with those who would restrain us, if for no other reason than to reflect on the shame of being seen to fight against the poor, who have this great advantage, that, even if they commit injustice, they're still shown mercy on account of their misfortune. 15. Think now of how they'll all fall before you: the poor and their caretakers as well as all the monks and virgins who supplicate on their behalf. Therefore, grant this favor both to all of them (since they're sufficiently afflicted, as is clear from those who beseech me) and, before everyone else, to me, who makes this request on their behalf. 16. If the fact that they dishonored me strikes you as a terrible thing, how much more terrible would it appear to ignore those who recommend this course of action to you. May God forgive the noble Paul for the violence he committed against us.

Gr. Naz., *Ep.* 159
383–early 384

To Theodore,

1. Let me introduce to Your Reverence my blood, your nursling, and one of God's precious possessions—my most respectable daughter the virgin Amazonia. 2. By respecting her faithfulness, giving relief to her bodily disease, and therefore fully extending your hand and feeling some regard for her, you'll perform a magnanimous act, one worthy of Your Reverence and, I'll add, our friendship.

Gr. Naz., *Ep.* 157
Late 383

To Theodore,

1. My spiritual business has come to an end. No longer will I proceed to annoy you. May you come together, may you fortify yourselves, may you contrive schemes against me! Let those who hate me declare victory! Let the canons be preserved with exactitude, starting with me, the most unlearned of all! 2. But exactitude isn't

subject to envy: let it not stand in the way of our friendship. The children of my most honorable son Nicobulus came to the city to learn how to write shorthand. Please see to them and everything else in an affectionate and fatherly way—for even the canons cannot stand in the way of this—and figure out how they might live near the church. 3. For I want them to shape their character in line with virtue by frequently running into Your Perfection.

Gr. Naz., Ep. 124
383

To Theodore,

Do you summon? I'm hurrying, but I'm hurrying only to be near you alone. Indeed, it's only from a distance that I embrace synods and assemblies, since my experience has been that most of them are, to put it mildly, corrupt affairs. What's left, then? By your prayers, help out my righteous yearning, that I get what I'm eager for.

Gr. Naz., Ep. 160
383

To Theodore,

1. For this reason,[82] you and I both intend for justice to come from Your Reverence to my daughter Eugenia, and for it not to let her be wronged by her heirs. 2. She would be wronged, it seems to me, if she were deprived of any part of what her grandmother—the woman whom, with utter dedication, she took care of—bequeathed to her as her granddaughter. And her grandmother left behind just a small estate[83] rather than the large one that she was promised and expected.

Gr. Naz., Ep. 161
383

To Theodore,

1. What I consider just, I've written in an epistle.[84] But if anything else not included in it comes to mind (indeed, I'm convinced that this would happen for the right reason), I would accept it too.
2. Otherwise I'd be committing a crime and transgressing piety itself, by introducing those who approach me now to a decider of justice by whose judgment I no longer abide. That's what most of the masses—terribly wretched and uneducated as they are—habitually do.

Gr. Naz., *Ep.* 115
383

To Theodore,

1. Your letter is also a festival, and something even better, because you anticipate the occasion by granting me a prefestival with your enthusiasm. 2. That, then, is what has come from Your Reverence, but as for me, I'm paying you back with something greater than my possessions: my prayers. 3. But that you may have a reminder of me, and also one of the holy Basil, I've sent you a volume, Origen's *Philocalia*,[85] which has excerpts from his useful works for lovers of eloquence. 4. With the help of effort and the Spirit, deign to accept it and to give me a demonstration of its benefit.

Gr. Naz., *Ep.* 152
383

To Theodore,

1. It's time I utter that scriptural passage "To whom will I cry out when I am done injustice?" [Hab 1:2]. Who will hold out their hand to me when I am oppressed? To whom will pass the weight of a church in such bad shape and broken down? 2. I testify before God and the elect angels [1 Tim 5:21] that God's flock suffers injustice by being without a shepherd and without a bishop, due to my mortification. 3. Yes, the disease is holding me down, and has swiftly led me away from the church, and now makes me wholly useless, always exhaling my last breaths and further crushed by routine business. 4. Well, if the province had any other chief, I should have cried out and testified to him, but since it's Your Reverence who sits in the highest position, I'm compelled to look to you. Think about the direction in which you want your church to go, and don't let it do anything unworthy of itself. 5. To leave all the other matters aside, what the Apollinarians[86] have imposed upon us—some of which they've already done, some of which they're threatening to do— you'll learn from my lords and fellow priests Eulalius the chorepiscopus and Celeusius, whom I've sent to Your Reverence for this task. 6. Keeping these matters in check isn't suited to my age or infirmity, but it is to your shrewdness and power, since God has allowed you, among other things, to also be strong in the universal protection of the church. 7. But if I'm not heeded even though I say and write these

things, may the only thing left come to pass: proclaiming to everyone publicly and establishing as a known fact that the church needs a bishop so that it is not struck down by my illness. As to the future, you'll know what to do.

Gr. Naz., *Ep.* 162
383

To Theodore,

1. Realizing that I'm writing an epistle about the same subjects that my lords the most honorable bishops wrote in a letter to Your Reverence, I exhort you, give your hand to the free women and don't let them be tyrannized and shoved about by the bullying tactics of a man against whom they had taken legal action. Rather, help them as it suits you, if you know why they suffer what they suffer. 2. But if you don't know, help them because they also suffer in this respect, that their injustice is neither familiar to you nor believed by you. But if anyone thinks that I'm meddling around, that I'm getting too involved with a lawsuit that doesn't affect me, let him prove it to me, and I'll be happy. 3. But now, I'm afraid that this isn't how it is. It's especially important that Christ and Christ's members haven't been divided [1 Cor 1:13] and that beneficence has no limits. But if anyone were to even imagine making divisions, I can think of two people who, in this case, would bear the brunt of justice's neglect: Your Reverence and myself. 4. Indeed, the condemned women live under the administration of us both. I also fear that he's brushing the truth aside with the persuasiveness of his eloquence. For that reason, participate in the judgment and in the trial's preliminary proceedings. Fight on behalf of my infirmity so that, even if my body's in this shape, I'm not reduced by necessity to fighting tenaciously for the truth with God and the cooperation of your prayers.

Gr. Naz., *Ep.* 122
383

To Theodore,

1. You owe me treatment even as I lie sick, if visiting the infirm is really one of the commandments [Matt 25:36]. But you also owe to the holy martyrs the annual honor that we celebrate in your Arianzus on the twenty-second day of our month of Dathusa. And at the same time, there are not a few matters of church business that require a

joint inspection. 2. For the sake of all involved, then, deign to come without delay. For if the effort is great, the wage will compensate for it.

> Gr. Naz., *Ep.* 168
> Summer 381–early 384

To Photius,[87]

1. "Everything that you have is mine" [John 16:15]—let me use God's voice for my introduction—but I say "mine" not only in the sense of our partnership in the Spirit but also because I contributed perhaps no small part to the present condition of the church when I was still engaged in public life and presiding over the community. Currently, I have only one concern—my exit—for which I've shrouded myself and for which I'm making preparations. 2. Indeed, let my things also be yours, regarded as shared in love. The best of what I have, though, is my most honorable brother and fellow priest Sacerdos, through whom I'm speaking to you and imagining that I see you.

> Gr. Naz., *Ep.* 169
> Summer 381–early 384

To Strategius,

1. What a strong wall blocks us from each other! Thus God has fated our affairs. The sacred hearth! The association! The common harbor for all who fear the Lord! Let other people take enjoyment from our noble pursuits; to me, only the memory remains, as well as my begrudging those who still partake of them. 2. That you may also partake of my noble pursuits, I'm making known to you my most honorable brother and fellow priest Sacerdos, about whom I know that once you lay eyes upon him, you'll say, "Gregory really is a lover of every noble pursuit!"

> Gr. Naz., *Ep.* 209
> Summer 381–early 384

To Castor,

1. How tyrannical and forceful you are! I just looked at your note, and it paid me no regard! But look, you've got the long-suffering[88] Sacerdos—your brother, my son and partner in sufferings. 2. So that I'm not completely defeated, return him—my comfort in life—to me as quickly as you can, since he will both be instructed and give instruction

in philosophical practice. Indeed, shared suffering is best for developing oneness-of-mind, and oneness-of-mind is best for deliberation.

Gr. Naz., *Ep.* 210
Summer 381–early 384

To Castor,

1. It seems to me that a foreign country is more beneficial than one's homeland. The one allows me to enjoy your friendship, while the other grants me nothing of the sort. I got this idea from my illness, which keeps me tied up and, in most cases, makes it hard or impossible to move, if I ought to speak truthfully. 2. Well, I'll put up with the hardship as long as it bothers me. What grievance can a human being not put up with? May you only be healthy and act in accordance with your rational capacity, and let your affairs reside in God's hand—and they will, if you genuinely grab hold of it! 3. As to the lady, our common sister, please send her back to me immediately, as she is the common support for reverent people and for my infirmity, or else I'll shout out many words against your Sacerdotis,[89] on whose account I've endured hardship, and I'll call her by her proper name. You'll know what it is by questioning her.

Gr. Naz., *Ep.* 81
After 372

To Gregory of Nyssa,

1. You dislike your travels, and you think that you're unsettled like bits of wood floating in water.[90] No, O Admirable One, don't be like that. For some cargo is carried about passively, but your travels are godly and there is stability in doing the right thing for the masses, even if you're not keeping stable in a particular spot. 2. If that's not true, let someone censure the sun for continuing its revolution while scattering its rays and giving life to everything that it lights upon, or let someone praise the steadfastness of stars and malign the planets, whose random wandering is harmoniously balanced.

Gr. Naz., *Ep.* 72
372–74?

To Gregory of Nyssa,

Don't let your distresses sting you too much, for the less we get distressed, the less distressing they'll be. There's nothing fearful about the heretics coming back to life; they've crawled out of their holes and act with confidence in the springtime, as you yourself write.[91] They'll hiss for a little while, I'm quite certain, and then they'll slink away when they find themselves at war with both the truth and the season—and even more so long as we entrust everything to God.

Gr. Naz., *Ep.* 73
After 372

To Gregory of Nyssa,

As to what you wrote in your epistle, here's how I'm doing. I'm not upset when overlooked, and I'm happy when honored. For I deserve the former, while the latter is fit for your ambition. Pray for me and forgive my brevity in writing. For certainly, if my letter is skimpy, at least it's ampler than silence.[92]

Gr. Naz., *Ep.* 74
After 372[93]

To Gregory of Nyssa,

1. Even while remaining here, I'm traveling abroad with you through love. Indeed, the act of yearning makes everything shared between us. I'm confident in God's beneficence and in your prayers, and so I have high hopes that everything will turn out for you according to plan, and that the sudden gust of wind will die down, and that God will give this reward for your orthodoxy, victory over your abusers. 2. Above all, I wish that I could see you soon and learn from you, as I pray. But if you linger because matters of business are impressing upon you, don't refuse, at the very least, to bring me gladness with a letter that tells of your affairs, and don't refuse your customary prayers for me. Let the good God freely give you—the universal support of the church—good health and good cheer in all things.

Gr. Naz., *Ep.* 76
Early 379

To Gregory of Nyssa,

1. This too was reserved for my wretched life, to hear of Basil's death and the departure of that holy soul, which left us in order to dwell with the Lord, having rehearsed for this his entire life. 2. But as

for me, because my body, still now, is in bad, even utterly critical, shape, I'm also robbed of this, among other things: rolling around in the holy dust,[94] being present with you while you philosophize appropriate things, and consoling our mutual friends. 3. Indeed, to anyone with a lick of good sense, experiencing the desolation of the church, shorn of such glory and shaken loose of such a crown, is neither a spectacle for the eyes nor a pleasant sound for the ears. 4. Even with many friends and words of encouragement, you seem to me to be consoled by no one so much as yourself and your memory of him. To everyone else you've become an exemplar of philosophy and something like a spiritual benchmark of self-composure in good times and endurance in grievous ones, since philosophy knows how to manage these two things, success with moderation and misfortune with grace. 5. These are my words to Your Dignity. What amount of time or word will console me, the writer of these words, except for your company and conversation, which in the place of everything else the blessed one bequeathed to me in order that I might think that I'm holding him as I observe his qualities in you, as if I were looking into a beautiful, pellucid mirror?

Gr. Naz., *Ep.* 197
Summer 381–early 384

To Gregory,

1. I rushed to you with all haste, even getting as far as Euphemias;[95] the commemoration that you performed for the holy martyrs there kept me back, and I couldn't participate in it owing to my sickness, and otherwise, my hoarse voice would have been wrong for the occasion. 2. I rushed both to visit you after so long a time and to marvel at you for the endurance and philosophy that you practice— yes, I'm learning about it—at the passing of our holy and blessed sister, 3. since you are a good man, accomplished, someone who stands beside God, who knows things divine and human better than everyone, 4. who judges to be the lightest what is heaviest to others in such situations: namely, living with the exceptional woman and then sending her off, entrusting to the only safe places as if a seasonably harvested mound of grain[96] [Job 5:26] (to use a phrase from divine scripture) she who shared in life's delights but escaped its distressing aspects by the [short] measure of her lifespan, she who, before being

mourned by you, was honored by you with the beautiful funeral owed to great people. 5. Know well: I'm longing for my own passing too, if not in the same way as you (for that would be saying too much), then in a way that comes close to yours. What feeling should we have in the presence of the long-prevailing law of God that now applies to my Theosebia (for I designate as mine the woman who lives according to God, since the spiritual kinship is superior to the bodily)? Theosebia— the church's point of pride, the ornament of Christ, the benefit of our race, the frankness of women![97] Theosebia—in such beauty, the most attractive and diaphanous among the sisters! 6. Theosebia—authentic priestess and yoke fellow of a priest, a woman equal in honor and worthy of the great mysteries! Theosebia—she upon whom the future moment will come as she lies among the immortal monuments with the souls of all those who now know her and will later! 7. Don't be surprised if I invoke her often, for I revel in the memory of the blessed woman. This is both my epitaph for her—a long one in brief—and my consolatory discourse for you, even though you can console others in such situations because of your philosophy in all things. 8. Currently, I'm deprived of your company (although I too yearn for it) for the reason that I mentioned, but we join each other in prayer: let us still remain on the earth, and let our common end, to which we draw near, not separate us. That's why we must tolerate all things, since we'll experience neither pleasure nor pain for too much longer.

Gr. Naz., Ep. 182

383

To Gregory,

1. "Woe is me that my sojourn is prolonged" [Ps 119(120):5]! My biggest problem is that my affairs are in a state of conflict and unrest and that we've not kept the peace that we received from the holy fathers. 2. I know, then, that it's you who will restore it in the power of the Spirit, which carries you and your affairs. 3. I exhort you, let none of our people nor any of the lordly bishops falsely state that they proclaimed another bishop to replace me against my will. Indeed, as of now, they've not cast me out and they don't bear animosity toward me like this. 4. But I need many things because of my mortification, and at the same time I fear the pressure of the church going uncared

for, and so I ask this favor from those bishops—one that won't contravene the canons and one that will give me relief—that a shepherd be given to the church, one given by your prayers, one worthy of Your Godliness, and one whom I'm putting into your hands, specifically the most respectable Eulalius, the most God-beloved bishop, by whose hands I would like to expire. 5. But if anyone thinks that we don't need to appoint one bishop while another is still alive, let him know that he won't prevail over me in this matter. For it's obvious to all that I was proposed as the bishop not of Nazianzus but of Sasima, if only for a short time, as I accepted the post as a foreigner out of respect for my father and my supplicants.[98]

Gr. Naz., *Ep.* 11
363–65

To Gregory,[99]

1. I've got a decent quality in my nature (for, of many qualities, I'll brag on this one [cf. 2 Cor 11:16, 18]): I'm just as disgusted with myself when I make a poor decision as I am with my friends when they do. 2. Accordingly, since all who live by God and conform to the gospel are friends and family members to one another, why shouldn't you hear from me with frankness what everyone whispers? 3. They're not commending your disreputable eminence (to speak like you),[100] or your steady decline into more despicable conditions, or your ambition, that most vicious of demons, about which Euripides speaks [E., *Ph.* 531]. 4. Why have you suffered this, O Wisest Man? Why do you condemn yourself by throwing away the sacred and palatable books that you used to read line by line to the people? Don't be ashamed at what you hear! Have you placed them over the smoke, like oars and shovels in the winter [Hes., *Op.* 629]? Have you taken bitter and unpalatable ones into your hands, wanting to hear the title of "rhetor" rather than "Christian"? 5. I find the latter better than the former—all thanks to God! But as for you, good sir, don't suffer this any longer but sober up, even if it is getting late, and come to your senses: defend the faithful and defend God, the altars, and the sacraments, from which you've gone far away.

6. And don't put these smug, rhetorical words to me: "What are you talking about? Wasn't I a Christian while I practiced rhetoric? Wasn't I faithful while I was hanging out with the young men?" Perhaps you'll

even bring in God as a witness. If I could issue a portion of a response, it would be "O Admirable Man, no, not to the extent that befits you." 7. Doesn't offending others with your current actions give those who are naturally disposed to vice an opportunity to suspect and say horrible things about you? Lies, no doubt, but what's the need for them? We live not only for ourselves but also for our neighbor. Convincing yourself is not enough if you don't convince others too. 8. Let's say that you participated in a public boxing match, or that you took punches to the head and dished them out too in the theaters, or that you twisted and contorted your body into disgraceful positions—would you still claim that you showed temperance in your soul? That line of thinking doesn't belong to a temperate person; accepting those words would be silly. 9. "Well, if you turned your life around, only then would I rejoice," as one of the Pythagorean philosophers said, lamenting a fallen companion. "If you don't," he wrote, "you're dead to me" [Pythag., *Ep.* 3]. I won't yet say this next line about you: "My friend has indeed become my enemy, despite the fact that he is still my friend," as the tragedy says [E., *Ph.* 1446]. 10. To say it more moderately, it will deeply pain me if you don't see for yourself the right course of action, something that belongs to the best of the praiseworthy, or follow the advice of the one who speaks well, something that belongs to the second best [cf. Hes., *Op.* 293–95]. 11. That's my exhortation. And agree with me, since I'm in deep pain on account of our friendship, burning equally for you and for the entire priestly order, and, I'll add, for all Christians. 12. If I must pray with you or for you, may God, who gives life to the dead, help your weakness.

Gr. Naz., *Ep.* 195
Summer 381–late 383

To Gregory the Governor,

1. I don't commend Hesiod for labeling those who share a craft "rivals" when he says, "Potter is angry with potter, and carpenter with carpenter" [Hes., *Op.* 25]. As my thinking goes, one shouldn't envy so much as run to, greet, and embrace a fellow practitioner of one's own craft. How much more does this apply to one singer getting angry with another [Hes., *Op.* 26], since a verbal expression constitutes the object of their efforts. 2. Having personally experienced this with Your Eloquence, if I was in good enough bodily shape that I could

indulge the urges of my soul, no one would have gotten ahead of me in running to you, hugging you, and pronouncing words of welcome to you. 3. However, a cloud blocks out the sun, as illness, this jealous chunk of flesh and my prison, does for me. Will you accept my epistle instead of my presence? Yes, you will, since you're eloquent and agreeable—I don't have to speculate on this point, because I'm certain of it. 4. And that you may know how confident I am in Your Excellence, look, I'm also bringing a request that is an absolute necessity for me, and I'm asking from Your Friendliness for the response that a friend would give. 5. From my right hand, I entrust to you Nicobulus, not as someone who will dole out justice but as someone who should receive it, along with his brothers and their mother—an untimely widow—and their household, formerly shining and admired when the senior Nicobulus was still with us. 6. Now, the already surging vices and expectations haven't allowed the chance to mourn, unless it occurs to you and your sense of justice to stand against the wicked demon, to pay honor to us, to respect our humanity, and to make your own office shining through your good deed for us.

Gr. Naz., *Ep.* 107
Lent 382

To Cledonius,

You ask what my silence means. It means moderation in words and quietude.[101] For one who rules over the whole will easily rule over the part.[102] Moreover, it tames the unspeaking but self-consumed heart.

Gr. Naz., *Ep.* 109
Lent 382

To Cledonius,

I'm not preventing a meeting. For even if my tongue is silent, at least I'll give my ears to your words, since listening to what one ought to do is no less honorable than speaking it.

Gr. Naz., *Ep.* 108
Lent 382

To Cledonius,

I maintain quietude in my speech while learning to speak what is necessary, and I'm training myself to prevail over the passions. If anyone accepts this, good for them! If not, yet another benefit of quietude is not having to respond to the masses.

Gr. Naz., *Ep.* 116
Lent 382

To Eulalius,

1. For me, even Lamis was a site for quietude and a school for philosophy, a place that I imagined while I was silent and that I want to see now that I'm talking, so that I may both fulfill the brothers' longing and exact revenge against you for your disparagement, you wicked interpreter of my head's signals. 2. For I'll be present, speaking in person, no longer someone subject to allegorical interpretation or conjecture but someone understood clearly [cf. John 16:25].

Gr. Naz., *Ep.* 117
Lent 382

To Eulalius,

I've had a new experience. Although I was silent in your presence, in your absence I'm yearning to impart a word to you and receive one back. Indeed, as in everything else, it's good to dedicate the first fruits of my eloquence[103] to the Word first, and then to those who fear the Lord.

Gr. Naz., *Ep.* 158
Late 383–early 384

To Eulalius,[104]

1. There is nothing stronger than the truth, as both Ezra and I believe [cf. 1 Esd 4:35]. Indeed, the virgin Alypiane, from whom I requested an entirely accurate account of her private thinking, as you ordered, speaks the truth openly and with purity, confessing her virginity and clinging to it more ardently than I expected, but more steadily than ardently—I mean, she does so with the zeal of a virgin and the answers of an elderly woman 2. The harshness of my interrogation seems, in the end, to have been useful, for she has quite clearly shown the firmness of her decision. And so, once you come to recognize these things, pray for the girl and cultivate—for the glory of God, for me, and for her entire order of devotees—the initial steps in salvation that she has taken.

Gr. Naz., *Ep.* 118
Lent 382

To Eugenius,[105]

1. The Ecclesiast says, "There is a season for everything" [Eccl 3:1]. Therefore, "I have placed a guard on my mouth" [Ps 38:2(39:1)] during that time, and "Behold! I will hinder my lips no more" [Ps 39:10(40:9)] once the time is up. 2. For the scripture says, "I am keeping quiet" [Ps 31(32):3, 49(50):21; Isa 42:14]. And will I keep quiet forever? No. I keep quiet for myself, but I will speak to others. If they were to speak what is necessary, good for them! If not, I'll block up my ears too.

Gr. Naz., *Ep.* 111
Lent 382

To Eugenius,[106]

You practice philosophy with isolation and thus with immoderate fasting, but I do so with quietude. Let's share the gift with each other. Whenever it is that we come together, let's sing to God together and produce just as eloquent a quietude as inspired a word.

Gr. Naz., *Ep.* 95
Summer 381–early 382

To Leontius,

O fortuitous disease and abuse from my enemies! Because of this, it is I who has been liberated from the Sodomic fire [Gen 19:24; Luke 17:29] and episcopal feebleness. How goes your progress to God? Let it be going well, but as for everything else, such as it is, let's put it out of our minds. I'll still see my abusers shortly, whenever our affairs are judged by fire [1 Cor 3:13]. I'm greeting you and, through you, our common friends. Remember my stonings.[107]

Gr. Naz., *Ep.* 239
Date unknown

To Epiphanius,

1. To the law that bids children be taught, I propose the law that bids fathers be honored [Eph 6:1–4]. Now, then, I'm guiding you to what is best: for example, receive my letter with the right hand of friendship! 2. If you were to write back, and would like to do so frequently, you might end up turning me into a spearman even as an old man, no more ignoble than Nestor.[108]

Gr. Naz., *Ep.* 20
Late 368

To Caesarius,

1. Fearful events are not unprofitable to those who understand them with the right perspective, and I would even go so far as to say that they're quite good and salvific.[109] For even if we pray that they don't come to pass, we nevertheless learn something from the events. 2. For an ailing soul approaches God, as Peter somewhere asserts most admirably,[110] and in everyone who survives a dangerous situation there lies a greater affection for the rescuer. 3. So let's not be upset that we partook of the evil event; instead, let's be thankful that we survived it. 4. Let's not appear to God one way in a time of dangers and another way after the dangers, but—whether at home or abroad, whether tending to our own affairs or acting in the public interest (for I must speak like this and not leave anything out)—let's adhere to the one who saved us and be on his side, thinking lightly of matters trivial and earthbound. 5. Let's also give to posterity a story, great for our own glory and great for the benefit of the soul. This very lesson—that danger is better than security and misfortune more desirable than prosperity—would be quite a good one for the masses too. At any rate, if before fearful events we belong to the world, let's have it that after fearful events we belong to God. 6. Perhaps I come off as burdensome to you by frequently writing you epistles about the same things, and perhaps you consider my words not as an exhortation but as a lecture. 7. For that reason, enough with them! But know that I'm eager to come to you, and I'm especially praying for it too, to rejoice together at your salvation and to converse more fully about these things, 8. and, if it sounds good, to receive you here as soon as possible to celebrate with thank offerings.

Gr. Naz., *Ep.* 7
Early 362[111]

To Caesarius,

1. We've become sufficiently embarrassed by you. What should I write to the person who knows best of all that we've even become distressed? 2. So as not to mention our concerns or the extent to which the rumor about you has filled us with despondency and, I admit, with fear, I wanted you to be aware, if it was at all possible, of

the words of others (acquaintances and strangers alike, known to us in one way or another, but Christians all the same), words that they are saying about you and me, not one speaking like this and another not, but everyone alike, one after another, since people like to philosophize about strangers more eagerly than about acquaintances. 3. Such topics have become for them, as it were, subjects of declamation. At one moment they claim that a bishop's son serves in the army; at another, that he yearns for external power and glory; at another, that he is a slave to wealth (at a time when the fire is kindled publicly and people are running the race for their souls [cf. Pl., *Tht.* 172e–173a]!)[112] and that he doesn't think the only glory, security, and welfare is valiant opposition to the times and getting oneself as far away as possible from every act of sacrilege and pollution. 4. How could the bishop warn someone else not to be swept away by the times or mixed up with idols? How could he censure those who go astray in some respect when he himself cannot speak with frank authority at his own hearth? 5. With some perhaps speaking in friendship and others attacking us acrimoniously, we hear these words daily, and ones even more hurtful than these—how do you think this affects us, and what kind of souls do you think we have as people who intend to serve God and look to future hopes, deciding that this is the only good thing? 6. By vouching for your intention, then, and persuading him that you won't put up with causing us distress for much longer, I somehow console our lordly father and guide his soul when he becomes so upset by the news that he wants to bid farewell to life itself. 7. But if our lady mother were to learn anything of what they utter against you (for up to now I've employed various schemes to hide it from her), consider how completely and inconsolably she would suffer, since she is a woman, fainthearted, and otherwise unable to moderate her behavior in such circumstances because of her intense reverence. 8. If you afford any account to both yourself and us, then set your mind to something better and more secure. Our property here is completely suited to an unencumbered lifestyle, at least to one not excessively insatiate and immoderate when it comes to the desire for more. But as to you obtaining an official position, I don't see what occasion we're waiting for by allowing the current one to pass. 9. If you keep to your same opinion, that everything is trivial compared to your ambition,

I don't mean to utter any further offense, but I offer the following prediction and swear that one of two things must come to pass. Should you remain a genuine Christian, you'll be ranked as the most dishonorable one and act in a manner unworthy of yourself and your hopes. 10. But should you aim at civic honor, you'll harm yourself in more crucial respects, partaking of the smoke if not also the fire.

Gr. Naz., *Ep.* 14
364–72?

To Caesarius,

1. Perform a service to both yourself and me, the kind that you'll not often perform, because occasions for such benefaction don't often arise. 2. Provide your most just patronage to my lordly cousins, considerably worn out because of a piece of property that they bought as both a convenient retreat and something that could provide them with sustenance for living. 3. But after they bought it, they fell into further difficulties, some pertaining to their dealings with arrogant sellers, others pertaining to being looted and plundered by neighbors. Consequently, their only chance for profit is to be released from the acquisition, once they've been refunded the down payment with the cost of expenditures, which were not a few. 4. So if it's all right with you to bring this bit of business to your attention, so that the contract can become completely thorough and secure with your close observation, this would be all the more pleasant for them and me. 5. But if not, the second-best option would be for you to at least position yourself against the man's meddling and arrogance so that he doesn't filch even one single thing from them, owing to their inexperience, by exploiting them should they retain possession of the property or penalizing them should they be released from it. 6. Well then, I'm embarrassed that I even have to write an epistle about these matters. Nevertheless, since I'm obligated to them because of both our kinship and their choice of career—indeed, for whom should we be more anxious than for such people, and at what should one feel more shame than failing to show eagerness in performing such services?—by all means, because of yourself, or me, or the men themselves, or all these factors together, perform this service for them.

Gr. Naz., *Ep.* 23
365–69

To Caesarius,

1. If what I'm asking is great, don't be surprised, since I'm asking it from a great person and the request should correspond in magnitude to the person being asked. 2. For it's just as inappropriate to seek important things from an unimportant person as it is to seek unimportant things from an important person—indeed, the former is unseemly, the latter frivolous. 3. By my own hand, I'm setting before you my most precious son Amphilochius, a man so remarkable in excellence and extraordinary for his age that I—an old man, a priest, and your friend—would love to be held in the same regard. 4. And if he gave way to a man's friendship and didn't suspect any fraud, why is that surprising? He didn't suspect the man of being bad, because he is not bad himself; he assumed that a correction of the man's speech rather than his character was in order. 5. That's why he took to working with him. Why would this strike sensible people as a terrible thing? Accordingly, don't let vice get the best of virtue, and don't bring dishonor upon my gray hair. Rather, respect my testimony and add an act of benevolence to my blessings, which perhaps have some account with God, before whom we stand.

Gr. Naz., *Ep.* 21
365–69

To Sophronius,

1. Gold is altered and refashioned on different occasions, molded into many decorations and modified by skill for many purposes. Nevertheless, it remains what it is—gold—and it's not the material that admits a change but rather the outward form. 2. Realizing that you thus retain the same excellence with your friends even as you advance to further positions, I'm confident in asking this favor, no more paying reverence to your position than trusting in your character. 3. Be kind to my most venerable son Nicobulus, who has a close relationship with me in all respects because of our kinship, his marriage, and, more than these things, his character. 4. In what matters, and to what extent? In whatever he'll need of you, and to whatever extent you think it fitting of Your Magnanimity. 5. As for me, I'll pay you back with the best of what I possess. I have eloquence

and can be a herald of your virtue, even if I'm far from your worth, at least as best I can.

Gr. Naz., *Ep.* 93
July 381–February 382

To Sophronius,

1. As I see it, retirement has an upside:[113] tranquility and freedom from politics. But the separation from your friendship and company—a great thing—is not so much an upside as it is a downside.[114] 2. Others are basking in your perfection, but to me it would be great if I could have just this, the shadow of a conversation in a letter. 3. Shall I see you again? Shall I embrace the person who made me so proud? And shall it be granted in what remains of my life? 4. If so, all thanks to God. If not, I would be, for the most part, already dead. As for you, remember your Gregory and tell others of my situation.

Gr. Naz., *Ep.* 135
Summer 382[115]

To Sophronius,

1. I practice philosophy in tranquility. This is the crime that my detractors have committed—how I wish they would commit another such crime so that I might know them to be my benefactors instead! For victims too can receive many benefits, and those who have been well off can be victimized. 2. Well, that's my situation. Even if I don't convince others, at the very least I want you before everyone else to know it, someone to whom I gladly submit an account of my affairs; moreover, I am convinced that you do know it and that you're persuading those who don't. 3. I exhort you: direct all your effort now, even if you haven't previously, toward creating harmony and bringing the wickedly divided sections of the world into unanimity, especially once you understand that the divisions are over not a point of faith but their own pettiness, something that I have personally observed. 4. The ability to do so would even be profitable for you, and my retirement would be undisturbed, if I appeared to take it not in vain but voluntarily, tossing myself into the open sea like Jonah of old, so that the billow would grow calm and the sailors be safely rescued [Jonah 1:12–16]. But if they are nonetheless lost to the storm, at least I tried.

Gr. Naz., *Ep.* 37
369

To Sophronius,

1. It's characteristic of devout people to honor their mother. Each has his own mother, but the common mother to everyone is their homeland. You've honored her with all the brilliance of your career, and you'll honor her now by having regard for me on behalf of those for whom I'm pleading. 2. What's the plea? You certainly know the rhetor Eudoxius, the most eloquent among his peers; to get to the point, his child, a second Eudoxius in both conduct and speech, now comes to you through me. 3. To make yourself more renowned, then, be kind to the man in whatever matters for which he needs your patronage. 4. Since you are the common patron of our homeland and one who has done—and, I'll add, will continue to do—good deeds for many people, what a shame it would be for you not to honor before everyone else the man best in eloquence and eloquence[116] itself, which it's right to respect in this case, if for no other reason than because eloquence is the means of praising your noble qualities.

Gr. Naz., *Ep.* 29
Late 369

To Sophronius,

1. You see what my affairs are like and how the cycle of human troubles goes round and round. Now some are flourishing, now others are withering; neither success nor misfortune remains stable for us (as indeed they say), but things shift and change for the worse in an instant, as though it would be better to trust in the breeze and in letters written underwater than in the prosperity of humans. 2. Why is this the case? So that, I think, we run all the more to God and to the hereafter while contemplating the instability and inconsistency of these things, and so that we pay some attention to ourselves, giving little consideration to shadows and dreams. 3. What's the point of my account? Surely I'm not giving this philosophical treatment offhandedly or vainly putting on a show.

4. Your Caesarius once belonged among the not-unseen and quite illustrious people (unless I, his brother, am deceived), distinguished beyond the masses by his learning and excellence, radiant in his abundance of friends, among them you and Your Nobility, first

among firsts, as he himself thought and persuaded me. 5. Surely this is old news, but through your own effort you'll add further epitaphs by honoring him and bestowing upon the departed something greater, which all of us, as human beings, have in our nature to do. 6. But here's the current news (and don't skim over my account without weeping, or, at the very least, weep to a good and useful end): he lies dead, friendless, deserted, pitied, deemed worthy of little myrrh (if even this much) and few burial coverings (it means a lot that he's been deemed worthy even of these!). 7. His enemies, I'm learning, have begun to attack; some plunder his possessions here and there with tremendous bullying, and others will do so later. What ruthlessness! What savagery! And no one will stop it. At the very least, the most beneficent person will bestow this one thing: invocation of the laws. And if I ought to speak concisely: I have become a tragedy, even though I was formerly considered happy. 8. Don't let this seem tolerable to you; rather, suffer and grieve with me, and give a gift to the dead Caesarius! Yes, in the name of friendship! Yes, in the name of what you hold most dear! In the name of your hopes, which you can make come true by appearing faithful and genuine to the departed—give this to the living and give them hope! 9. Do you think that I'm upset about his possessions? By my lights, it would be more unbearable than shame were it to seem that Caesarius, alone among everybody, had no friends when, in fact, he believed he had many. 10. So that's the favor and those the reasons, since perhaps my affairs too are not a secondary concern to you. In what matters, through whom, and how you will help, the troubles themselves will suggest and Your Sagacity will scrupulously consider.

Gr. Naz., *Ep.* 39

369

To Sophronius,

1. I want everything to be copacetic with my friends. When I say my friends, though, I mean the noble, the good, and those joined to me in virtue, since I too make some claim to it. 2. Believe you me, as I investigated these things just now as to what was the best possible thing that I could bestow upon my most venerable brother Amazonius (for the conversation I recently had with him made me particularly happy), I concluded that one thing before all ought to be

bestowed upon him: your friendship and patronage. 3. For in a short period of time he demonstrated much learning, the kind for which we used to strive when we could barely see clearly and the kind for which we now strive instead of the other, once we began to look to the height of virtue. 4. If I came off as at all virtuous when I was with him, he would know. So in return, I'm showing him the best of what I possess, friends to a friend. Counting you as first and foremost among them, I want you to appear to him as such—something our common homeland demands and my own longing and reason desire, since I promised to him your solicitude before all.

Gr. Naz., *Ep.* 22
365–69

To Sophronius,

1. Just as we recognize gold and stones by sight, so too should we immediately spot in men those qualities that are good and those that are not, without needing any deeper investigation [cf. E., *Med.* 516–19]. 2. For then I wouldn't need much eloquence when I intercede for my most honorable son Amphilochius before Your Magnanimity. 3. I would have expected something incredible and astounding to happen sooner than him acting, or even intending to act, ignobly for money. Everyone agrees that his inclination toward excellence is great and that he possesses a soundness of judgment mature beyond his years. 4. But why should he suffer? Nothing escapes envy, because some disgrace has fastened even on to him, a man who ran into an accusation because of his simplicity rather than because of the viciousness of his character. 5. Watching him be torn apart by slanderers, however, shouldn't seem tolerable to you. No, I beg your sacred and great soul: honor your homeland, give assistance to virtue, respect me, who has been glorified by you and through you, and, before everything else, be with the man by adding willingness to your influence, since I know that all things pale in comparison to your virtue.

Gr. Naz., *Ep.* 189
Date unknown

To Eustochius,

1. Imitate Alexander for me, O Admirable Man. Just as he was generous in order to please the Athenians and therefore named

Athens the eternal theater of his kingdom [cf. Plu., *Alex.* 60.6], so too should you, regarding my business to be important if for no other reason 2. than eloquence and Athens itself, paying respect to our shared fathers in eloquence,[117] be eager to double your zeal for eloquence in support of the noble Pronoius. 3. Whatever you bestow on the young man, you will by all means bestow on me: I deserve to receive benefits from you, and I am, perhaps, not a bad praiser of your eloquence, even if I sit far below the sophistic thrones now that I have imposed upon myself the safe prerogative of verbal stillness [cf. Simon., frag. 66 Bergk].

Gr. Naz., Ep. 190
383

To Eustochius,

1. O Odysseus, how fiercely you strike me down [*Il.* 14.104], chiding me for being a Stagirist[118] [cf. D., *Or.* 18.294] and most officiously quibbling with me! Even as I praise that frankness of yours with which you write what you write[119]—for it's better to divulge the source of distress than to convict the ignorant by default—I also have something to rebuke. 2. Nevertheless, to maintain the courtroom custom, I'll give my defense first and then make my own accusation, doing both with an equal amount of goodwill.

3. My Nicobulus approached the good Stagirius without my consent [*Il.* 9.108], lest you suspect that he had it. Thus I forgot neither Athens nor your friendship and companionship. But he went of his own accord as well as that of his father, who wanted it so, although I did recommend him by letter. Why was this unfriendly or loathsome?

4. Now that you have my defense, accept my accusation too. I do not praise your "doll makers" and "Telchines,"[120] terms that you hurl against your rival, since you have succeeded in calling rivals those who share your craft. How long will these things go on for? And how will I tolerate the sophistic abuse? How far must it go? Until death breaks us from this depravity? 5. In these matters, [Stagirius] is young, he yields to ambition, he lays claim to any advantage, and, to temper my words now, he is probably worthy of forgiveness [D., *Or.* 21.66], if I may speak to Your Grace a bit like Demosthenes. But in this case and at your age, engaging in the giving and taking of head butts is totally contentious and inappropriate, not only because it's

undignified and entirely uncivilized but also because it's all too easy to jump into the fray. Whatever you would say is what you'll hear [*Il.* 20.250] (to deploy Homer again), like a stream doubling back: "claw me, claw thee" [Sophr., frag. 149]—this is entirely irreproachable.

6. What, then, is the wisdom by which we can become preeminent in virtue while being defeated by or even prevailing with the assistance of vice, which is far worse? But I also blame the judges, truth be told, in this respect: when acting as hearers, they praise the very things that they punish when acting as judges. 7. Not only this, but they also have many accomplices who kindle vice and have divided themselves into partisan rivalries up to the point of not commending a claim if it is not believed and insisting that it be tried in the public court if it is believed. Or like this: if a claim is false, the accusers ought to be punished, but if true, those against whom the claim is made ought to be punished. Playfully toying with the reputations of those who have done well for themselves is not as important as an actual lawsuit.

8. Well, if you're persuaded by me—indeed, my account goes for both [you and Stagirius]—say farewell to such words and censures, if for no other reason than to pay respect to my gray hair, or even because you've grown exhausted in these most shameful affairs. For your part, resolve to honor the ancient exhortation that bids virtue be cultivated whenever someone has a sufficient way of life [Pl., *Resp.* 3.407a]. 9. And also don't contrive plots against yourselves, but aim at the hopes of the young men, who certainly might suffer the most terrible things were they to learn vice while training in eloquence— and this would not be undeserved, since they have you as a teacher not of virtue but of vice.

10. But if I seem to be burdensome to you by writing these words, shoo me away with equal ones and advise a useful course, so that either you benefit in being persuaded or you rebuke me with your resistance.

Gr. Naz., *Ep.* 191

383 (after Gr. Naz., *Ep.* 190)

To Eustochius,

1. How ignorant I am! So stupid and uneducated! I admonished a sophistic man! What insanity! And I wasn't even disciplined by the

common proverb: as a bald man, I shouldn't doze off in front of a ram or rouse a nest of wasps against myself—that is, a tongue readier to speak with viciousness. 2. Well, that hardly bothers me—for I've been added to a roster of many people, as I'm learning, and if you keep on living, many more will come after me—but this really does, that I wasn't believed to be acting in the spirit of friendship. 3. Nevertheless, I hope that you are strong in both body and soul, and that you'll restrain your tongue if possible. But in the meantime, at least, I'm still fond of our relationship.

Gr. Naz., *Ep.* 100
July 381–February 382

To Gigantius,

1. Pleased at the invitation, I'm even more pleased at what you write, not because I am praised (a trivial thing indeed) but because you are thinking in the right way. The bond of your love for me is our hope in the same things and our genuine adoration of the Trinity— 2. we speak about it even more than we breathe, both in and out of danger, letting everything else come and go with the times, however they want, but retaining this immovable thing within our souls, the only treasure not subject to envy and, really, our very own. 3. For my part, when I ponder anything else—the great tribulations that surrounded and still surround me, the capriciousness of vices whirling up and down around me, and the war being waged against me by everyone, even though I do no wrong—I focus on this alone, that I was deemed worthy of becoming the truth's herald, while the sound teaching was rejected and spit out on to the deserted, untrodden, and desiccated earth, as it is written [Ps 62:2(63:1); cf. Jer 2:6]. To get to the point: I'm letting loose all my anguish, but I'm also quite pleased to have been deemed worthy of things better than I deserve. 4. Why am I writing these words? To make it clear that the only sure thing for me is friendship and fellowship with people of like mind. But who in their right mind would intentionally abandon people of like mind? Is any celebration greater than celebrating with such people? 5. If illness and winter weather impede my enthusiasm, I'll deal with the loss. But as for you, forgive me and pray that we have another opportunity to meet.

Gr. Naz., *Ep.* 228
Date unknown

To Pansophius,

1. Who doesn't praise a plant before it teems with blossoms? Who isn't made happy by a grainfield just before it's bundled into sheaves and promises a ripe crop? Or by a recently initiated soul just before it's beautified by God and begins to shake off its earthly shackles so that it may join God and see the truth of what we currently see as shadows [Pl., *Resp.* 7.514a–517e]? 2. For these reasons, then, I'm especially rejoicing at my beloved brother and fellow deacon Evagrius as I watch him approach philosophy not without valiance, since philosophy is also the passionate desire for wisdom. 3. I'm also rejoicing, though, because he is procuring your friendship for me, and I'll rejoice even more if you send me an epistle and repay me with even more tokens of friendship.

Gr. Naz., *Ep.* 229
Date unknown (after Gr. Naz., *Ep.* 228?)

To Pansophius,

1. A great distance stands between the Iberians and me[121]—the journey is not a few days. Friendship, however, makes neighbors of those who are far away from each other. How pleasant are the symbols of the festival! How pleasant is your invitation, and your yearning for my company! 2. Well then, in return for them, what equally good thing should I wish for you? May you be as good as you are! If I ought to say something even better, may you surpass yourself!

Gr. Naz., *Ep.* 230
Date unknown

To Theodosius,[122]

1. I imitate painters, who make an initial outline of their subjects' bodies with shadowy sketches, then make it more precise with a second and third go-round, and finally finish it up by adding colors. 2. What's the purpose of my example? We have a pure and unadulterated friendship with each other—something especially rare nowadays, and found among few people—and it was neither a family connection nor a commonality of homeland nor what Homer calls

"lovely companions" [*Il.* 3.175] that created it for us so much as the fact that we have similar ways of life and that we enjoy the same things, which builds friendships quite well and makes them stronger. 3. Our families are also now joined together (let this word be with God!), so that our friendship gains an addition and we belong to each other even more—and it was God, our helper, who enacted it with a lawful love spell. 4. And so, hold on to me through my sweetest son Euphemius and I'll hold on to you through your sweetest daughter. 5. In the future, I don't know about whom or to whom I should speak—about the young man to Your Dignity, or to the young man about your affairs. For a father's affection should extend with equal intensity to his children. 6. I'm praying for you, moreover, that the union turns out best in every way and proves to be as good a match as possible, since God has joined them together.

Gr. Naz., *Ep.* 174

383

To Eudoxius,

1. Let me conquer you with friendly letters. Indeed, I am writing you first, as you see. And know well that I wouldn't make a show of myself—for that's not my style—if I didn't regard your friendship as a great thing and think it necessary to prod you to write, as one does a colt with a strap. 2. Would that you be spurred especially to this, if you were to take note of who I am and to whom, about whom, and with which words I am writing, and that it is indeed fitting for children to inherit a friendship as they do their father's property. 3. Moreover, it's good to consider this, that while you are in your philosophical prime [Isoc., *Dem.* 3],[123] it is I who am the father of philosophers, and virtue should be paraded before me like the most valiant of athletes before their trainers. 4. Should I say something even better than what I just said? You have no small pledges of my philosophy: you're educating my blood and the blood of my nearest [kin]. You know of whom I speak: the children of Nicobulus, my most legitimate and honorable son. 5. Whatever you do for them, think to remember me, who is worse than no one (if I must trust those who say so) in judging eloquence, testing effort, and making decent teachers all the more exalted with plaudits.

Gr. Naz., *Ep.* 175
383

To Eudoxius,

1. Again my Nicobulus comes to you, and again I'm going all out in pushing you to be very excited about him too. Since he is too slipshod somehow and needs incentives—even though the young man possesses a decent nature (unless my desire deceives me), something that is, for the most part, yoked to the well groomed—confer upon him your own work ethic. 2. To speak like one of your people:[124] complete the song by imitating and becoming for your Eunomus the mythical cricket, substituting for the broken string.[125] Thus, I think that you will gain glory in the young man while giving the greatest of gifts to me, who doesn't come before you and Your Eloquence too much.

Gr. Naz., *Ep.* 176
383

To Eudoxius,

1. What should I say that you have against me, O Admirable Man? What is your reason for not writing? I won't accuse you of disregard, laziness, or not having something to write about; such qualities are not like you. 2. Perhaps you're holding a grudge against me for my iambic verses, which Valentinus—he who is destined for a bad end—spat out, even though you wanted them. 3. For it's not fitting for one man, a rhetor, to get up in arms against another man, a clever one, just because someone dared to compose such iambic verses earlier. But "tame your great wrath, Achilles" [*Il.* 9.496], and once again set your stylus, that ashen spear of yours [*Il.* 20.272], in motion for me. Don't expect to come across big problems, [such as] the episcopal lifestyle, just because you've experienced some little ones. 4. Ride, hunt, go about however you want, at least for my sake; I will write nothing further, nor will I play around with you. These words should suffice: I value your friendship immensely. 5. Such a game, then, has gone on for long enough. Here's something that no longer concerns game players but rather hard workers: again I entrust you with my sweetest son Nicobulus. 6. Would that you receive him from me now as if from me personally, so that you will show his father a rhetorical work and me a sophistic one.[126] For I know that if you are

willing, the task will be easy for you. Only let go of your scorn for the admirable sophists, and [quit] fighting for more [students].

Gr. Naz., *Ep.* 187
383

To Eudoxius,
1. You accuse me of not writing, while you, I think, are not one of those who write as often as possible, if the disease is not making me delirious and forgetful of the benefits that I've received. 2. Yet if nothing else, Your Eloquence owes me an epitaph, the craft for which is speaking and writing, as I lie dying. So that's my rebuke, for those who offer friendly rebukes should not do so beyond the bounds of friendship. 3. The words that you write about my sweetest son Nicobulus[127] are terrific, admirable, and enough to secure his father's contentedness, which easily believes what it wants. 4. But [as for me], I'll see the truth in your words as soon as the young man provides me proof and appears not unworthy of either your promises or my hopes.

Gr. Naz., *Ep.* 177
383

To Eudoxius,
1. How's it going with respect to your virtue? Have we made any progress toward God? I suspect that this, more than everything else, is what suits you. Indeed, I love to ask and hear about these things. 2. However, let's allow other things to bring us joy in whatever way they will. Yet even if we want these to turn out well too, we want it for this one reason, that you keep away from what you disdain and practice a superior philosophy to superior ends. 3. Reply to these words of mine and be as great as I hope you are for the noble Nicobulus. Should I ask for more, satisfy my greed as if you were an ambitious man.

Gr. Naz., *Ep.* 178
383 (after Gr. Naz., *Ep.* 177)

To Eudoxius,
1. In Athens there used to be an ancient and, I would say, most excellent law: once young men reached their sixteenth birthday, they would be introduced to professional crafts and introduced like this. 2. The tools of each craft would be set out in a public place, and the

young men would be brought to them. Whichever [craft's] tool each one was delighted with and ran to, this was the craft that he would be taught, since in most cases what is natural turns out well, while what is unnatural utterly fails. 3. What does this anecdote mean to me? I'm saying that you—indeed, you're made for philosophy—ought to neither disregard it nor push yourself toward anything that doesn't fit you, but rather that you should cling to the skill toward which you're inclined, not only because it's the best but also because it more naturally suits you. 4. Don't fight against a river's current, the proverb also bids us [Sir 4:26], and poetry does not want the person skilled in horseback riding to sing.[128] Why not? Because you would utterly fail in both riding and song.

5. But what is your aptitude? Well, at least as it appears to me, who has put some thought into it, it is first your character: the gentleness of your disposition, your sincerity, and your aversion to these vicissitudes of life. Next, the natural suitability of your soul, your high-mindedness, and your facility in contemplation. Third, your care for the sick and bodily weakness, since even Plato thought that this was no small contribution to philosophy [cf. Pl., *Phd.* 66b–68b]. 6. And besides, you've reached such an age that the passions are already receding. I also think that you're no more bowed down than beautified by poverty, and you know how to feel shame, unlike [other] rhetors. 7. But neither do you have a repulsive voice, nor have you become wicked, nor are you vulgar, nor—to speak concisely—do you possess any of those qualities with which Aristophanes fashioned Agoracritus for demagoguery [Ar., *Eq.* 5.140–229]. But given that you are called "rhetor," you rank among the rhetors in every respect, aside from your character. 8. Accordingly, don't dismiss the amount of philosophy with which you've already started out and hold second place among those who hold second place rather than first place among the greatest. Even if I were to give you the first place among folks around here, you wouldn't put up with being the best jackdaw when you're able to be an eagle.

9. For how long are we going to be puffed up by trivialities and things that concern those who go around on earth? For how long are we to play among juveniles and fictional compositions[129] and be lifted up by applause? From now on, let's make a change, let's become men, let's cast aside the dreams, let's run past the shadows [cf. Pl., *Resp.*

7.514a], let's leave to others the delights and particularly the pains of life. 10. Let envy, time, and fate—what they call the instability and irregularity of human concerns—gamble with, turn upside down, and play with others. Bid farewell to thrones, positions of power, riches, distinctions, vanities, calamities, this cheap and expectorated little reputation by which someone, elevated rather than ridiculed, would dishonor the games and shows of this great tent! 11. For our part, let's grasp the Word and before everything choose to possess God, our only and lasting good, so that we, who are still trivial and still seek this out, might have a good reputation here,[130] or one altogether from there,[131] since the prize for virtue is becoming God [cf. 4 Macc 9:8] and being illumined with the purest light, which is contemplated in the threefold monad, whose luster we now possess in but a moderate way. 12. Come to these conclusions, make progress, give wings[132] to your thought, seize the eternal life, never let your hopes stand still until you come to the coveted and blessed summit [cf. Pl., *Phdr.* 247a]. I'm certain that you'll even be praising me, only slightly right now but quite a lot soon, since you see yourself in what I'm promising, and in my promises you're finding no vain blessing or imaginative representations [cf. S.E., *M.* 8.354] but rather the truth of real things.

Gr. Naz., *Ep.* 179

383 (after Gr. Naz., *Ep.* 178)

To Eudoxius,

1. What are you saying? Am I persuading you with these words? Will you change over from teaching and take your station with us, formerly your opponents but now, if I'm allowed to say it, your advocates? Or must I sing for you a little longer? No, O Admirable Man, don't put this off. 2. For it's shameful for one who has the greater portion to abandon the whole. For if the beginning is half the whole [Diogenian., *Paroe.* 2.97], what else is more than the half except the whole? Well, if I'm sufficient in my exhortation, these words should be good and nothing more should be sought out. 3. If you need an even better adviser, though, it is Solomon who admonishes you to drink wine with deliberation [cf. Sir 31:27] lest you be diverted by life's drunkenness and dizziness, while it is I who utters a bit of advice, although altering it: take counsel with God and do not completely fail in what's required of you.

Gr. Naz., *Ep.* 180
383 (after Gr. Naz., *Ep.* 179)

To Eudoxius,

1. You come from a good father, beloved child [*Il.* 21.109; *Od.* 21.335];[133] this is the kind of thing that I'm learning about you. Only rise up, prosper, and reign [Ps 44:5(45:6)]. And as for me, I'm in good spirits, even if you don't yet confess your philosophy. 2. I pay attention more to what you say than to what you do, since not confessing your philosophy is itself quite philosophical too. Here is what the critic Dionysius says about the rhetor Lysias: his lack of craft is very much a craft [D.H., *Lys.* 8].

Gr. Naz., *Ep.* 32
Date unknown

To Philagrius,

1. It's good that you practice philosophy in your sufferings and become for many a model of endurance amid pains. Just as you used to mortify the body when everything was perfectly fine, when you were healthy, so too should you take advantage of this situation now, since you're already infirm and idle, but not, so to speak, in an idle way. 2. For you're practicing philosophy, and what they claim that Diogenes said a long time ago, while feverish and fighting through it, this is what you also hold out for others to see: the wrestling match between soul and body. 3. This is fitting for my Philagrius, to be neither made soft nor bowed down in the face of sufferings, but rather to despise the mud, to allow the body—which, either now or later, by the law of nature, will be dissolved completely (for as it wears down, it will depart, owing to either disease or time)—to undergo its own sufferings, to keep the soul itself up high, to be stationed by God's side in your thoughts, and to know that it's absurd for us to practice philosophy outside of dangers while appearing unphilosophical in times of need and cheating ourselves in the undertaking.

4. Obviously, you have gone over all of this in your thought—so many of our ideas, so many of outside ones[134]—since you're a man trained in both and a teacher of other people and you've collected the cure for the human condition from all of them by your own effort. 5. Let me philosophize with you for a bit, if you don't mind: I don't approve of that captious statement of Aristotle, who, in defining

happiness for us, went in the right direction only up to a certain point by declaring it to be a soul's virtuous activity and included it in the perfect life on account of the mutability and instability of our nature—an especially wise point [Arist., *E.N.* 1.7.9–15]. 6. He proceeds no longer magnificently but instead quite abjectly, however, because he also adds external prosperity [*Nico. eth.* 1.8.15–17], so that if someone happens to be poor, disease ridden, lowborn, or exiled, he is blocked from happiness by virtue of that condition. 7. But I do praise the vigor and high-mindedness of the Stoics, who say that nothing external prevents happiness but that the exceptional person is blessed, even if Phalaris's bull holds him while he's being burned.[135]

8. That's why I also admire those among us who stood in danger on behalf of the good or vigorously endured misfortune,[136] although I also admire anyone like them on the outside,[137] such as that Anaxarchus, Epictetus, and Socrates, lest I say too many. 9. The first, while his hands were being crushed on a mortar block as the tyrant so ordered, directed his torturers to bray the sack of Anaxarchus.[138] What did he mean by this? Our flesh is in a sorry state: the real Anaxarchus—his philosophical soul—was not pulverized, a distinction that we refer to as the outer and the inner person [cf. 2 Cor 4:16; Eph 3:16]. 10. The second practiced philosophy as though in another's body while his leg was stretched and twisted, and it appeared that his leg had broken before he even took notice of the violence. 11. As for Socrates, after he was sentenced to death by the Athenians and while he resided, as you know, in prison, he continued to lecture his students on that other prison—the body—and disdained the possibility of escape [Pl., *Phd.* 82e, 117b–c]. When the hemlock was brought forth, he was quite happy to take it, not as if taking it for death but as if making a toast to friendship. 12. I also would have added our Job to these, except I knew that you were far from his sufferings, since you are and will be with God.

13. I think that you're soothing yourself, my divine and sacred captain, and when you heal yourself like this, it's also easier for me to cheer up as your praiser and beloved friend, 14. since you're neither bowed down by the disease nor thwarted by the peace of sinners and their bounty in this life, which the divine David says [Ps 72(73):3], but rather purified, if it's right to say this about you, and treating infirmity as the stuff of virtue.

Gr. Naz., *Ep.* 87
July 381–February 382

To Philagrius,

1. The reason that we're unable to be with each other is the same for each of us: your body assaults you as it does (to say nothing more about it), and you know that I'm quite miserable. For, know well that once I returned from my journey, I would not have delayed in running to, embracing, and providing a counselor on certain questions to you before everyone, an intelligent man and a friend exalted in piety. 2. That which remains for us—mutual conversation by letter—you have done and are doing well and I, for my part, am also doing. The subjects of your letter are not trivial to me, nor do they deserve a short treatment; that's why, after examining them neither casually nor superficially but quite carefully, I've come to the following conclusion. 3. I have grown tired of struggling against jealousy and the sacred bishops who dismantle the common unanimity and treat their rivalries as a natural consequence of the faith. 4. Therefore, I know to turn the ship back (as the saying goes), to draw down into myself (as they say of a fishing boat when it senses a storm), and to watch from afar others throwing and taking punches while I pack up for things over there.[139] 5. If it's precarious to abandon the church, as you write, how so? If with respect to my church, even I would admit this, and it would be rightly stated. But if with respect to a church that has nothing to do with me[140] and has not been proclaimed to me as a penalty, I bear no responsibility. Should I be overcome by the fact that I had charge of it for a time? May so many other people be overcome too, whoever has had charge of things that did not belong to them! 6. While there is certainly a reward for the work, one cannot be blamed for refusing it. Have no fear for me regarding liability; instead, fear this, that I may sustain some injury.

Gr. Naz., *Ep.* 92
Date unknown

To Philagrius,

1. How is your body holding up? Or do you give it too little account, obviously, to know how it holds up? Concerning your soul, I won't ask how it is. For I know that it's also doing quite well, given that you are philosophically bearing your body's sufferings with

valiance, welcoming the situation as a test of your virtue and not just an inconsistent movement of material existence, so that suffering is more blessed for you than health is for others. 2. You're giving me a sufficient enough proof of your philosophy as to issue me such commands and on such subjects.[141] I boldly write to others on these matters, but it's not safe to risk doing so before a judge like you. Moreover, I'll try not to contradict the one giving out orders.

Gr. Naz., *Ep.* 33
Date unknown (after Gr. Naz., *Ep.* 32?)

To Philagrius,

1. I sense that some fault you for being enthusiastic about your only possession and loving to work in so severe a bodily condition. There's no surprise here, given that it's easier to philosophize amid strangers than amid your own people. 2. For my part, though, if I saw you doing this beyond the point of moderation by devoting yourself to philosophy in a competitive or extreme way, truth be told, I would rebuke you too, without respect for our friendship or education. 3. On the other hand, if you work hard but not beyond moderation, and if you use what you're hard at work on for what's right, and if your suffering comes to occupy your thoughts and convinces you that bodily matters pertain to the body, I don't have it in me to not rebuke your rebukers, having acquitted you of the charge. 4. Moreover, I'm persuading myself that there's no one better than you—whom everyone employs as a teacher and likewise a counselor, privately and publicly, for their own problems—to devise calculated thoughts about practical matters and to ponder the soul in a philosophical way. 5. But if watching over health or restoring it to the body is within the ambit of the physician alone, who would be so daring and uneducated as to admonish you when it comes to these things? 6. Let the masses rejoice, then, and let them be the jackdaws who evaluate the flight of eagles. As for you, consult your own counsel, and God too, about your suffering and whatever pertains to your suffering, and don't fail in what's right.

Gr. Naz., *Ep.* 34
Date unknown (after Gr. Naz., *Ep.* 33?)

To Philagrius,

1. I remember your company when we were together with each other a while back at my Mataza[142]—for what I call mine I also

assume is yours—as well as the philosophy that you practiced then, which gives me chills even now as I call it back to mind. 2. I interpreted for you the seventy-second psalm (for you bid it and I couldn't refuse), in which David grows dizzy and vexed at the wicked people who continue to thrive [Ps 72(73):3]. Then, directing his thoughts toward the punishments over there[143] and the retribution reserved for our lives, he thus withstood the disturbance, and his distress was cured. 3. And I drew my exegesis toward suffering as much as I could, using both our own and outside concepts[144] to philosophize them, because I was talking to a great and educated man, because the Spirit bore us along together like this, and because the feeling of pain incited us, for nothing is more conducive to ingenuity than suffering. 4. Anyway, my speech was running its course. You, however, jumped up in the middle of my speech as if from the starting line of a race, holding out your hands toward heaven and gazing to the east as much as possible (for you weren't able to see). "I give thanks to you, Father, O Maker and Disciplinarian of Your Humans [cf. Heb 12:7–10]," you cried out, "because you treat us well, who are unwilling, and you cleanse the inner person by means of the outer [cf. 2 Cor 4:16; Eph 3:16], and through countervalent forces you guide us to a blessed end, for reasons that only you know!" 5. And why should I mention all the things that you philosophized before I was there and while I was there, as if rejoicing in your disease? You too had a teacher for a student. 6. But why am I reminiscing about these things? So that, by crying out and proclaiming to everyone through you that, from my perspective, the wicked should lament the internal disease more than we lament the external one and that philosophical disease is better than unbridled health, we may be like this.

Gr. Naz., *Ep.* 35
Date unknown (after Gr. Naz., *Ep.* 34?)

To Philagrius,

1. Earlier I wrote you encouraging words for your suffering,[145] since you had indeed fallen down. But now I think it's you who is encouraging me while I'm in just as bad of shape. 2. For being friends, we shouldn't be separated in these things. You've already given much more encouragement, describing the endurance with which you endure.

Gr. Naz., *Ep.* 36
Date unknown (after Gr. Naz., *Ep.* 35?)

To Philagrius,

1. I feel pain in the disease and I'm glad, not because I feel pain but because I'm a teacher of endurance to others. 2. Since I can't not suffer, from my suffering I've at least sneaked away with this: forbearance and thanksgiving as much in joy as in pain, since I'm convinced that none of my efforts are lacking in reason—even if it might seem so to me—next to Reason.[146]

Gr. Naz., *Ep.* 31
Date unknown

To Philagrius,

1. What is upsetting to you is completely [upsetting] to me too. Indeed, we treat all things as shared between friends, whether or not they are good; that, in fact, is the very definition of friendship. 2. Yet if it's necessary to philosophize about them and to discuss fitting subjects with you (as is necessary, of course, and as the law of friendship imposes), I neither wish nor suppose that it's good for you—being Philagrius and eminently trained in divine things—to suffer in the same way as the masses, or to let your body degenerate, or to lament your sorry plight as fatal. 3. Instead, you ought to act philosophically in your suffering, to cleanse your faculty of thought now more than ever, to appear better than your shackles, to regard the disease as an opportunity for training in what's profitable (that is, despising the body and bodily things, as well as destroying every flux and tumult), to belong wholly to the upper part,[147] 4. and to live for the future instead of the present, treating life here as practice for death—this is what Plato says [Pl., *Phd.* 81a; *Grg.* 493a]—and, as much as possible, releasing the soul from the body, or tomb, to speak like him [Pl., *Cra.* 400c]. 5. Should you, O Excellent Man, treat these things philosophically and be like this, you would derive the greatest benefits, and ease my mind with respect to your situation, and teach the masses how to philosophize their own sufferings. 6. Moreover, if it's of any concern to you, you would gain no small thing—namely, the admiration of all. 7. But of the books that you requested, I've found one and eagerly sent it to you (I mean the volume of Demosthenes). The other one I've lost. I don't have what you want, the *Iliad*. 8. Don't lose your trust in me, though,

because there's only one of them that I confess to enjoy, and the only ones that I deservedly own are those that you partake of and those that you can use as if they were your own.

Gr. Naz., *Ep.* 30
Late 369 or early 370

To Philagrius,

1. I don't have Caesarius. I'll admit it, even if my suffering is not philosophical. I cherish Caesarius's possessions, and whenever I see a reminder of Caesarius, I embrace it and kiss it; it's even as if I expect to see him, to be with him, and to talk with him. 2. I've gone through something like this even now with respect to your letter. As soon as I read the opening address of your epistle, the name "Philagrius" and the very fact that it was actually you were sweet to me, and all the good times of yesteryear came back to me: the cities, the lectures, the table,[148] the poverty, "the things proper to the lovely time of life," as Homer says [*Il.* 3.175], whether games or studies, the sweat of eloquence, the teachers we had in common, the height of our hopes—however someone might denominate the good things back then, at which I especially rejoice, even in recollecting them. 3. Well, so that, thanks to you, we may converse about these subjects in further detail, put that stylus of yours into motion and indulge yourself in the writing of a letter. To me it would be no small thing at all, even if jealousy were to snatch away my greatest asset—your company—by making my affairs distressing.

Gr. Naz., *Ep.* 80
Summer 381–early 382

To Philagrius,[149]

1. You ask how my affairs are. They're quite bad. I don't have Basil, I don't have Caesarius: my spiritual brother, and my bodily one. With David, I'll say, "My father and my mother have forsaken me" [Ps 26(27):10]. 2. My body is in bad shape, and old age shows upon my head. I have a combination of anxieties: there are raids into my business, I have no trust in my friends, and the church is without a shepherd. Virtues bid me farewell [X., *H.G.* 1.1.23], vices are laid bare; I am a ship in the night, nowhere is there a beacon—Christ is asleep [cf. Matt 8:24]. 3. Why must I suffer? For me, there is just one end to

vice: death. Judging by the things on this side, I will find the things on the other side even more terrifying.

Gr. Naz., *Ep.* 224
Before 383

To Africanus,

1. What is it that most delights horses? Horses, of course. What about eagles? Nothing but eagles. You've also heard the proverb that a jackdaw feels comfortable with a jackdaw. 2. You must certainly conclude that, in the same way, Attic men delight an Attic man, and an adherent and patron of excellence delights someone who lays claim to it. 3. What makes a leader, it seems to me, is being a supporter of virtue and an opponent of vice, whether that leader holds a bloodless office as I do, or [is] one endowed with sword and belt. 4. Indeed, knowing that you are a master in virtue, someone who doesn't compel his subjects with force but chastises vice with fear rather than deed—the very definition of the best governance—I won't offer you blood. 5. In fact, that's why I was eager to meet you—and still am now! However, since I cannot get this, because of an illness, I necessarily come in a letter, and it's best that I'm addressing you through a man of my household, a friend and family member, Nicobulus, by my lights the most honorable in all respects; for me, he will also make a formal defense to you—the man is trustworthy, if he is anything, inasmuch as he knows me—and through me, he will make himself known to Your Perfection.

Gr. Naz., *Ep.* 227
Date unknown

To Ursus,

1. It's pleasant to address friends, and even more pleasant to do so through friends. Among them is my most honorable son Anysius; he'll give you some good news about my health (if by "health" I mean a slight tilt toward feeling better) and share information about whatever he thinks right. 2. Know well, though, that I find it most pleasant to be with you and enjoy your affection, which you're requesting in a friendly and genuine way,[150] and that I have no other desire except that those to whom I extol you know your kindness. 3. If it's also possible or, better yet, plausible, Your Sagacity will determine, so that I'm not accused of bad timing and so that I

don't appear burdensome to anyone, as if I were showing up with no explanation and for no reason. 4. Since I'm not successfully persuading the masses that I'm innocently practicing philosophy, I'm giving all that I have to God.

Gr. Naz., *Ep.* 225
Date unknown

To Hellebichus,[151]

1. What punishment the illness inflicts on me! I should run to embrace you and reminisce about our old friendship and intimacy. 2. My body, however, isn't up to it. That's why I'm coming to you by letter and greeting you with a salutation. 3. Since I should also be bearing gifts, this is what I offer: the lector Mamas, whose father is a soldier and who has, because of his disposition, dedicated himself to God. 4. Leave him alone for God and for me, and don't count him among the deserters; write him a note of discharge lest others subject him to abuse. You'll be giving yourself auspicious hopes for your war and command. Yes, I exhort you, show concern for him. 5. Indeed, showing special concern for God and his auxiliary force over there[152] belongs to those who have the greatest power in hand and decide everything.

Gr. Naz., *Ep.* 237
Date unknown

To Macedonius,

1. I'm not greedy for good treatment from my friends, even if you're extravagant in providing it. That's why I've sent the cantor back to you, per our agreement. 2. He's really quite good, in that he's a quick study, and he's pleasing to you perhaps because of his psalm singing, which is always suggestive of God and salvation. 3. And if you were to perform another service, whenever it pleases you and the time seems right, you would do something better, and it would be even more characteristic of your friendship.

Gr. Naz., *Ep.* 155
Autumn 382

To Asterius,

1. Why am I suffering this? You're leaving office and forsaking me while I'm ill and afforded by envy no chance to utter obsequies for

you.[153] What a loss and act of cruelty! 2. Let me risk saying something audacious: why should I even bother laying hold of the good if it won't remain? For the presence of delightful things does not cheer me up as much as separation from them brings me grief. 3. I've been honored by you; I've been glorified; I've taken advantage of your office; I took my fill of your beneficence. I haven't forgotten, and I won't forget, these things—let me sooner forget myself than you! 4. In the place of my words, what will you have from me? Could it be anything other than my noblest possession? I have prayers, which might offer you salvation and great esteem. If I'm lucky enough to live a long life, I hope that you might see me again.

> Gr. Naz., *Ep.* 147
> Summer 381–autumn 382

To Asterius,

1. Who is more just than God [Job 4:17]? Yet even though he is the maker and lord of all things, he regards his own people as chosen, gives them the name of Israel, and couldn't care less that he might be thought unjust for it. 2. Why is it shocking, then, if I, concerned for everyone under my protection and patronage, also more adamantly defend my son Nicobulus, whom I recognize as my caretaker in old age and sickness, whom I have had thrust under me like a crutch and staff for my weakness? 3. I am putting him into your hands, and through yours into the governor's, since I think it totally strange to use my connections to acquit other people of serious charges—even as those initial ones now become his bitter accusers—4. and not be able to free him from abuse and obtain for him, by my own efforts, the same honor that I obtain for strangers. He must be having the same experience as eyes, which see other things but not themselves, or as deep-lying springs, which provide water to faraway places but don't flow to nearby ones. 5. Let these little boys have their terrible—beyond terrible!—acts of brazenness, even though they will make few to no discoveries so long as the investigation's timing does not put us under duress. 6. However, why should this concern lords who have no share in what happened? And what sense is there in seeking restitution from some for the sins of others, and in now fretting about the public good when a private conflict is the source of distress?[154]

Gr. Naz., *Ep.* 148
Summer 381–autumn 382

To Asterius,

1. What's this? Perhaps you'll say, "Gregory is writing to me again? Epistles again? Requests again? What greediness, which I myself have set in motion!" 2. Of course not, O Admirable Man, don't have that reaction. For whom are harbors if not those caught in a storm? For whom are drugs if not the ill? May I not be robbed of these things, and by much more, rather, let me trust in my influence with you! 3. Indeed, I'm no longer asking but demanding that one favor always summon forth another favor. Nicobulus—which is the same as saying myself, for he is what props me up—stands amid abuses. 4. And how can I remain silent, not be burdensome, and maintain a strong philosophical disposition? Give your hand to the oppressed so that you may also obtain God's hand, since you need it, inasmuch as you're human. 5. Submit yourself to all friendship, to our union, and, with the help of God, to your influence in my affairs. For neither does a red-hot iron need many strikes against a stone to reveal the fire within it, but the flame flashes as soon as it is stricken, nor do you need a longer exhortation—and this one on my own behalf!—since the power of my persuasiveness is strong and your participation in an official position is so legitimate. 6. I'll also say one more quick thing: while some have received favors through my connections, I need this one for myself, a point that should win over Your Eloquence even more.

Gr. Naz., *Ep.* 150
Autumn 382

To Asterius,

1. I rejoice at writing and at being rebuked for not writing, were it to ever happen, for your rebukes are also useful. Furthermore, I know that I've written often and on many subjects, and, to be sure, I know that I get what I need from you. If nothing else, my letters bear witness to the host of your favorable reactions. 2. If you, with respect to our friendship, were more generous than anyone could pray for and I were more craven in my requests, then you would have virtue's first-place prize (I beg your pardon as I avoid being vulgar, given that the wise man's saying acknowledges that all moderation is best).[155]

3. Moreover, thanks be to God for entrusting you with success and thereby setting before us a common benefactor and colleague. Since, through this epistle of mine, I am even now entrusting to you my brother and fellow deacon George, one of my most remarkable men and someone most useful to the church, I think he deserves to obtain your confidence in matters where he disagrees with some individuals and to not be carried away by an act of tyranny.

Gr. Naz., *Ep.* 156
Autumn 382

To Asterius,

1. Heracles was great among human beings, as the story goes (that I might remind you, being eloquent, of something of yours). He would not have been so great, however, had he not had Iolaus as a fellow combatant, especially against the Hydra, that bitter and multiheaded beast whose heads the former severed and the latter cauterized, just as you do with the heads of vice. 2. The sons of Actor drove past many people on their chariots, as Homer believed [*Il.* 23.638–41]. Indeed, they were twins in their bodies and skill, dividing up the job of driving with each other, one on the reins and the other on the whip, thereby making mutual contributions to the victory. 3. A captain keeps many sailors safe, but he would not do so in the same way were he not helped by a good lookout man, someone to examine the winds, point out in advance things under the sea's surface, and generally act as the ship's eye. 4. From my perspective too, that's what your position has been. Yes, the governor is radiant by himself, but you enhance his radiance with your cooperation. Praising you for many things, I especially admire that, while maintaining your strong goodwill in public matters, you leave room for friendly letters, demonstrating precision not with a roughness of style like many unmeasured writers but by smoothing the roughness of your office with gentleness.

Gr. Naz., *Ep.* 204
Date unknown

To Adelphius,

1. So far, so good! The first steps have been really quite nice for us: we praise virtue; we both bow our heads to God; we've not been

constrained by things below us except when utterly necessary; we embrace a better and more divine friendship; we've clasped hands and pledged our trust [*Il.* 6.233]. 2. Come now, for the next step in our relationship, let me make an intercession with you, since I've placed God at the beginning of my account and moved in lockstep with him, whom I regard as the patron of my every deed and word. 3. Don't be surprised if I entrust so important a matter to a letter, for it is your kindness most of all—but also the simplicity of your demeanor and your liberality, which one finds rarely and in very few people—that stirs up my confidence in these matters. 4. Yet I'm not committing everything to a letter—I'm not so old-fashioned as to do big things in a small way or serious things in a cursory way—5. but now, as Pindar says, let's "use golden pillars to support a strong-walled palace," and a little later "we'll erect a shining house" (Pi., *Olymp.* 6.1, 3), whenever God permits, by joining deed to word, as they say. 6. Many of the noble families in your region are approaching (yes, I'm convinced that many approach—who wouldn't appreciate you and your connections?); many of the high-browed are extending their property to you, as well as their family, friends, civic influence, imperial influence, and all the playthings of the times that amount to irrational distractions, falling to some people at one time and others at another, tossed about and moved around from one place to another like pieces on a game board. 7. For my part, I'm introducing you to one person before everyone else—me!—and indeed I'm seeking out one person before everyone else: you! Should anyone be better than me or from a better place (I acknowledge it, since this is my position), at least they won't surpass me in this one respect (this shall be averred in God): faithfulness and authenticity in affection, where, more than anywhere else, people with good sense, at any rate, should begin drafting their composition. 8. That should suffice for Your Perfection, and perhaps it exceeds the appropriate length of an epistle. In closing, let me issue a prayer for both you and me: would that God, who dispenses these and other things to those who love him, bring into your mind whatever is best and beneficial for me as much as for you, who above all deliberates on matters of importance.

Gr. Naz., *Ep.* 205
Date unknown

To Adelphius,

1. We shouldn't dishonor a son, but we also shouldn't distrust a father. For that reason, don't distrust me when, in my own defense, I claim that illness and spiritual leisure—not any timidity or contempt, which perhaps you suspect of me—are what prevent me, summoned above all with great earnestness, from coming to Navila[156] and participating in the synod. 2. Well then, I'm still being overpowered by the infirmity now. But were God to give me health, I would also offer up a self-defense through deeds by running to Your Nobility and restoring the full measure of blessings to my household. Indeed, I want and pray that mine be yours.

Gr. Naz., *Ep.* 206
Date unknown

To Adelphius,

1. I'll still call you honorable, even though you're not deliberating on honorable things. Accept my frankness, as I'm impelled by fatherly affection and, because of my good feelings for you, I cannot exercise restraint. 2. It's far better to give as much help as possible to someone in distress than to let someone chasing pleasure put a bounty on his own head. Eli was a priest and he reproved his impious children, saying, "It is not a good rumor, O Children, that I've heard about you!" [1 Sam 2:24]. Yet because he did not issue a more forceful reproof, he received a forceful rebuke, and a pious father paid the price for his children's transgression.[157] 3. This example makes me fear for myself, and so I come to this exhortation. I don't know what happened to you! 4. What sort of moral blindness has come over you? How can you bring shame upon your own family? Are you also bringing shame upon my gray hair and the hopes that I had for you when we ran into each other at Navila,[158] after conversing with you and convincing you, as I believed, of every good thing? 5. How do you not hear scripture saying, "Do not give your wealth to women and your possessions to second thought" [Prov 31:3]?[159] 6. For know well that soon you will rue these words, whenever your flesh consumes your body [Prov 5:11], as it has been written, and whenever

your mind, as if parting the clouds, can look to God and purely meditate on his benefits. 7. Watch for the trap [Ps 140(141):9]! Don't let your own eyes carry you away [Prov 6:25], but if they do, keep sober! Don't lend support to the chatter that you stole away her mind with love spells, since licentiousness is clever in the contrivance of wicked acts. 8. It is indeed a grievous thing that a great house, brought together by great toils, would dissipate and instantaneously come undone like this, especially in the initial stages of a professional career, when each individual, by his own efforts, lays the foundation for a good or bad reputation. 9. But far more terrible is the defilement and rape of these women, virgins, whom you and your parents consecrated to God, as you convinced me; you are already detaining some and terrifying others by convincing them of the same fate. 10. Well then, since you fear the God that you adore, and since you respect me, keep yourself from every other bad decision. If you could get some perspective and recognize the ill repute that you've brought down upon all of us, perhaps you wouldn't need another exhortation, but reckon this shame as an index of your actions. 11. I could write words more pleasant than these, but none more advantageous. I'll leave off writing more, since I know that my words can have little or no effect if the fear of God does not discipline you. It's easy to scratch wax with iron, but it's more difficult to scratch iron and still more difficult to scratch a diamond with even the hardest object, because of the inexorability of its nature.

Gr. Naz., Ep. 233
Date unknown

To Ablabius,

1. I'm learning that you're passionate about the sophistic art and that your form is admirable—that is, you speak impressively, hold a strong gaze, walk proudly and loftily, keep your focus there on Marathon and Salamis (these, of course, are your embellishments), think about nothing except Miltiades and Cynegirus as well as Callimachus and Lamachus,[160] and, given that you're as close to the enterprise as you are, dress yourself up entirely in a sophistic way. 2. Well, if you were to use it to craft an account of virtue, you would be my kind of sophist and reports of your good reputation would travel ahead of you down the road. But if you turn out to be a

run-of-the-mill sophist and forget our friendship, during which we often discussed the good with each other, I won't say anything else that annoys you, except this, perhaps putting it in as moderate a way as I can: 3. know that you play among the boys for a brief period but you will play in your own class whenever common sense comes to you—but let's leave that for later.

Gr. Naz., Ep. 173
Summer 383[161]

To Postumianus,

1. With respect to education, you stand on high in the language of your choosing and in whatever form of eloquence you choose. In one language I hear only of your fame, since I am neither Roman in my language nor skilled in Italian affairs, but in the other I've got enough experience as to recognize it in others, if I can claim to judge how great they are—and not a few people say I can make that claim.
2. You were elevated to not a few offices, or rather you rose, to use a more accurate word, to not a few. You came to the summit of authority, receiving it not as a gift of fate, as many might say, but as a prize for virtue, so that it has become more august and the emperor merits praise for deciding on you. 3. Even still, I'll add some of my own trivial words. First you were initiated in piety, and then you took responsibility for it. Indeed, I remember your eloquence, and my ears still ring with admiration. If you also added remembering your friends to these qualities—and I'm sure you will, to the extent that I can make out from past events—I would admire you even more.
4. This is the limit of human happiness or blessedness, and I trust Pindar, who philosophizes that human beings cannot experience the region beyond Gadeira[162] [Pi., *Nem.* 4.69]. 5. Since you have obtained great things, you are also obligated to great things. God has treated us well, by first making you our own and then putting you in charge of us. At the same time, it would be inappropriate for me not to put the most important requests to so great a man—accept me when I make this exhortation. 6. Since there is another synod of bishops (I don't know why or how they're convening), consider that there is nothing so proper to your office as bringing peace to the churches by you or through you, even if you're bound to punish the rebels with ferocity. 7. Don't be surprised if I appear to be over-the-top, having

withdrawn from public affairs without curbing my interest in them. For I may have abandoned to whoever wants them my claim to thrones and pride, but not my claim to piety. But now I'm even more trustworthy, as I think it seems to you too, since I care for the community and for nothing of my own.

Gr. Naz., Ep. 132
Summer 382[163]

To Saturninus,

1. You require friendly letters, I know well, even if writing it is especially audacious.[164] Like a good slave [cf. Matt 25:21–23], you dispense authority to outsiders but license to speak frankly to us, who are deemed worthy of approaching God. 2. That's why I am addressing you and presenting my affairs to you, who craves this. All is well for me with God except for one thing, my concern for the churches, so troubled. 3. Whatever contribution you can make for them, don't shrink from advocating for universal concord in both word and deed, since again there is a synod of bishops and again a dread that we might be put to shame, if this one comes to a bitter end too, like the last one.[165] 4. I'll leave my affairs to God, who knows how to recognize and judge all things, even if I gladly yielded to envy and to those who wish for it [to come about], by sidestepping an affair that appears beneficial to many people but is actually precarious and by arriving, as if from a frightening and harsh storm, at a calm and safe anchorage.

Gr. Naz., Ep. 181
382–83

To Saturninus,[166]

1. Even if the height of your office is inaccessible, your friendliness is still beneficent, for which reason I'm confident in bringing this entreaty to you. 2. To all the good things that you've done for me, add this too: deign to look pleasantly, at least, upon my most eloquent son Eudoxius, a man worthy of your virtue in both conduct and speech, and deem him worthy of your own patronage concerning what he requests of Your Excellence. 3. For my part, I'll pay you back with prayers, the only means by which I can repay my benefactors.

Gr. Naz., *Ep.* 133
Summer 382[167]

To Victor,

1. I'm not acting audaciously by writing to you now, but actually timidly, because I didn't do so sooner. Really, that's not even true. For I don't have an abundance of people through whom I can send letters, although you can imagine how I yearn for it as I spend my time in a country somewhere far from your lodging and care for my body there. 2. Now that the time is right, I both address you and think that you, by letter, ought to bestow on me the same honor that you used to bestow when I was present, even though I'm absent now, and not be timid in comforting me, so distraught at the separation between us. 3. Since there is again a synod, again a fight—and this between my enemies as they carefully observe all my affairs—give your hand to the general establishment of order so that the church doesn't get the worst portion, and don't neglect everything consumed by the conflagration currently surrounding the church. 4. Rather, administer whatever flame retardants you can and command others to do the same, so your situation turns out well as the community pursues the better course.

Gr. Naz., *Ep.* 134
July 381–February 382

To Victor,

1. You're truly a conqueror and completely a commander, O Admirable Man! Indeed, just as you used to conquer your enemies with weapons, now [too] you conquer all things with kindness as much as you can. 2. Therefore, I'm confident in bringing this address and, with the address, my most honorable son Hyperechius, whom I know you'll honor because of his disposition, should you get any experience of the man, and because of me, to whom you know everything should be given. 3. Also, urge him to take confidence in you as a reminder of our friendship, for which, I'm convinced, you have great respect.

Gr. Naz., *Ep.* 136
Summer 382[168]

To Modarius,

1. You are my kinsman, relative, and any other such word that one might use. For piety joined us together, as well as the glory of virtue,

which I observe in you, who show plainly that "Greek" and "barbarian" is a distinction between bodies, not souls, and a contrast between locations, not character or conduct.[169] 2. Truly, were my race to imitate Your Excellence many times over, I'm certain that everything—both public and private affairs—would be good for me. 3. I exhort you: just as you, with your own hand and intelligence, valiantly brought the foreign war[170] to an end while standing over us, so too put an end to our [war] to the extent that it is within your power, by striving to bring about a peaceful conclusion for the currently convening bishops. 4. Indeed, they come together often but find no limit to their vices, always compounding troubles with further troubles for an increase in shame, something that you too know.

Gr. Naz., *Ep.* 137
July 381–February 382

To Modarius,[171]

1. For a while, I have yearned to speak with Your Dignity, and thanks be to God for giving us the occasion! While searching for a way to repay the person who is handing you my epistle, I realized that it would be best to commend him to Your Authority. 2. Partially on account of me, deign to look upon him with pleasure, since he is both mine and yours—my companion but your soldier (I mean Theodore, the one now approaching you through me)—so that he might get a feel for the honor you've always paid me and still now pay me.

Gr. Naz., *Ep.* 70
372–73

To Eutropius,

1. What's this? Eutropius the Great in my neck of the woods? I'm hearing about it, but I'm not taking enjoyment from it. Was Tantalus of old any different than this, wasting away by thirst while standing in a pool of water? 2. You yearn for my company, as you write, and rightly so! Being who you are, indeed, you ought not to despise your friends, but you ought to treat us well, even if you must do so cursorily, and pay honor to the same things after your term of office that you deigned to honor while in office. 3. How am I doing, you wonder? And how is my soul holding up, which yearns for you, if not in a great way, at least not in a bad way, as is reasonable since I'm

shackled by illness (for the greater the respect, the greater the yearning)? 4. As for you, be for me the Egyptian drug—whether this is the word [we might use] or some other—with which Homer soothed souls in their distresses [*Od.* 4.219-29]. 5. How will you turn into this [for me]? First by excusing me, for kindness materializes in a pardon; then by educating me with what you would write in an epistle. In that case, I would then be obliged to admire you in your office more for your virtue than for your authority.

Gr. Naz., Ep. 71
372–73

To Eutropius,

1. Let one person praise one of your characteristics and let another praise another (certainly, there's enough of you to go around for many tongues). As for me, I'll say what I've admired most. The by-product of your immense excellence and eloquence is that, all by itself, it can make you friends, some of whom are reputed to be important. 2. In addition to all the honors you paid me when you occupied the highest throne—still an object of envy—and in addition to our encounter in Asia, if you remember (and I'm certain that you do remember, since, with your perfection in every regard, you're also an expert in matters of friendship), you saw me as, among other things, most pleasant and you bid me to write, honoring me with your eloquence. 3. And not only that, but you also deigned to write me first, imitating good artists who train their students with lots of demonstrations. 4. So, by doing it well, you've now done [precisely] this! Don't hesitate to show me kindness in the future, even if the thrones thrust you up high again (they'll thrust you into higher office, not into higher virtue, because, in this regard, you cannot go any higher, having already reached the peak). 5. But as you act in the common interest, don't neglect your friends. [Be] like those Homeric youths who were motivated by friendship in the middle of a war, since even your Homer embellishes his work with this point.

Gr. Naz., Ep. 94
July 381–February 382

To Amazonius,

1. Should one of our common friends—I'm convinced that they are numerous—ask you, "Where's our Gregory now? What's he up

to?," say with boldness that he practices philosophy in tranquility, concerned as much about those who wrong him as about those who are not even known to exist. Thus he is unconquered. 2. Should the same person ask you again, "How does he bear the separation from friends?," say, no longer with boldness, that he practices philosophy but that he does so in quite the second-rate way. 3. Each person has a particular weakness: for me, it's friendship and friends. One of them is the admirable Amazonius. Perhaps you would provide me comfort and make me feel better if you were to remember me, and persuade me that you're doing so, in a letter.

> Gr. Naz., *Ep.* 38
> Late 360s

To Themistius,

1. The spear distinguishes the Spartans, the shoulder blade the Peloponnese, eloquence the great Themistius. Indeed, even if you're superior to all people in all respects, I know that this is your most remarkable feature. 2. It has also joined us together from the start—if indeed my own ability in eloquence amounts to anything—and has now convinced me to take confidence. 3. If you were to learn, though, about the man for whom I intercede, you would immediately approve of my confidence. Let me present him to you: Eudoxius, the child of the famous Eudoxius but my most outstanding son in conduct and speech, as you'll discover for yourself when you bring the stone up to the measuring line, as the proverb goes (and what measure could be fairer than you?). He is my friend in the highest degree, no less because of his virtue than because of my friendship with his father. 4. Please guide him onward, then, since you'll be doing a good deed for me and honoring our eloquence by providing the man this service. He needs to be distinguished for his eloquence and get himself a career based on his eloquence. He'll present what it should be and how it should happen in person, and Your Eloquence and Intelligence will determine what it will be and how it should happen.

> Gr. Naz., *Ep.* 24
> Late 360s

To Themistius,

1. Eloquence is in danger and the opportunity is yours, if you are indeed the king of eloquence. Besides, my Amphilochius is a friend

to you by virtue of his father, and I'll add that he is the type of person who won't bring shame upon his forebears or our friendship, unless I'm a poor judge of such qualities. 2. And here's the most important thing, especially for a philosophical man like you: he is having legal troubles despite doing nothing wrong. Coming off as uncaring might be the most unimportant thing to someone else, but to me, on the contrary, it would be a most serious matter. 3. So I do the only thing I can: I intercede in the presence of those who can act well. Given my current condition, I can do nothing else. 4. As for you, confirm the argument of your Plato when he said formerly that cities would not put an end to their vices until power consorted with philosophy [Pl., *Resp.* 4.473c–d; cf. Pl., *Ep.* 7.326a]. 5. For you are sufficiently both.[172] Lend your hand to one who needs it, advise a prudent course of action, and help him out. 6. There's no better philosophy that you could practice than now joining us in the fight for a just outcome, with the result that we—your praisers (so long as you provide us material to speak about) and friends—will act well too.

Gr. Naz., *Ep.* 112[173]
Lent 382

To Celeusius,

1. I received you even during my quietude, so that you would learn that the stylus speaks the word of quietude. Let me say what befits friendship and such an occasion. You, a judge, are committing a crime by not fasting—how can you guard over human laws while thinking lightly of divine ones? 2. Purify your courtroom lest one of two things happen: you either become wicked or are considered wicked. Allowing disgraceful spectacles is the same thing as putting on a spectacle. Here's my main point: you'll commit less sin once you recognize that you're judged as a judge. I've got nothing better than this to offer you.

Gr. Naz., *Ep.* 113
Lent 382

To Celeusius,

Don't judge me for practicing silence, since I don't judge you for speaking, which is the law that Paul issued regarding meats [Rom 14:3]. But if you must judge, fear lest my tongue be set in motion against you first, if it takes you to be deserving of quietude.

Gr. Naz., *Ep.* 114
Lent 382

To Celeusius,[174]

1. Since you prosecute my quietude and rusticity, you chatty and sophisticated man, come and let me tell you a not unrefined tale, if I could somehow hold you back from prattling on about this, at least. 2. Swallows laugh at swans for not wanting to converse with humans and publicize their music, for instead spending their time around meadows and rivers, for embracing isolation, and for singing just a few notes while singing what they do sing among themselves, as if they're ashamed of their music. 3. "The cities, the human beings, and the bedrooms are ours," [the swallows] would say, "and we speak to humans and tell them our stories, these being indeed ancient and Attic: Pandion, Athens, Tereus, Thrace, the departure, the anxiety, the violence, the excision, the letters, and above all Itys, and how we became birds from humans."[175] 4. And the swans thought little of the swallows, abhorring the glibness of their speech. When they deemed it right, they would say, "O Swallows, it's because of us that, when we allow our wings to blow something sweet and harmonious to the western wind, someone comes upon our isolated spot, that they may listen to our music. Therefore, not singing many songs and [not being] in the presence of the masses is best for us, because we treat each part of the song philosophically, with due measure, and we refrain from mixing our music with noise. 5. But human beings bring difficulties to you who dwell among them, and they turn away from your singing—and rightfully so, since you cannot cut out your own tongue to keep quiet! Don't you lament your dissonance and the suffering you've caused? Aren't you still noisier than good speakers and musicians?" 6. "Realize what I'm telling you," says Pindar [Pi. frag. 105a Maehler], and if you find my voicelessness to be better than your sweet-sounding tongue, stop prating against my quietude, or I'll utter an especially true and especially concise proverb to you: the swans will sing their songs when the jackdaws keep quiet.

Gr. Naz., *Ep.* 138
Late 381 or late summer 383[176]

To Bosporius,

1. As old-fashioned and naïve as I am, I was thinking that you owe me an explanation about what happened. But since you're not letting up in your war against me, instead always fighting old battles and devising one outrage to add to the others—I don't know the reason, whether because you hate me or because you're freely allowing others to dishonor me—2. I'll leave it to God to perceive and decide; nothing that exists escapes him [Job 34:21], which the divine scripture says, even if we muddy up the face of truth for the sake of looking good for the masses. 3. I've made my announcement to Your Reverence: I have been defeated and, should God grant it, I won't recoil from worrying about what could happen to the church (since you are fighting with me about this, especially now that time is becoming urgent, owing to our opponents' expected attack, as you yourself write).[177] 4. I will, however, submit this humble body to God until he supplies nourishment and I gain strength, so that neither would I thus bear the burden of being judged by you, and of being decried by every clergy member who crushes me with every sort of complaint, and of watching the church go uncared for, and of harming the masses because I looked past the affairs of the church, nor would you have to put any more work into dishonoring me. 5. Let me do this with your prayers, if you are indeed backing away from presiding over the church, as you tell me and the facts persuade me. For it's better to die with those worries than with these, since we must always be miserable when God shapes our situation like this.

Gr. Naz., *Ep.* 153
Late 381 or late 383

To Bosporius,

1. Twice already have I been tripped up [cf. Gen 27:36] and deceived by you in this (you know what I'm talking about). If you did this justly, may the Lord smell a pleasing fragrance from you [Gen 8:21]. But if you did so unjustly, may the Lord forgive you. 2. It's fair that I speak about you like this, since we've been commanded to put up with being wronged. Besides, just as you're the lord of your own

opinion, so too am I of mine. Gregory the Burdensome will no longer be burdensome to you. I'll retire to God, who is the only one pure and unadulterated. I'll contract into myself. 3. I've prescribed these measures for myself, for the proverb allows only fools to stumble on the same stone twice [cf. Plb., *Hist.* 31.11.5, 31.12.2].

Gr. Naz., *Ep.* 89
Late 381 or late 383

To Bosporius,[178]

I appreciate the conscientiousness of your invitation, but I would be quite ashamed of myself for not telling the truth. I'm afraid that I am done with public life. I bring such shame to my gray hair, to our common altar, and to the labors that I started in my youth by having you regard me as worse than even the worst and by having those whom I would have least expected dishonor me.

Gr. Naz., *Ep.* 240
Date unknown

To Meletius,

1. I haven't received a letter from you at any point in a really long time; how could you know that I'm yearning for one? But neither have I written one, although I'm convinced that you too yearn for one. 2. How negligent, lest I say inconsiderate! I was falling asleep in such a way that even Arganthonius[179] in his slumber was of little account to me. Where is my old fraternity? Where is our shared eloquence, and the assemblies, and the sweet and bounteous spring from which we used to draw water? 3. Well, as for me, I'm rousing myself, shaking off the dust like Achilles's horses [*Il.* 17.457], albeit a bit late, I hesitate to admit, and shaking out my mane. 4. Don't suspect me of writing a comedy. If our friendship matters to you at all, it will be evident in what you write.

Gr. Naz., *Ep.* 226
Date unknown

To Anysius,

A letter came to me from you telling of your health and that your departure went according to plan. All thanks be to God! Should I have anything important to write in a letter about my own affairs, let there be greater thanks!

Gr. Naz., *Ep.* 90
May 381–February 382

To Anysius,

1. You ask me how things are going. I'll respond with a story. They say that the Athenians sent an embassy to the Lacedaemonians back when they were ruled by a tyrant; the embassy came about so that the former might receive an act of goodwill from the latter. 2. But as soon as they returned from their embassy, someone asked, "How did the Lacedaemonians treat you?" "As slaves, quite well," they replied, "but as free people, quite horribly." 3. Well, that's what I can write myself! I experience more goodwill than the destitute but more hardship than those concerned with God. Yes, the ailment still bothers me, or bothers me even more than before, and my friends have not stopped doing bad things and harming me in whatever ways they can. 4. Pray, however, that the Divinity might be compassionate with me and that I might get one of two things, that I'll either escape dreadful things altogether or endure them. Even this would be a mild attenuation of my misfortune.

Gr. Naz., *Ep.* 193
381–82

To Vitalianus,[180]

1. I can sense your reproaches and silence. Perhaps you would say, "We were giving a wedding feast, and one for your golden Olympias! A group of bishops was there, but you, a proper gentleman, were not, because of either disdain or timidity." 2. Neither is the case, O Admirable Man. However, I think that it wouldn't have been possible for a tragic actor to offer a comic panegyric while at the same time being completely unattractive and unmatrimonial, with two gouty feet staggering about, the object of ridicule amid dancers (to banter a bit with you in a connubial way). 3. Well, at least in my intent I'll be present, celebrating with you and joining the young couple's right hands together and both with God's. Since you have every other good thing, it's fitting that the union have the best outcome, and one in accordance with our common prayers.

Gr. Naz., *Ep.* 194
Summer 381–early 384?

To Vitalianus,[181]

1. Look! You've got a second son-in-law! You're removing the sweet burden and doing it well. I'm idle, as you might say, but the real story is that I'm weak, not idle. 2. Besides, I'm succeeding in godly affairs. Yes, I've left the excitement to others, but we'll enjoy philosophical practice as soon as you've limited your focus to God and exist entirely for the things above. 3. Even now, I'm contributing my prayers to the newlyweds, if I must give you the most beautiful gift.

Gr. Naz., *Ep.* 75
Date unknown

To Vitalianus,[182]

I'm not frequently in conversation with you. The reason is that you're surrounded by the masses, in whom I take virtually no pleasure. If you extract yourself from the masses and keep virtue as a companion, you'll see the lame start to run, as the proverb goes [cf. Aesop, *Prov.* 182]. For I promise you this and, with God, I'll enact it.

Gr. Naz., *Ep.* 207
Date unknown (probably after Gr. Naz., *Ep.* 208)

To Jacob,

1. If my body were in good enough shape for exertion, I would have satiated my yearning for your company by coming to you in person, and I would have told you about what I wanted. For my account isn't about trifles. 2. Since I'm restrained by illness, though, I come to you in a letter out of necessity. I'm bringing to Your Nobility my most discreet daughter Simplicia, formerly the wife of the noble and good Alypius, the ornament of my entire homeland, with the lamentable names of widowhood and orphanhood,[183] so that she may get justice from you in whatever way she needs your help. 3. Just look how bad her misfortune has been. She hasn't stopped singing dirges yet; she agonizes over her orphaned children; she travels down long roads in so weak a body and with little experience in legal matters— she who is accustomed to not even peeping out of her house! 4. Is anything more pitiable than this? She has no place to sing dirges, and suffering is destroying the modesty of her nobility. Well then, after

you've mulled these things over and shown respect to my exhortation, don't wait for someone else to become a judge of you, the great and beneficial Jacob. 5. Don't force her to make longer journeys, since she is confident in the justice of her cause, as she is persuading me and many others. Once you've looked through the epistles, however, and examined her justice with complete uprightness, send back to me a more cheerful woman, having taken to heart before everything that it's from God that you've got great influence, money, glory, and a path to greater success [cf. Pi., *Olymp.* 8.13–14]. Guard over them for yourself during the present act of beneficence; as a father of children and someone who has gotten yourself out of some dangers and then stepped right into others, thus keep all this in mind, and use the present situation to engender for yourself favorable hopes with God.

Gr. Naz., *Ep.* 208
Date unknown (probably before Gr. Naz., *Ep.* 207)

To Jacob,

1. I know Your Dignity through hearsay, but I admire that, despite so few people having conversed with you over tremendous distances,[184] the account of Your Excellence is terrifically grand in all corners. 2. For this reason, I'm confident in making this intercession. The admirable Alypius, the universal patron of friends and guardian of orphans, has left us behind. This is no small misfortune to me. 3. It turned out thereafter that even his most discreet wife came to care for the orphans. 4. Give her consolation now with an act of beneficence, and give your own children security through a good deed for the orphans, and show her affection beyond what is owed to strangers. 5. Giving this favor to me will have an added bonus: whatever honors you'll have rendered me, you'll have rendered to God, whose servant and attendant I've been deemed worthy to be, even if I'm less than deserving.

Gr. Naz., *Ep.* 82
Date unknown

To Alypius,[185]

1. I'm writing you this first letter and making this first request; therefore, it would be right that, in this case, I get your help in the matters that I describe. What am I describing? With violent attacks, and no one there to help, the noble Palladius tears apart my house,

which I've learned is in your jurisdiction. 2. Indeed, it's good for you to be concerned about a man especially when he is present but even more when he is absent, so that my property, deteriorating and diminishing, may not completely vanish because of the utter lack of anyone there to prevent it, and so that, with no prize for their struggle, the aggressors will have nothing more for themselves.

Gr. Naz., Ep. 83
Date unknown (after Gr. Naz., Ep. 82)

To Alypius,[186]

1. I commend you for exercising concern for my affairs. I commend you further for informing me through an epistle that you are doing so. You granted a favor to justice in the earlier case[187] but to me in this one. 2. But to keep you from growing weary of me as you do the right thing in the following situation, I hope you shine ever more brightly by adding to your effort so that we may admire you even more! 3. My son Euphemius is not yet present, but he is expected to be soon, and I suppose that if he shows up, he'll not need too much work from you.

Gr. Naz., Ep. 86
Date unknown

To Alypius,[188]

1. How you tyrannize me with friendship! I'm sifting through our doctrine on vows, and I approve of the cloak wearers.[189] I am not, however, transgressing the law as badly as those specialists in erotic love among the Greeks. 2. For they not only make offerings during the throes of passion, as if to a god, but also consent to the annulment of oaths because of erotic love. If I too transgress a law because I'm in the throes of friendship, I'm not committing any sin. 3. Come to me, then, if you please, as soon as you've changed your clothes, so that things turn out best for me in both respects: I get to meet up with you, without straying too far from our doctrine. If you don't come, it would owe entirely to your cloak. Should anyone charge me with transgressing the law, I would openly declare to the utmost degree that you were among the vow's performers, not among those summoned. 4. If one of the people with me didn't accept this response, how would he respond to this, that I summoned you as an orphan? This is how you'll [again] tyrannize me once you have the

opportunity. 5. My third, and most important, response [would be that] you could summon me to a vow as if to participate in the vow. Well, that's how I'll receive you [when you come]: by speaking like a rhetor. 6. With respect to your sister, no one would censure us for her presence; on the contrary, they would censure her and us if she did not show up. So let her come voluntarily. For your part, cheer up and, with confidence in me and my vow, come meet me so that you make my festival all the more joyous. After all, with God's help, you supplied the food sufficiently—or should I say, as befits an orphan—with valiance and quite in accordance with a vow.

Gr. Naz., Ep. 84
Date unknown

To Alypius,[190]

1. Fortunatus, the one delivering this epistle to you, is a member of my household. If you need an additional credential, he is one of my praiseworthy deacons. These are the things you should learn from me. 2. I'm certain that you'll add further credentials by appropriately and attentively seeing to the man in whatever he requests of Your Reverence. In whatever way you do well by him, you'll be performing me a service.

Gr. Naz., Ep. 85
Date unknown

To Alypius,[191]

1. Make my affairs your own, just as you've previously done and demonstrated through deeds. Make my beloved brother and fellow priest Lucianus your own, deigning to look upon some of his concerns with pleasantness and impelled to show concern for the house of my kinfolk over there,[192] 2. since, with God's help, my business is coming to a tidy conclusion because of your decision and the beneficence of the Mightier.

Gr. Naz., Ep. 61
372–74

To Aerius and Alypius,

1. Just as it is a right and sacred thing for truly loving parents to dedicate the first fruits of their harvest, their winepress [cf. Exod 22:28–29], and their children to God—because both we and our

possessions come from him—so too is it with your recent inheritance, so that the portion eagerly given may provide security for the greater whole. 2. Accordingly, don't wait to show us kindness after everyone else, but rather before everyone show kindness to God, on account of whom you'll also show kindness to everyone else; once you've tossed aside the external conventions, come serve ours, giving this fruit of eagerness from yourselves. 3. We'll get donations from other people but eagerness from you, to whom God can offer a massive return on your current investment, not only in this transient and fluctuating life but also in the eternal and enduring one. Our only security lies in looking to that and aiming all our hopes at it. 4. Well, in order to receive something great from God for yourselves, be the same to the poor! With neither pettiness nor stinginess but with terrific lavishness and eagerness, fulfill the wish of the departed woman, whom you thought would be present with you and observing the current events! Bring her rest through the bestowal, so that you not only possess property from her but also procure a mother's blessing, which supports children's households [Sir 3:9], 5. taking to heart, as it is written, that a small portion with righteousness is better than a large one with stinginess[193] [Prov 16:8] (lest I say something slanderous),[194] and that many people offer to churches everything their household can afford. Of their own volition, they give their entire estate and occupy themselves with the noblest business—becoming poor on account of the wealth over there.[195] 6. That you may reap abundantly, then, do not sow sparingly [2 Cor 9:6] but freely give this good lot [cf. Ps 15(16):5] both to yourselves and to your beloved, stealing nothing from what has been written but bestowing everything with pleasure and joyousness, as though returning what properly belongs to God, as if you would only gain whatever you spent for your own souls. 7. For why should you hoard it up for bandits and thieves [Matt 6:19] and for the vicissitudes of the times, which change erratically and whisk unstable prosperity all about, but not deposit it into vaults secure and stronger than the attackers? 8. Display your frugality, then, in other circumstances and to other people (for I also pray that you're powerful with kindness), but fight the good fight [2 Tim 4:7] with us. Will one person prevail over another with piety and the blessings that God owes to the generous [Prov 10:6]? 9. So convince me that you are genuinely

Christians, and even more than that, since you began from so noble, pious, and just a starting point, you may continue to think with one mind in this case and others too, so that you are made glad by each other and me by you, who in other situations have become for the entire church a good example of generosity in these matters.

Gr. Naz., *Ep.* 3
Date unknown

To Evagrius,

1. Being praised gives me pleasure. Indeed, to think well of my son Evagrius is to think well of me, for the virtue of children is the glory of fathers. 2. For my part, I'm certain that your son took no benefit in eloquence from me (well, perhaps a bit), since I have no great ability with respect to eloquence. I won't deny, though, that I have bestowed upon him the single greatest thing before everything else: the fear of God and the conviction to despise present things. 3. And so I've prayed, and continue to pray, that he have the best, so that the initial fruits, which he received from me, may reach their full maturity and so that I may share in some of the fruits of my labor. 4. Special thanks are due to Your Dignity because you deigned to remember me and to honor me with reminders of our friendship. I was happy to accept them, since they are no small things.

Gr. Naz., *Ep.* 55
Mid-360s

To Nicobulus,

Due perhaps to the laws of love, you're running from those who chase you to make yourself all the more enticing.[196] Come then, and now make up for the damage done to me by so long a time. Even if something should detain you momentarily, you'll leave again, so that, again, you'll become a more august object of desire.

Gr. Naz., *Ep.* 12
Mid-360s

To Nicobulus,

1. Oh, you extraordinary man! So unspeakably great! So mighty in form and courage! You make fun of my Alypiane, that she's small and unworthy of your greatness. 2. Yes, now I know that the soul can be measured and virtue weighed, that stones are more valuable than

pearls and ravens more respectable than nightingales. 3. Go ahead, take enjoyment from her size and her measurements, and leave nothing for Aloeus's sons of old [cf. *Od.* 11.306–12]. For you're guiding the horse, brandishing a spear, and taking care of animals. 4. But there's no such work for her, because carrying the weaver's shuttle, managing the distaff, and sitting at the loom don't require much strength; that's the privilege of women [cf. *Il.* 4.323]. 5. If you were to add to her qualities that she has clung to the ground in prayer and always keeps company with God in the superior movements of her mind, why does her height or the measurements of her body matter to you? 6. Observe her timely silence, listen to what she says, note her disregard for personal appearance, how manly she is among women, her housekeeping, her spousal affection. Once you do so, then you'll also affirm the truth of that Laconian saying: "A soul cannot truly be measured, and the outer person should keep its focus on the inner person."[197] 7. Were you to look at her like this, you'd stop joking around and mocking her as small, and instead you'd congratulate yourself on the union.

Gr. Naz., *Ep.* 97
July 381–February 382

To Heraclianus,

To me, you're always the noble Heraclianus, one who speaks with and listens to education. The noble Constantinople is with me because of you, even if temporarily, since Envy wanted it to be like this. But if Gregory should also be noble to you, it would be better for both of us. You'll prove it by letters that you'll send me, which is the only possible way.

Gr. Naz., *Ep.* 128
July 381–February 382

To Procopius,

1. After a long delay, I, whom you used to deem worthy of great favors when I was present and whom, I'm certain, you'll deem worthy of the same things when I'm absent, am addressing you as the one who, as I see it, is before everyone and in front of everyone. 2. Let my son Anthimus, the minister of this epistle, get a great reward for his great service. Who is he? Someone who might obtain your patronage in whatever he needs. 3. The most important factor in my intercession

is that this very man left an illustrious military appointment; perhaps he is even known to you for his great deeds, as his bodily defect will also persuade you as soon as you see it. 4. By itself, his departure is hard to bear, but even harder to bear is the fact that it's seemingly undeserved. When added to these facts, I'm certain that my entreaty will also rectify what has attracted my attention.

Gr. Naz., Ep. 129
July 381–February 382

To Procopius,

1. If my body weren't treating me poorly and I didn't have poor prospects for its continued existence, first and foremost I would reap a profit from an encounter with you and your company, something that I entirely owe[198] to you. Second, I would have completed this act of intercession through my personal presence. 2. Given that I'm completely bedridden and unwillingly punished, shackled by sickness, the next-best thing that I could do is approach you by letter, give you my right hand, embrace you, and confidently ask about my fellow deacon Eugenius, whom I'm asking back from Your Magnanimity. 3. So if there's no crime, then, in his association with the sacrilegious Regianus (for he seems, at least, to have committed no other crime), then [send him back] because of justice itself, whose referee and patron you are. 4. If you decide that he has committed a crime, then [send him back] anyway, on account of the God whom he serves and on account of my gray hair, which you know to be an object of respect for many fearers of the Lord. I exhort you, then: give this gift to both me and the entire clergy, and make your prospects with God favorable for yourself by liberating this person from abuse. 5. In return, you'll get something with no less value (lest I call it a great thing) than what you're giving: my prayers.

Gr. Naz., Ep. 130
Summer 382[199]

To Procopius,

1. If I must write the truth, here's how I'm doing: I'm staying away from every convention of bishops because I don't see any happy ending to a synod that leans toward an increase in vices rather than a decrease. 2. Yes, the contentious and power hungry will always be around, along with—don't assume I'm being petulant when I write

like this!—those who are [supposedly] superior to reasonable discourse. Anyone who passes judgment on vice in others is prosecuted for it no sooner than he puts an end to theirs. 3. Therefore, I've contracted into myself and come to think of tranquility of soul as the only sure thing. And now I have an illness that protects my decision; I'm nearly always breathing my last and unable to make myself of any use. 4. Therefore, let Your Magnanimity agree with me, and let the most pious emperor[200] be persuaded by you not to condemn me as indifferent but to recognize the infirmity for which I need retreat before any other benefaction—something which he knew and conceded to me.

Gr. Naz., *Ep.* 9
July 363–February 364

To Amphilochius,

1. "Use golden pillars to support a strong-walled palace," as Pindar has it [Pi., *Olymp.* 6.1–2], and from the start make yourself known to me on the right side in my present concern so that you might build a spectacular palace and appear glorious within it. 2. How will you make it stand out? By honoring God and godly things. What could be greater and more exalted to you than that? How, and with what, will you show him honor? By this alone: caring for God's devotees and ministers[201] of the bema. 3. One of them is also my fellow deacon Euthalius, from whom—I don't know how—some agents from the governor's office are trying to levy gold because he transferred to a better position. 4. Don't think this tolerable! Lend your hand to the deacon and to the entire clergy—and before all others, to me, for whom you care—or he might be the only one among humanity to suffer the most terrible things by not obtaining the benevolence of opportunities and the honor given to priests by emperors,[202] suffering instead an insult and a fine due in equal measure to my own inferior position. 5. It's good for you to not acquiesce to them, even if others bear ill will.

Gr. Naz., *Ep.* 13
365

To Amphilochius,

1. I praise Theognis:[203] he doesn't praise friendship that stops at drinks and pleasure, but he does praise it when it comes to lawsuits. What does he write? "Next to bowls of wine, one's close friends are

many, but amid a serious lawsuit, they are fewer" [Thgn., *El.* 1.643–44]. 2. Now then, we have not shared bowls of wine with each other, because we haven't spent a lot of time with each other (although we more than everyone should have[204] done so, on account of ourselves and our fathers' friendship[205]), but we do request goodwill in deeds. 3. At hand is a struggle, even the greatest of struggles: my son Nicobulus finds himself amid unexpected troubles, from quarters where one would least expect to find litigants. 4. We therefore ask that you come and help us as soon as possible by joining his case and advocating for him, if you find that we've been done wrong. If not,[206] don't sell out your freedom, which I know everyone always testifies about you, and let the opposing party gain the advantage.

Gr. Naz., *Ep.* 63
374

To Amphilochius,

1. Are you in pain? Clearly, I'm quite delighted. Are you crying? As you can see, I'm celebrating and priding myself on the current events. Or does your son, seized and honored for his virtue,[207] cause you distress? Is it so bad if he won't be present with you, if he won't tend to your old age, and if he won't help out in day-to-day affairs as he usually does? 2. Isn't my father bringing me grief now that he has made his final departure, from which he will never return to us or be seen by us?[208] For my part, then, I'm not accusing you of anything or demanding from you the obligatory consolation, since I realize that one's own problems present no chance to deal with those of other people. For no one is so loving and philosophical as to be above the passions and exhort someone else while needing exhortation himself. 3. For your part, though, you throw one punch after another by bringing charges against me (as I'm learning) and thinking that your son and my brother is being neglected or, even more serious, betrayed by me but that I don't perceive the damage done to everyone, kith and kin alike, but particularly to myself more than everyone, since I placed the hopes of life [Titus 3:7] in him and assumed that he was my only support, my only good adviser, my only sharer of piety. 4. And why do you imagine this to be the case? If because of the first things [I mentioned], keep in mind that I came all the way to you of my own volition because I was disturbed by the rumor and

eager to share my opinion with you while there was still an opportunity to deliberate on these matters. And you shared everything with me—except this particular concern, either because it's uncomfortable or because you had something else on your mind that I wasn't aware of. 5. But if because of the latter, certainly my suffering as well as the honor and rites that I owed to my father, over which I could prioritize nothing, did not permit me to meet with you again, since the suffering related to those things was fresh, when practicing philosophy and transcending human nature at the wrong time would be not only impious but also wholly inappropriate. On top of that, I thought that I was preoccupied by the business that consummated in him,[209] which is what seemed right to the One Who Guides Our Affairs. 6. Indeed, that's how it was. But now let go of your grudge against me, since, I'm convinced, it's the most unreasonable of all passions. And if a greater one comes up, show it to me so that you do not cause grief to me in part and to yourself, and overly suffer from something unworthy of Your Excellence by bringing charges against me, whom you used to consider as your sole benefactor instead of others, even though I have done nothing wrong and in fact have been equally tyrannized, to tell the truth, by common friends.[210]

Gr. Naz., *Ep.* 25
After 370?

To Amphilochius,

1. I didn't ask you for loaves of bread, because I wouldn't ask for water from the inhabitants of Ostrakine.[211] But if I were to ask an Ozizalean man[212] for vegetables, of which you have an abundance and we a great dearth, it wouldn't be surprising or even out of the ordinary. 2. Deign to send me, then, the largest and finest vegetables, or as many as you can, since even small things are great to the poor but especially since I'm welcoming the great Basil. You've had experience of him as a full-bellied philosopher, but you don't want to experience him like this, hungry and grouchy.

Gr. Naz., *Ep.* 62
Date unknown

To Amphilochius,

The command of Your Inimitable Virtue is not barbarian but Greek and even Christian. The Armenian, though, on whom you entirely pinned your pride, is an undisguised barbarian and stands at a distance from my point of pride.

Gr. Naz., *Ep.* 26
After 370? (after Gr. Naz., *Ep.* 25)

To Amphilochius,

1. The vegetables that came from you to me are so tiny! What else could they be except golden vegetables? Yet your wealth consists entirely of orchards, rivers, groves, and gardens; your land bears vegetables as others' land bears gold; "you live among the meadow's foliage" [Theoc., *Id.* 18.39]. 2. Your grain, the mythical blessing! Your bread (in fact, the so-called bread of angels [Ps 77(78):25]), so welcome and incredible! 3. So share them with me ungrudgingly, or I'll make no other threat except that I'll withhold my grain and we'll see if crickets truly feed on dew alone [cf. Theoc., *Id.* 4.16].

Gr. Naz., *Ep.* 27
After 370? (after Gr. Naz., *Ep.* 26)

To Amphilochius,

1. You're playing around.[213] For my part, I know the danger of a hungry Ozizalean, especially when you've been out in the field. 2. This one is the Ozizaleans' only praiseworthy quality: even if starvation makes them decay, they still smell nice and get a dazzling funeral. How so? They're located among the many multicolored flowers.

Gr. Naz., *Ep.* 184
Late 383

To Amphilochius,

1. May the Lord fulfill all your petitions [Ps 19:6(20:5)], and may you not refuse a father's prayer. You sufficiently refreshed my old age by coming all the way to Parnassus[214] per invitation and rebuking the slander pronounced against the most honorable and God-beloved bishop,[215] since the wicked love to turn their own flaws against their rebukers. 2. For, on the one hand, stronger than every accusation are the man's age, his lifestyle, our having heard from him the same things that we also taught, and those whom he has recovered from error and added to the common body of the church. 3. On the other hand, however, the timing was bad, and because of his

revilers and maligners a more precise demonstration was required, which you personally gave to us, [or] rather to the more capricious [among us] and those easily deceived by such things. 4. But if it should please you to bear witness to these things in person by taking upon yourself a greater journey and, with the rest of the bishops, to arbitrate between those involved in the dispute, you would be doing a spiritual deed and an act worthy of Your Perfection. I and all those with me greet the monastic community with you.

Gr. Naz., *Ep.* 28
After 370? (after Gr. Naz., *Ep.* 25–27)

To Amphilochius,

1. While inspecting the mountainous cities that border Pamphylia, I fished out a seabound Glaucus[216] there among the mountains, not dragging the fish out of the deep with the mesh of a fishing net but ensnaring my prey with a love for friends. 2. As soon as Glaucus had learned how to walk, I dispatched him as a letter carrier to Your Goodness; kindly host him and deem him worthy of the hospitality made famous by the scriptures—with your vegetables [Prov 15:17].

Gr. Naz., *Ep.* 171
374–early 384

To Amphilochius,

1. Hardly ever looking up from the toils of illness, I have run to you, the guardian of my remedy. For a priest's tongue that philosophically speaks of the Lord lifts up the weary. Accordingly, perform the superior act of your sacred functions and dissolve the magnitude of my sins as you undertake the sacrifice of the resurrection. 2. While I'm awake and asleep, your affairs are my concern; you've become my good plectrum[217] and you have implanted in my soul a harmonious lyre; with your countless writings, you have thoroughly trained my soul for full knowledge. 3. But don't hesitate, Most Godly One, to pray for me and intercede on my behalf when you draw down the Word with your own word, when you divide the lordly body and blood with a bloodless division, using a voice as the knife.

Gr. Naz., *Ep.* 234
Date unknown

To Olympianus,[218]

1. I couldn't arrange for the return of the little volume that you got from me, Aristotle's epistles, but I could let it stay with you as a gift appropriate for an eloquent person and a nice reminder of our friendship. 2. But so that, as a most fearsome rhetor and the best judge, you don't deliver an indictment against my transgression and insult to your position, that I tried to corrupt a judge who is so unassailable and who is above every bribe, let what I've given you come back to me. 3. I seek no reward from Your Eloquence—what would you even give me, who practices the philosophy of possessing nothing?—other than the very act of writing an epistle, so that your return gift would be proportionate, paying off a debt of gratitude for epistles with epistles.

Gr. Naz., *Ep.* 67
Autumn 374[219]

To Julian,

1. I have many reasons for my friendship with you, and if there is no other, at least there's eloquence: the masses hold nothing more respectable and engendering of familiarity. There's no basis for hostility between us, and may there never be! For the troubles that have sprung up against my brother Nicobulus, or because of Nicobulus, are no more my business than what happens among the Indians, except that I was displeased at what transpired. 2. Accordingly, don't hold the following words against me, and don't resolve on the worse course for yourself because of this. Instead, perform the same effective act of beneficence here that you supplied to the poor. Liberate the clergy around me—they are the ones on whose behalf I'm making this petition—from the tax registry, once you've mulled over how very inappropriate it would be for some people to dedicate all their property to God but for you to not want to be freely helpful, and for all those who hang around the bema in other cities to be given the relief but not those with me and assisting me, and for these things to happen to your closest acquaintances [such as myself], a fact of which, it happens, I'm not ashamed. 3. It's good for me to send you these words, but I cannot meet with you until the right time, since my disease impels me to Tyana,[220] where I'll find treatment. Pardon me

for this. In my place you have God, present and giving assistance to the poor, something far more respectable than my presence.

Gr. Naz., *Ep.* 69
Autumn 374 (after Gr. Naz., *Ep.* 67)

To Julian,

I've got your promise, and I'm confident in your character; for that reason, I've also got the gift.[221] Well then, the Great Dissolver of Debts knows better than everybody the measure of the donations and recompense, but if it were up to me to settle these important accounts, I would say that I made the sacrifice, while you performed the act of beneficence. Let's each get our portion of recompense.

Gr. Naz., *Ep.* 68
Autumn 374 (after Gr. Naz., *Ep.* 69?)

To Julian,

1. You summoned me to your abode—a nice thing to do!—so that I might be a partner in planning for the assessment, and indeed the matter is no small concern. If I were in good health, I would meet you with enthusiastic eagerness, but I'll come when I can, God willing. But for now, let me render my presence by letter. 2. I know that you come from holy parents and that from the beginning you have grown up with divine fear. Well then, obviously you do what you know to be good for you in terms of both excellence and the security of your soul, even if I weren't to write it. 3. But if I should make some contribution, I would tell you this: before any other way of life that Christian souls offer to God, this one has now been prescribed to you. So long as you keep your concern for the community and rectify whatever has been poorly managed in the past, you'll store up great things for yourself too. 4. The one greatest thing for your security (which you should watch over first and foremost) is to receive co-workers whom, in both conscience and character, you know surpass others. For what good is a competent captain who hires terrible oarsmen?

Gr. Naz., *Ep.* 64
374

To Bishop Eusebius of Samosata,

1. When Your Godliness was passing through my country, I couldn't even stick my head out of my bedroom, because I was tarrying in a

recent illness. The disease that induces fear about the end, though, was not as bothersome to me as being robbed of your holy and good company. 2. I had so great a desire to see your precious visage that I was like someone who needed treatment for the wounds to my soul and hoped to get it from Your Perfection. 3. But even if my missing your company at that time was a product of my own sins, now I am able to ameliorate my troubles through your goodness. 4. For if you would only deign to remember me in your acceptable prayers, then I would have this stock of every blessing from God, both in this life of mine and in the age to come. 5. For with respect to such a man—bravely struggling for the gospel's faith like this; enduring terrible persecutions; preparing great license for himself to speak frankly with God, Dispenser of Justice, through the endurance of tribulations; and deciding to become my patron through prayers—I'm convinced that whatever power he has would be mine, and it would be as if from one of the holy martyrs. So I exhort you to remember your Gregory unceasingly in those things that I pray deserve your memory.

Gr. Naz., *Ep.* 44[222]
Autumn 370

To Bishop Eusebius of Samosata,

1. Where will I begin your encomiums? And what is the proper name by which I should address you? Pillar and bulwark of the church [1 Tim 3:15]? A star in the world [Phil 2:15], to use the same phrases as the apostle? The crown of boasting [1 Thess 2:19] for the portion of Christians that is saved? God's gift [John 4:10]? Your homeland's support? Canon of faith? Ambassador for truth? All of these together and more? 2. Let me also corroborate my excess of praises with things that were seen. What timely rain came like this to a thirsting earth [Ps 146(147):8; Job 5:10]? What kind of water flowed out of a stone to those in the desert [Exod 17:6–7]? What great bread of angels did a human being eat [Ps 76(77):25]? 3. As they were being submerged at a critical time, did our common lord Jesus appear to any of his disciples to tame the sea and rescue those in danger [Matt 8:24–26] in the same way that you appeared to us, who were worn out, dejected, already shipwrecked? Why should I say anything else? You filled the souls of the orthodox with great exuberance and pleasure and dissolved the despair of so many.

4. But our mother church—I mean the one in Caesarea—is now really taking off her widow's garments [Gen 38:14] at the sight of you and putting on the robe of gladness,[223] and she will shine even more now that she has received a shepherd worthy of herself, his predecessors, and your hands.[224] 5. For you too can see for yourself what my affairs are like and how much your zeal, sweat, and frankness with God worked miracles. My old age is renewed [cf. Ps 102(103):5] and my illness conquered; the bedridden leap [Matt 9:2–7; Mark 1:29–31; Luke 5:18–25; cf. Acts 28:7–8] and the weak gird themselves with power [1 Kgs 2:4]. With these examples, I would guess that my own affairs will also turn out as I wanted. 6. Well then, for himself and me too you have my father, who will put this noble finishing touch on his entire life and his venerable gray hair with this current struggle for the church. And I know well that I'll welcome him back stronger and more invigorated by your prayers, in which confident people[225] should entirely trust. But if he should be brought down by anxiety, he would incur no damage from this kind of conclusion to these kinds of matters. 7. But I exhort you: please excuse me if, having tried a bit to escape the tongues of the wicked, I should later run to you, embrace you, and make up with my personal presence for whatever shortcomings my current acclamation has.

Gr. Naz., *Ep.* 65

374

To Bishop Eusebius of Samosata,

1. Already in every way precious to me and among my genuine friends, my most respectable brother Eupraxius appeared more precious and more genuine because of his affection for you. Even now he is thus rushing to Your Godliness, just as—to use one of David's expressions—a deer quenches his great and unbearable thirst with a fresh and pure spring [Ps 41:2(42:1)]. 2. Blessed is the one deemed worthy to be near you, but more blessed is the one who sets atop his sufferings for Christ and his sweat for truth so great a crown, which few of God's fearers have obtained. 3. For you put your not untested virtue on display: not only did you sail the straight course and lead the souls of others during a season of fair weather, but you also shone forth during the trials' difficulties and became more

exalted than your persecutors by valiantly leaving the land that bore you.²²⁶ 4. Others have the soil of their homeland, whereas we have the city above. Others perhaps have our throne, whereas we have Christ. What a bargain! We've acquired so much for despising so little! We went through fire and water [Ps 65(66):12], but I trust that we will also come to refreshment. 5. For in the end, God will not abandon us, and he'll not stand by as a spectator to the persecution of right doctrine, but rather his consolations will bring us joy [Ps 93(94):19] in proportion to the multitude of our pains. This, then, is what we trust in and pray for. For your part, I beg you, pray for my lowliness, 6. and whenever the opportunity arises, don't hesitate to grant me a blessing with a letter and to cheer me up by informing me of your situation, which you have deigned to do even now.²²⁷

Gr. Naz., *Ep.* 231
Date unknown

To Eusebius,²²⁸

1. This is my dearest Evopion. It's time for her marriage, and it will be the groundwork for her life, and her parents' prayers will be fulfilled. As for me, I'm absent, and it would most certainly be right for me to be there praying with them. 2. What's more is that I promised you I'd be there; indeed, hope laid beneath my yearning. Yet willingness is enough for self-deception. Drawing back as often as I headed out, I've been defeated by illness at last. 3. Well, let others invoke the gods of love [Simon., *Epig.* 25.3] (since playfulness also characterizes a wedding). Let them write about the bride's beauty and then extol the groom's grace and cast them with eloquence into the bridal chamber among the blossoms. 4. For my part, let me sing you my nuptial song. May the Lord bless you from Zion [Ps 127(128):5]! May he join the union! May you see sons of your sons [Ps 127(128):6], and—it's not too much to say—may they be superior to you! 5. This is the prayer that I would have made for you in person, as I'm doing now. You'll take care of the rest, and let her father place the crown on her, as he wished.²²⁹ For even if I could somehow attend weddings, here's what I've decreed: there are crowns for some but prayers for me, which I know to be unconfined to physical locations.

Gr. Naz., *Ep.* 42 (= Bas. *Ep.* 47)[230]
Summer 370

To Bishop Eusebius of Samosata,

1. Who will give me wings like a dove [Ps 54:7(55:6)]? Or how will my old age be renewed [Ps 102(103):5] that I may be able to make the trek over to Your Charity, to satisfy the yearning that I have for you, to recount the distresses of my soul, and to find in you some consolation for my tribulations? 2. For it's no small fear that has taken me at the death of the blessed bishop Eusebius:[231] those who used to lie in wait for our metropolis's church, intending to fill it up with heretical tares [cf. Matt 13:25], are now seizing the opportunity to use their own wicked teachings to uproot the piety sown in people's souls with much toil and to chop up its unity, something that they have also done with many [other] churches. 3. And when the clergy's letter came to me,[232] encouraging me not to abandon them at this crucial moment, I looked all around and remembered your love, your upright faith, and the zeal you always have for God's churches. 4. Therefore I have also sent the beloved Eustathius, my fellow deacon, to exhort and entreat Your Solemnity [to direct] all your efforts on behalf of the church, to put your seal on the present letter, to refresh my old age with a meeting, and, with my cooperation (should I be deemed worthy to help you out in the good deed), to restore the famous piety to the orthodox church by giving it, according to the Lord's will, a shepherd who can guide its people. 5. For before our very eyes we have a man of whom you're not ignorant.[233] If we're deemed worthy to obtain him, I know that we'll procure great license to speak frankly in God's presence and dedicate the greatest benefaction to the people who invoke our assistance. But again, and often, I encourage you, having put off every hesitation, to meet with me and get here before the difficulties of wintertime.

Gr. Naz., *Ep.* 66
374

To Bishop Eusebius of Samosata,

1. You bring me joy by writing, remembering me, and, more than anything else, granting me a blessing in your letter.[234] For my part, if I were worthy of your sufferings as well as your struggle for Christ and because of Christ, I would also have been worthy of coming to you to

embrace Your Godliness and to receive a model of endurance in the midst of sufferings. 2. But since I'm not worthy of this, troubled by many afflictions and engagements, I'll do the next-best thing: I am greeting Your Perfection and asking that you not grow weary of remembering me. 3. For being deemed worthy of your letter is not only a profit for me but also a boasting point and a source of pride in front of the masses, because I have an account with a man so great—who has virtue and a strong relationship with God—that others too can conform to his word and example.

Gr. Naz., *Ep.* 141
Spring–autumn 382

To Olympius,[235]

1. An opportunity for beneficence comes again, and again I dare to trust to a letter an exhortation about such an important matter. For the disease emboldens me even though it won't let me come out, nor will it allow you to pay a decent visit. 2. So what's my request? Accept it from me with both gentleness and beneficence. A man's death is terrible (how could it not be?): today he exists, but tomorrow he won't, and he'll not return to us [Sir 10:10]. How much more terrible is it for a city to die, one where kings have sat, one where ages have stood firm, a place that a long succession has closely guarded! 3. This is my argument on behalf of Diocaesarea,[236] previously a city but currently not a city unless you consent to lenient treatment. Imagine her falling before you through me, and let her have a voice, let her don mournful garb, let her cut her hair as if she were performing in a drama, and let her craft this bit of eloquence for you: "Give your hand to me as I lie on the ground—help the infirm! Don't help time lay siege to me, and don't let the ruins of the Persians be destroyed.[237] 4. It's more proper for you to lift cities up than to tear down those that succumb to fatigue. Play the city founder either by adding something to what's already here or by simply preserving what exists. Don't tolerate my being a city only during your term of office and no longer existing after you. Don't tolerate giving to time the sad story of how you took me as numbered among your cities, only to abandon me as an uninhabitable place, a former city, distinguished only for its mountains, cliffs, and forests."

5. Let the fictional city craft and speak those words to Your Beneficence. Accept an exhortation from me as a friend. Please put

some sense into those who violated the ordinance of Your Authority, for I won't take a bold tone with you when it comes to that, even if their boldness did not stem from a common concern, as they claim, but was an irrational urge of young men. 6. Rather, let go of your anger and deploy superior reasoning. They were cut to the quick by the execution of their mother,[238] and citizens cannot bear to be called, or to actually be, cityless. They lost their minds, committed crimes, despaired of their own preservation; the unexpectedness of the experience made them senseless. So should a city not be a city because of this? Of course not, O Admirable One: don't sign off on this. 7. Rather, honor all the citizens, decurions, and civic officials who lie prostrate before you. Think how the misfortune would affect everyone alike, even if they acquiesced to the greatness of Your Authority while groaning, so to speak, on the inside. 8. Honor my gray hair too; it would be terrible for me to not have a city now when I previously had a great one, and for the temple that I erected for God and my beautification of it to become a habitat for wild animals after your term of office. 9. For it wouldn't be too terrible, even if others think it is, if statues were slated for demolition—and don't think that I'm making an argument about them; my focus is on more important matters—but it would be terrible if an ancient and gloriously enduring city were slated for demolition along with them while I, honored by you and thought to have some clout, live and see [*Il.* 1.88]. But that's my argument about such things.

10. If I were to say more, I wouldn't find anything stronger than your own thoughts, by which so great a province is led—and may you lead more and greater ones, and in greater offices! It's necessary, though, that Your Magnanimity know this about those who have fallen before you: they're utterly wretched, castaways, and they had no share in the disorder of the sinners, as many of those present at the time persuaded me. 11. In addition to these things, think hard about what you consider to be beneficial to both a good reputation here and your hopes for over there.[239] I'll put up with whatever you recommend, albeit not without disappointment—but I'll put up with it. Indeed, what else could I do? If the worse option prevails, I'll freely offer this alone: I would lay down tears for the former city.

Gr. Naz., *Ep.* 142
Spring–autumn 382

To Olympius,[240]

1. Even if my yearning for your company burns hot and the need of your petitioners is great, the disease remains still unconquered. Therefore I'm confident in trusting this request to a letter. 2. Pay respect to my gray hair, to which you've already shown respect, doing it well and often. Pay respect to this illness as well, to which my sweat for God has contributed to some degree, if I can make a youthful boast. 3. And for this reason, spare the citizens who look to me, since I've got the freedom to speak frankly with you. Spare the others who are under my care. For your business suffers no loss because of beneficence, since you use fear for correction, while others use punishments. 4. In return for these things, may you obtain a judge as great as you are to your petitioners and to me, who makes this request.

Gr. Naz., *Ep.* 105
Spring–autumn 382

To Olympius,[241]

1. Time is swift, the struggle is great, and the disease brings pressure that nearly immobilizes me. What's left except to rely upon God and supplicate Your Beneficence? May God guide more good decisions to your mind, and may you not quickly reject my plea 2. but receive with gentleness the wretched Paul, whom justice has perhaps brought under your power in order to, by the magnitude of your gentleness, enable you to become more glorious, and in order to commend my prayers—if they're anything of value—to Your Beneficence.

Gr. Naz., *Ep.* 104
Spring–autumn 382

To Olympius,[242]

1. I know that I've gotten so many other great favors from Your Clemency, and may God pay you back for them with good things from himself, and may one of those good things be to finish out a splendid and glorious term of office! 2. But in what I'm asking now, I come to give rather than to receive [cf. Acts 20:35], if it's not too

coarse to say. By my own means, I bring to you the wretched Philumena, who is falling prostrate before your judgment and putting on you the tears with which she crushes my soul.[243] 3. Well then, as to what crimes she has suffered and at whose hand, she'll tell you in person, for it wouldn't be safe for me to accuse anyone, although I must say this: to everyone with a lick of good sense, especially those whose wife and children have been left exposed, widowhood and orphanhood deserve assistance [Jas 1:27]—they are our great guarantees of mercy—given that we, being human, decide between humans. 4. Pardon me for making my request through epistles, since I'm currently laid low by illness.

> Gr. Naz., *Ep.* 143
> Spring–autumn 382

To Olympius,[244]

1. What's the benefit of human beings having many experiences, and good ones too? It teaches them beneficence and inclines them toward their petitioners. For there's no technique as good at teaching people how to act with mercy as having previously received it. 2. This has happened to me too. I learned sympathy from experience. And do you see my generosity? Although I need Your Clemency in my own affairs, I'm making this request on behalf of others and I'm not afraid of exhausting your beneficence in others' concerns. 3. I'm writing these words for the priest—well, rather the ex-priest Leontius. If he deserved to suffer for what he did, let's leave the matter there so that his punishment doesn't become excessive. 4. But if he has still got some retribution coming to him and the rebukes are not yet equal to his sins, grant him pardon because of me, because of God, because of the bema, and because of the whole college of priests among whom he was once numbered, even if he has now proved himself unworthy by what he did and what he experienced. 5. It would be best if I convinced you, but if not, I'm sending you a more respectable intercession, a partner in your office and glory.

> Gr. Naz., *Ep.* 144
> Spring–autumn 382

To Olympius,

1. Rash action is not entirely praiseworthy. That's why, in this particular case, I've deferred the decision about the most respectable

Verianus's daughter, allowing time for amendment and surmising, at the same time, that Your Goodness doesn't condone divorce, the investigation of which you've entrusted[245] to me, whom you know not to be rash and thoughtless in such matters. 2. Well, I have therefore restrained myself until now, and, I suppose, not without reason. Since I have come to the end of the appointed time, though, and since I must inform you of the examination's result, I'll do just that. 3. The girl seems to me to be of two minds, divided between respect for her parents and consideration for her husband. Her words are with the former, while her thought—I don't know if this is of any importance—is with the latter, as her tears indicate. 4. Clearly, then, you'll do whatever commends itself to Your Justice and to God, who directs you in every respect. For my part, though, I've given my opinion to my son Verianus as sweetly as I can, that he should bypass many of the important points of debate so that he does not ratify the divorce, which stands completely at odds with our laws, even if the Roman ones decide otherwise.[246] 5. For it's incumbent upon you to guard justice, which I always pray for you to say and do.

Gr. Naz., *Ep.* 145
Spring–autumn 382 (before Gr. Naz., *Ep.* 144)

To Verianus,

1. State executioners do nothing terrible, for they too are subject to laws. Nor is the sword illegal with which we punish the wicked [cf. Rom 13:4]. Nevertheless, neither should the state executioner be praised, nor should the murderous sword be received with gladness. 2. For my part, I couldn't endure being an object of hate like this were the divorce to be confirmed by my own hand and tongue. For it's better to stand amid unity and friendship than separation and dissolution of life. 3. It seems to me that the most admirable governor took this to heart when he entrusted an inquiry about your daughter to me as someone who could come to a dissolution neither precipitously nor dispassionately.[247] For, obviously, he appointed a bishop, not an accountant, and made me a mediator for your sudden reversal of circumstances. 4. Accordingly, I exhort you to find my timidity acceptable. If the better course prevails, then use me as a servant of your will—I'm even glad to receive commands in such matters! But if the situation turns toward the worse, toward

the utterly perverse, toward that which, before today, I've not undertaken, then you should seek out another, more fitting person for this task. 5. That I might show favor to your friendship (even if I know that I pay the most honors to you in all respects), I've got no leisure to offend God, to whom I furnish an account of my every movement and thought. 6. Truth be told, though, I'll trust your daughter when she can escape her veneration of you so as to speak the truth with frankness. Her current suffering, at any rate, deserves pity, for her words are separating her from you, while her weeping is separating her from her husband.

Gr. Naz., Ep. 131
Spring–autumn 382

To Olympius,[248]

1. More oppressive than the illness itself is your not believing that I'm ill and commanding so great a journey, thereby pushing me into the midst of troubles, the withdrawal from which I cherished, nearly therefore confessing gratitude for my body's mortification. 2. For untroubled tranquility is preferable to the pomp of public life. I write this epistle even though I previously received the same order from your most admirable deputy. And now, let Your Magnanimity deign to write an epistle on my behalf, which I would have as a trustworthy witness to my illness. 3. Even the damage that I now incur is convincing, since I'm unable to run to and enjoy you, you who governs with virtue so decently and admirably that the first part of your term of office would be preferable to the distinction of others' entire tenure.

Gr. Naz., Ep. 125
Early 382

To Olympius,[249]

1. Even gray hair can be taught something [cf. Sol., frag. 18], and old age, it seems, is not entirely a trusty indicator of sagacity. Since I was familiar with the Apollinarians' idea and impiety best of all and observed their unbearable insanity, I thought that I might be able to tame them with long-suffering and mollify them little by little, for which I even held out my hopes. 2. But it seems I was oblivious to the fact that I made them worse and harmed the church with my ill-timed philosophy. For reasonableness does not win over bad people. 3. Even now, if I could have taught you these things on my

own, know well that I wouldn't have hesitated to get myself moving, beyond my capacity, to fall before Your Dignity. 4. But since my illness has advanced further and I must make use of the Xanxarian baths[250] on the counsel of physicians, I'm crafting a letter in the place of myself. 5. In addition to everything else, the wicked and wickedly perishing people have dared to summon bishops condemned by every eastern and western synod or to misuse those who showed up (for I can't speak about the matter with any precision), and to rise up against all the imperial commands and your own precepts by granting the name of bishop to a certain person among their impious and fraudulent members, emboldened, I suspect, by nothing as much as my mortification (indeed, I must admit this). 6. If these things are tolerable, let Your Steadfastness tolerate them. I'll tolerate them too, just as I've done many times before. However, if they're burdensome and unendurable to the most pious emperors themselves, deign to take vengeance on the offenders, even if you must do so less than their insanity deserves.

Gr. Naz., Ep. 140
Spring–autumn 382

To Olympius,[251]

1. Again I'm writing to you when I should be present. However, I have confidence in you, O Referee of Spiritual Matters (to mention the first thing first) and Corrector of Public Affairs, both of which [offices] are from God, since you've received the reward for piety—namely, that official business proceeds according to plan and that what is unattainable by others is attainable by you alone. 2. For intelligence and manliness guide your office: the former discovers what must be done, while the latter finishes with ease what was discovered. And your greatest quality is this: the purity of your hand, which directs all things. 3. Where is your ill-gotten gold? It doesn't exist, since, like a tyrant on the lam, it was the first thing that you sentenced to banishment. Where is the enmity? Condemned. Where is the gracefulness? Well, you indulge in this a bit (for I must make a small accusation against you), but only to imitate God's beneficence, for which even now your soldier Aurelius asks through me. 4. I call him a foolish deserter and a prudent supplicant, because he put himself into my hands and through mine into yours, submitting in

his defense, like an imperial image, my gray hair and priestly position, which you've often professed to respect. 5. Look! The same hand brings him to you that has both offered bloodless sacrifices and written many words of praise for you—and will write even more, I'm sure, if God were to extend your office (and I mean yours and that of your co-worker, justice).

Gr. Naz., Ep. 106
Spring–autumn 382

To Olympius,[252]

1. Look! Another pretext for a letter to you, which, truth be told, you provided in that you solicited it by paying [my letters] honor. Look! Another supplicant to you, this one a prisoner of fear, my relative Eustratius, who falls before Your Goodness with me and through me. 2. He refuses to rebel against your office forever, even if a just fear has stricken him with panic, and he opts not to fall before you through someone other than me, so that he might render your beneficence toward himself more august by using intercessors such as myself, whom you, if nothing else, will make great by accepting their exhortations like this. 3. Let me say one more quick thing: the other gifts, the first ones, you gave them to me, but this one you'll give to your own judgment, since once and for all you've set your mind to comforting my old age and infirmity with such honors. I'll add that you always make the Divinity more amenable to yourself.

Gr. Naz., Ep. 126
Spring–autumn 382

To Olympius,

1. I had a good dream. I had been brought up to the lodging to get some comfort from the bath and hoped then to have your company. I wasted several days, as if I had already held this good thing in my two hands, before I was suddenly carried away by an illness that vacillated between bothering me and threatening me. 2. And if I should find something comparable to the experience, I suffered like octopuses, who, when forcefully ripped from the rocks, often risk losing some of their suckers on the rocks or taking a bit of the rocks with them. 3. Well, that's my situation. What I asked of Your Excellence when I was present I'm also confident to ask for when absent. I found my son Nicobulus to be quite cramped in his anxiety about the

public post and his close attention to its station, a person both weak and unaccustomed to such responsibilities,[253] unable to bear the solitude. 4. Please assign him to any other task that's dear to you, for he's eager to serve Your Authority in every way. If possible, though, free him from this anxiety. If nothing else is available for him, honor him as my sick nurse, since, although I've requested and obtained many favors from you for many people, I also need to use Your Clemency for my own situation.

Gr. Naz., Ep. 146
July 381–autumn 382

To Olympius,

1. When I obtained your courtesy in all things and insatiably took my fill of Your Clemency, I used to say, as if by some prophecy, that I was afraid of depleting your beneficence in the affairs of other people. 2. For in this case, the struggle is mine (if what concerns my family is in fact mine) and I'm not crafting my eloquence with my usual frankness. First of all, because it's my problem, it requires greater humility to make petitions on my own behalf, even if it's more effective. 3. In the second place, I'm wary of causing satiety, that it may dissolve any pleasant feeling toward me and oppose all noble things. That's how things stand, then, and I imagine that's really how they should be. Nevertheless, confident in God, before whom I stand, and in Your Generosity to do the right thing, I'm also confident in this supplication.

4. Let Nicobulus be the worst of all, he who did wrong only in this single respect: because of me, he is an object of envy and more liberal than he ought to be. Let my antagonist be the most just of all human beings. Indeed, I'm ashamed to accuse a former ally of mine in the presence of Your Uprightness, 5. but I don't know if it appears just to you to seek punishment among some for the crimes of others, to seek punishment [of Nicobulus] for crimes unrelated to [him] and even done against his will, while [my antagonist] so incites his slaves and gets them so agitated as to make [Nicobulus] yield to his accuser more eagerly than he intended. 6. But must Nicobulus or his children be enslaved, which seems right to his abusers? For I would be ashamed at the grounds and timing of the insult if it were to come about while you were in office and while I've got some influence with

you. Must we now assist the government? Must we now increase the roster of decurions when [my antagonist] is upsetting my private affairs? No way, O Admirable One—don't let it appear just to Your Purity! 7. But once you've understood with the swift flight of your thought the malice from which these things emerged, and once you've shown respect to me, your praiser, present yourself as a beneficent judge to those who were incited, since today you're passing judgment not merely on human beings but even on virtue and vice, to which governors who favor virtue like you do should give greater attention than the average person. 8. In this case, not only will you have prayers from me, upon which I know that you don't cast scorn, like the masses, but I'll also make your office famous among everyone to whom I'm known.

Gr. Naz., *Ep.* 154
Autumn 382

To Olympius,

1. You'll be our governor even after your term of office (for I judge matters differently than the masses do), because you've gathered within yourself every virtue appropriate to governance. Indeed, to me, many of the high thrones are down low—those whose hand humiliates them and enslaves them to their subjects. On the other hand, many are exalted and buoyed up despite being down low—those whom virtue places up high and makes worthy of greater offices. 2. But why do these things matter to me? No longer is the great Olympius with us, and no longer does he stand at the helm! We've come undone, we are betrayed, and we revert to being Second Cappadocia, since First Cappadocia is with you.[254] 3. Why should I speak about the concerns of others? Rather, who will tend to your Gregory's old age, and cure his infirmity with honors, and put him in a more honorable position by procuring from you beneficence for the masses? 4. Well, go down your path now with a better procession and pomp, leaving my many tears behind and bringing with you the kind of great wealth that most rulers don't possess: glory and inscriptions on the souls of all—pillars that are not easily moved.[255] 5. If you come to over us again with a greater and more glorious office (yes, my yearning predicts this!), we'll no doubt offer up more perfect gifts of thanksgiving to God.

Gr. Naz., *Ep.* 196
Date unknown

To Hecebolius,

1. I'm going to howl against myself, and forgive me, someone in agony, for speaking like someone in agony! O wicked and malicious chunk of flesh! What vicious things you do to me! What vicious things you concoct! There is a man nearby whom we should have just pursued even if he were far away, because of his virtue in governance and his general mildness. 2. For your part, you're doing poorly; you're even, dare I say, paralyzed—you're neglecting, on the one hand, some who partake of the good and, on the other hand, me, who takes the hit. Such, then, is the content of my accusation. 3. But since merely complaining about what I'm suffering isn't enough, I need a remedy for the wound. I've found it in my confidence in this epistle and sketching my presence in the letter. 4. And if you, teeming with goodness, are also looking for a way to do right by me, I confidently bring before you my household, pitiable and worthy of your beneficence: a widow with her orphans, the tears still warm on their faces. I mean my niece and her children, who came from a good father—in arms, he performed many labors for emperors, not anonymously but quite famously, but he also served governors like yourself in many ways (perhaps you've heard of a certain Nicobulus). They now stand in danger of suffering terrible calamities. 5. For they[256] are attempting to abuse the orphans again now, even after [the orphans were made to] surrender their friends and swear oaths during the course of investigation.

Gr. Naz., *Ep.* 238
Date unknown

To the most reverent and completely-adorned-in-Christ ascetic community of the blessed Leucadius at Sannabodae,[257] to the monks and virgins sanctified by Christ Jesus, Gregory sends greetings in the Lord.[258]

1. What happened by God's dispensation is a matter for thanksgiving—a combatant leaving the stadium after the good fight in which he fought and being taken up by the referee to receive the crown of righteousness [2 Tim 4:7–8] and, by his own efforts, to go farther than the chorus of angels—and not a pretext for tears to those

who are otherwise sensible.[259] 2. This and all other great things are the beginning of joy and cheerfulness for those who look to the truth according to the gospel. 3. Since some custom dictates that we should bear a sad countenance at the passing of the saints and appreciate an exhortation from the beloved, I am therefore neither letting myself say anything sad and downcast nor intending to prop up my hearers with these sorts of words. 4. I am, though, performing the requisite exhortation in counseling Your Proprieties to always look at him by looking at one another. For I pray that each man and woman be conformed to the blessed man's life, so that you might get assurance whenever you see each other, because you would be staring right at his defining feature. 5. Conform your life to his purity, his freedom from anger, his humility, and his effective philosophical practice, as well as his way of keeping his soul always directed toward God and his way of not being carried aloft by the deceptions of life. Consequently, as you see these qualities in one another, you shall etch a memorial for him within yourselves and neither you nor he will exist in a state of death. 6. Indeed, his living will always be placed on display in your life, and, through your good citizenship, you will make yourselves foreigners to death's community. 7. Farewell, and move onward in soul and body! In the power of the Holy Spirit, may the Lord provide shelter to those who remember me in their prayers.

Gr. Naz., *Ep.* 149
Spring 382–autumn 383

To George,

1. My ailment is healing, but it's not beaten. Of course, I'm stunned at how my fellow deacon Euthalius, neither respecting the rank nor honoring our relationship, beat with chains and blows the wretched Philadelphius, as the marks from the blows indicate. 2. Accordingly, don't accept the episode in a casual manner, but, after you've gone in person, present me with the result [of your investigation]. Let the deacon also be present to offer a defense against the accusation and to give you an impression of the beaten man's well-being. Indeed, I don't tolerate such bad behavior being dared nearby under my purview.

Gr. Naz., *Ep.* 199
Date unknown

To Nemesius,

1. If I seem burdensome to you by writing lengthy epistles, don't be surprised, or I'll denounce you before the just judge—you!—and I'm certain that you'll acquit me of the charge. 2. You are personally responsible for my confidence, since you invite my request in your eagerness to grant it. This too isn't surprising. For there are many reasons that you would eagerly grant me a favor: my old age, my illness, our partnership in eloquence (if any word of mine resides in eloquence), my very yearning for your company despite being prevented [from it] by infirmity and being utterly incapable of such a deed. 3. Who is my ambassador? Even if he were in the wrong, I wouldn't be ashamed of so great a man, but if he is in the right, give him your assent eagerly. 4. My most respectable son Theodosius comes again to Your Eloquence—he is mine and yours, mine as a scout and yours as a supplicant. And he comes to make a request about a pitiable situation: orphans are imperiled and the human intervention on which they depend is uncertain, and I fear the passing of a father who relieved their orphanhood in many ways. 5. Deposit one favor for all of them: give your hand to this misfortune, which you will personally scrutinize. 6. Your office requires no addition in eminence, for the morning star doesn't need any addition in brilliance. But if you're looking for an addition, know well that there is nothing better or more brilliant than doing this [favor], as many of those willing to tell the truth will teach Your Excellence.

Gr. Naz., *Ep.* 198
Date unknown

To Nemesius,

1. Some praise Pythagoras of Samos[260] because when they compelled him to make a sacrifice (since he didn't generally approve of sacrifice), he averted any consequence by sacrificing a ceramic cow, on the grounds that one ought not to purify corpses with corpses, by which he meant bodies. 2. You're doing the right thing by imitating him, O Admirable Man—since you've been forbidden from imposing any additional penalty, and you alone among [all] the governors, or with just a few of them, instill fear in your subjects without resorting

to punishment—and not seeking damages from Valentinianus, who is both yours and mine (for I'm making this request on behalf of family members), but limiting his penalty to pretending to utter an additional punishment. 3. Indeed, he's not standing trial because of his personal carelessness, if I must come right out and say it. Being able to convince you as a judge would be best, but if I can't do that, let me appeal to our friendship and recite to Your Eloquence what someone supposedly wrote to his friend: 4. "As to so-and-so, if he has committed no crime, then release him on account of justice. But if he has committed a crime, release him to me."[261] Certainly, release him once you've realized that, on the one hand, an additional penalty of two horses would bring no substantial boost to the public treasury but, on the other, the favor would be registered to my account. 5. And let me add this: to the utmost degree, give your assistance to the misfortune of a man afflicted by circumstance.

Gr. Naz., *Ep.* 200
Date unknown

To Nemesius,

1. From my perspective, you've been treating governance as a philosophical discipline, and I know that you'll continue to do so if God cares about our affairs. 2. Nevertheless, it would be absolutely wonderful to be with you now that you're coming into some downtime from public duties, something for which you used to yearn, and now that I could, in tranquility, take pleasure from Your Sagacity, of which I partook for a brief time yet failed to obtain for any long stretch, just as one's sight cannot hold on to a flash of lightning. 3. This would be a great thing to pray for, but it won't be something easy to get, since my body is in the shape that it's in. 4. Well, if I could get a meeting, I would have it all! (In fact, based on your promise, you also owe me a meeting on the topic of my doctrine, a promise that somehow you left unfulfilled.) If I can't get it, I'll put up with the loss, albeit unwillingly. 5. As for you, know that you are with me wherever you are, and may you be guided by my prayers. For as long as I draw breath, know that you remain with me, on whom you've engraved yourself, me who is no less valuable than any pillar. You'll engrave yourself still more deeply when you join with God and openly become one of ours, or at least when I become yours, to put it more sweetly.

Gr. Naz., *Ep.* 201
Date unknown

To Nemesius,

1. What happened? You passed through my area with no advance notice and I couldn't catch you, any more than those who believe that they stand next to the source of an echo when they're actually deceived by the echo's repercussions. No doubt, this is the only time of all the others that I've acted tyrannically. 2. At any rate, however, please write me an epistle, O Admirable Man, and I'll have it in the place of you, a shadow, as it's said, in the place of a body.

Gr. Naz., *Ep.* 242
Late 381 or late 383

To Peter,

We've been far away from each other for a while now, neither associating face-to-face nor having conversations through epistles. I'm confident, though, that the distance concerns [only] our bodies and not our spirits. Now that I've got an opportunity, however, I'm addressing Your Reverence and asking you to pray for me, worn down as I am by old age, disease, and the agony of my lifestyle and my departure.

Gr. Naz., *Ep.* 164
July 381–February 382

To Timothy,

1. I've always been a noble hunter of noble qualities (to write with a youthful insolence). I discovered your eloquence, hidden and evading detection under the cover of philosophy. [I found it] with my own eloquence, which ferrets out [eloquence in others], and made it known to further people; to use one of our expressions, I put the light under the bushel on the lampstand [Matt 5:15]. 2. To leave aside your other noble features—your education and piety, as well as the mildness and moderation of your character (it's tremendously difficult for one person to possess them all)—look how tremendous what I have here with me is![262] 3. You remember me, you welcome my letter, and you heap praise upon praise, not for the sake of [merely] praising me (for I'm aware of your philosophy) but to make me better and lead me forward, even though I'm disappointed that you suspect I find such things important. 4. Well, my affairs are at an end.

I've succumbed to envy, and now I'm practicing philosophy in tranquility with God, keeping company with prayers by myself, and feeling free of worldly agitations and tumults. 5. As for you, stay manly for me, be stalwart [Ps 30:25(31:24)], and fight for the Trinity as best you can. And be the meek fighter [cf. Luke 22:36], which you used to see me doing too. Indeed, I don't want baboons to enjoy a good reputation while lions keep quiet. 6. Pray for me too while I work diligently to obtain a peaceful exit, something to which I've already given my assent.

Gr. Naz., *Ep.* 188
383

To Stagirius,

1. Are you Attic in your education? I'm Attic too. Do you sit before youths? I do so before people of every age. Do you mold them for speech? I do so for character. 2. We have a lot in common with each other. In the place of and before all else, though, there's this one thing: my sweetest son Nicobulus, who stands between us.[263] 3. By treating him well, you'll show off your education and our friendship, if it matters to you. 4. I think it does, for even elderly athletes are honored by younger ones, so that, since the former give the victory prizes to the latter, they are regarded as being faithful to the customs of the contest.

Gr. Naz., *Ep.* 165
Date unknown

To Stagirius,[264]

1. I'm learning that you're unphilosophical in the face of suffering—and I don't praise it. For I must write the truth, above all to a beloved man and someone who lays claim to excellence. 2. That's how I am when it comes to these things—at least, that's what I tell myself, and quite correctly. I don't praise either excessive passionlessness or extreme emotionality: the former is inhuman, the latter unphilosophical. The one who treads the middle path, however, ought to appear more philosophical than those who cannot control themselves at all, but more human than those who practice philosophy without moderation. 3. And had I written to anyone else, perhaps I would have also needed longer arguments: sympathy would be required in some cases, exhortation in others, and perhaps

censure in others still. For grieving together is suitable for consolation, and illness requires treatment from a healthy individual. 4. As I am crafting my eloquence for an educated man, it should be enough to say the following: be under your own control and that of the books with which you have daily conversation, where there are many lives, many ways of life, many points of pleasure and smoothness, as well as many points of misery and roughness, as is reasonable. 5. For God intertwines them, it seems to me, so that sadness won't be incurable and glee not undisciplined and so that we look to him alone when we contemplate the instability and inconsistency of these things. I apply these words, then, to your experience as a rule and norm. 6. And if you know anyone praiseworthy of those who have utterly collapsed under pains or anyone who has remained upright amid the pain, use the sad person and enjoy his sorrow—no one is jealous of lamented misery. 7. But if he plays the coward and deserves censure, the proverb states, "The one who wounds is healed" [*Mantiss. prov.* 2.28], although now it would be good to say, "I have been wounded." Besides, it is both shameful and unusual for me to imitate the masses in such situations, 8. since the Word makes me even more exalted than the present times and convinces me that they're fleeting, like shadows [Col 2:17; Heb 8:5] and riddles [1 Cor 13:12], and that I should consider neither sadness nor glee as truth but live elsewhere and keep my gaze over there,[265] and know that vice is the only cause of sadness, and virtue, as well as appropriation to God [cf. Pl., *Resp.* 10.631b; *Tht.* 176b], the only cause of gladness. 9. Sing these words to yourself and it'll be easier, but even more, know that you would have already started and continued to sing even if I hadn't written these words.

Gr. Naz., *Ep.* 166
Date unknown (after Gr. Naz., *Ep.* 165)

To Stagirius,[266]

1. I derive some benefit from your epistle,[267] O Admirable Man, and perhaps not a small one, since you're a clever healer of such things. Censure repelled your sadness, blushing replaced your suffering, and you valiantly rose up to the altercation like quite the sophist. 2. You even seem to me just like Achilles's horses in Homer: you lifted up your head and shook off the dust when it was time to

stop mourning Patroclus [*Il.* 17.457]; you began to desire the plains, weapons, and exhibitions again. Thus, your letter to me was shining, ambitious, and even somewhat striking, if I'm understanding you. 3. Only, act like a man and practice philosophy against the suffering! For my part, I'll admit that judging sailors from the shoreline is no great feat and that struggling against miseries by yourself is a greater challenge than cheering from the sidelines,[268] unless someone were to say that you didn't need to either struggle or set sail (if philosophy is stronger than those in whom it currently exists). 4. The battle lines have drawn close to me in many respects and often, throughout the whole of my life, I suppose. There are many who could attest whether I, in these situations, acted in a stupid or unmanly way while I cheered from the side or struggled by myself.

Gr. Naz., *Ep.* 192
383

To Stagirius,[269]

1. I'm going to be frank with you. Indeed, it's my nature to be so, and that's how I like it. If you don't hand Nicobulus over to me, you'll do me wrong, for I will have clashed with a friend and I'll get nothing further from you. 2. However, if you give me what I hope you will, you'll show a conciliatory spirit and we'll have the best possible outcome in two regards: I'll get to make my apologetic defense before him, and I'll get to praise you. If you allow me to admonish you in a fatherly way, though, without spitting on my advice because you're used to being in charge, accept a word from a man unfamiliar with such matters. 3. At some point, put down the weapons—the slings, the fearsome ashen spears [*Il.* 20.272], the tongues with which you attack and wound each other—and do so in view of your partisan praisers. 4. And put them down all the more because it's easier than taking up actual weapons, so that you don't lead the young men to vice—if not by your words, then at least with your actions—instead of virtue. For one quietly counsels the outcomes that would make one happy. 5. Do this, and you'll do yourself a favor, keep me as a friend, and not prove false the expectations of those who have trusted you. This would be the reward for your labors regarding Nicobulus. If I were to get full confirmation of it, I would even pay you back for these things with a fuller acclamation.

Gr. Naz., *Ep.* 96
July 381–February 382

To Hypatius,

1. I've sustained damage for a long time now, since the first among cities[270] does not hold the first among men. Good needed to be spread abroad, I suppose, and the common benefit needed to come about for everyone, inasmuch as you sow concord from on high just as those who cultivated the crops with seeds, at least as it appears in the myths and stories.[271] 2. But intense agony stays with me, because I enjoyed this only for as long as it takes for lightning to flash quickly within the field of vision before I was defeated by envy and contracted into myself, having left to others authority over the church, along with its finer trappings (because of those who haphazardly play games that shouldn't be played, so to speak). 3. But you, O Best of All, preserve your same attitude toward me, which is that of a magnet drawing iron to itself.

Gr. Naz., *Ep.* 232
Date unknown

To Diocles,

1. I wasn't invited to the wedding of my daughter, yet I'll still be present, celebrating, sharing in the excitement, and wishing you all the best. 2. One of the most important things is that Christ be present at the wedding (where Christ is, there is orderly behavior) and that water become wine [John 2:9] (for everything can be transformed into something better). Just as things that cannot be mixed should not be mixed, so too should bishops and buffoons not meet in the same place, nor prayers and applause, nor psalm singing and instrumental concerts. 3. For the marriage of Christians, like everything [else] they do, should maintain orderliness; the conduct should be solemn. These words are my wedding gift. For your part, may you give me back ready obedience. As to the bridegroom, if he abides by these words, you've got a son; if not, a soldier.

Gr. Naz., *Ep.* 10
362–63

To Candidianus,

1. Where are the sophists now? Why do the poets lay silent? What better words, what more illustrious subject do they seek? Every

musical and harmonious tongue should now be roused for you, and every oratorical tongue should resound with loftiness and intensity, not only because the most righteous obligation of all is to celebrate an upright ruler with eloquence but also because it's most appropriate to adorn with both arts[272] the individual who is best at both.

2. Had I not laid eloquence to rest prematurely (for now—yes, now—I feel this way) and decided with more haste than wisdom, one might say, to neither deliver panegyrics nor make public appearances while I practiced philosophy, I would probably have outdone even the Tyrrhenian war trumpet [cf. S., *Aj.* 17; A., *Eu.* 567; Pi., *P.* 1.72] (for I'll say it with no fear of Momus's jagged stone, as Pindar has it [Pi., *Olymp.* 8.55]), had I not been condemned to an untimely fate of silence.[273] 3. But what I have experienced just now because of you, what my condition is—perhaps you might know it from an image: I'm stamping the ground with my feet, as it were, like the most impetuous of horses, champing the bit, cocking my ear, chuffing hot breath from my nostrils, gazing with ferocity, shaking off the froth, yet still remaining within the corral, since the law does not permit me the race.[274] 4. What then? Since this is how things seem to be, what will I do? Shall I toss aside eloquence altogether and stand awestruck at your deeds in silence, leaving the acclamation to others? Of course not! Let each person, though, acclaim your deeds however each wants and can. 5. Without a doubt, you'll satisfy many speeches and panegyrics if each separately acclaims a portion of your qualities. Some would treat your administration of public affairs, as well as your understanding and diligence in them—for who is more resourceful as a discoverer of the necessary or more effective in enacting what is discovered? 6. Others would treat the scales of your justice, and how you adjudicate conflicts as though under a bright light, a sublime man sublimely taking pride in what is right. 7. You've got a terrifying sword for striking, but since it does not strike, it has become an object of reverence. You prevail over criminals not by punishing them but by working to keep them from committing crimes in the first place and by making everyone subject to your way of thinking rather than to the display of raw power so characteristic of others, for whom brashness is legal. 8. Let others admire the power of your speech and, if you wish, your entire way of speaking, a product as much of your judgment of what to say as of your own

ability to say it. For he who is competent to judge a speech is even more capable of pronouncing it himself—one may compare the former to the golden pebble or to that Homeric balance by which the equality of Eumelus's horses came to be judged [*Il.* 2.763–67], but as for your ability to speak, [your words] are more plentiful than snowflakes on a winter's day [*Il.* 3.216–23]—just as now, in a similar way, you preside over the games in which you formerly participated. 9. Let others praise your resolve, mixed with mildness but not to the point of falling into softness, like the pounces of lions. Let others praise you for affording no honor to mighty and valuable gold, with its august appellations [cf. Pi., *Olymp.* 1.1–2, 13.78], and for making it yield swiftly to your justice: of everything else, this fact alone is loftier than what is both heard and believed. 10. Let some poet, free and independent with his skill, gather a chorus of farmworkers and sing to you a rustic tune [Ar., *Ach.* 674]. Let him reap the ripe crop and weave a most pleasant garland. Let him raise vines, plaited with ivy and grapes, to your head. 11. These are the first fruits of farming [Theoc., *Id.* 7.128–57], which, through you, have returned to human beings. Let stones give flow to milk and springs to honey [cf. Deut 8:7]. Whether native to our region or growing in the mountains, let every plant at once abound in cultivated fruits, as it is in the compositions of poets whenever they address the earth's reception of some beneficence. 12. As I have said, let other people say and fashion these words. For not only does one's own situation weigh one down, as seems true to the lyric poet [Pi., *Nem.* 1.53], but it also engenders preponderant gladness. For my part, I'll tell you which features of yours I especially admire and embrace. You stay above the adversity of the times. 13. You're Greek with respect to worship, and you serve the current imperial administration[275] with its political operation not like the flatterers of our time but rather like the high-minded friends of virtue. You eschew the attendance of the former, maintain goodwill toward your homeland, and produce undying glory through mortal action. 14. This too ranks among your praiseworthy features, that you pay respect to friendship in the great dignity of your office and that you devote your time away from your accomplishments not only to remembering but also to honoring your friends by letter, to confessing your yearning for them, and to drawing close to you those who are far away. 15. In return for these things, I wish for you nothing greater in terms of your reputation (for your virtue has no room left for improvement, even if your position does) but rather, before all else, the one greatest thing, that you join us and God at some point and belong to the class of the persecuted instead of the persecutors,[276] as the latter is carried away in the impulse of our time and the former possesses immortal salvation.

Gr. Naz., *Ep.* 15
360s or early 370s?

To Lollianus,[277]

1. It's good that you're returning to me—after a long time, yes, but nevertheless (and what's better than this) you've liberated me from my anxieties about you because you've done so intentionally. 2. I consider everything [I have] as shared with you, both grief and gladness; that's what friendship is. 3. Seeing that you are returning, "share your good fortune with your friends," as the speaker says [E., *Or.* 450]. 4. You would share it if you were willing to look at my lordly cousins Helladius and Eulalius as kinsmen (I may say "kinsmen"—for I don't know what better word I could use—so long as you don't regard me as a stranger to yourself) and not put up with them needing any further patrons. 5. Instead, make yourself available to them in all ways: as a useful friend, a kind neighbor, a valiant defender, and (lest I continue to spell them out one by one) as the noble Lollianus, known for his integrity. 6. If you were you to talk with them further and observe the height of their philosophy, I can promise that you would intercede for them before others. I'm quite confident in your character, and I have so many reasons to expect that I will not disappoint you with respect to those for whom I'm personally interceding.

Gr. Naz., *Ep.* 203
Summer 381–early 384

To Valentinianus,

1. To change it up a bit and borrow a phrase from tragedy, I was banished from Karbala[278] in the most accursed way [E., *Or.* 24]. By no means was I banished by a word, but by a deed [E., *Ph.* 389]—and a truly appalling one at that. 2. It would have been much better to announce my removal with a formal proclamation than with the women whom you united in opposition to me, thereby mutilating

the solemnity of my life and yoking it to the daily disgrace and
blasphemy of those who all too easily abuse people like me, who
chose to live like this. 3. If it's not too audacious to say, you have used
Eve to cast me too from paradise [cf. 1 Tim 2:13–15]. For it would
have been easier to use a pretty word to propitiate me and to utter
fair statements that would lead me to believe that you weren't
expelling me, that you were actually paying me honor, you who so
wished to be my neighbor. 4. Perhaps you would add that you were
welcomed like kith and kin and took enjoyment from our friendship.
That's how to do it with a word and not a deed! 5. Indeed, when you
visit my place, I welcome and greet you, but oh, how I recoil from the
women running your household, as if from the attacks of vipers! 6.
Well, my ordeal has come to an end. I was outwitted, I drew back, I
imposed upon myself a penalty of abandoning my manual labors, my
hopes, and making long apologetic speeches to the holy martyrs. 7.
Even if, no doubt, these activities are severe and difficult, they're still
the means of practicing philosophy along the path of my life, and
they're not yet so burdensome as to make me move from one city to
another [cf. Matt 10:23] (a situation that I've been ordered to tolerate). 8. May you dwell in your place for longer than its previous
inhabitants, and more prudently than I might hope, so that you don't
offend the holy martyrs or strike yourself down because of the
neighborhood. 9. Before all else, though, fortify yourself against this,
and keep away from the devotees of the martyrs, lest you devise a
bad turn of events for yourself and your affairs by disrupting the
status quo with a bad interlude.

Gr. Naz., Ep. 98
Date unknown

To the Decurions,

1. It seems to me that you wouldn't hold yourselves back from
even the wallet of Diogenes of Sinope,[279] were it up to you. Instead
you would accost him, designating as his handiwork his cloak
and staff, not to mention his lack of possessions, which stemmed
from philosophical conviction and the way he supported himself
by going from one door to another, aimlessly, wherever he
happened to be. You seem this way to me because you're trying
to impose a fine on my brother Theotecnus for his handiwork.

2. What are the first, most important points of justice that I should utter on his behalf? That he's a deacon, or that he's helpless, or that he's a foreigner who has more in common with others than with us, or that his lifestyle is respectable and that he's a priest for the martyrs and a sojourner?[280] 3. Know that he also exercises hospitality beyond his means. Perhaps his only fault is this: he alone, of everyone around here, forces himself to be useful! 4. Judge for yourselves which of these reasons will best serve his case, but give the man a full pardon, lest you come off as inflicting serious damage while providing minimal benefit to the community, as if [you were] stripping the naked, like [the scripture], in fact, states, rather than offering clothing [Matt 25:43].

Gr. Naz., *Ep.* 78[281]
April–November 380

To Theotecnus,

1. I know that it's hard to accept rational arguments when there was an act of injustice and anger still brews. For anger and grief are blind, especially when righteous indignation is present. 2. All the same, since I was among those subjected to the injustice and outrage and, no less, indignity, I've therefore got justice on my side as I counsel you to not bring me dishonor. 3. I've suffered terrible things; if you'd like, you could even add, what no other human has suffered. However, let's not for that reason also commit injustice against ourselves, and let's not hate piety to the extent that we bring harm upon ourselves. 4. Your wife is great and your daughter precious— but not more precious than your soul. Consider, on the one hand, that you were recently deemed worthy of grace and cleansed of your sins in the bath[282] but, on the other, that sullying your gift with blood and requiring another purification all over again poses no ordinary danger. 5. Let's not lay traps for ourselves, then, and cast away our ability to speak frankly with God by coming off as bitter toward those who committed the injustice and indignant beyond measure. Let's leave the person to God and to the punishments over there.[283] Let's get ourselves a beneficent judge by coming off as beneficent [ourselves], and let's forgive so that we are forgiven [cf. Matt 18:35]. 6. Let no vain argument deceive you into thinking that legal prosecution and handing the transgressor[284] over to the laws is irreproachable.

There are Roman laws, and then there are our laws; the former are immoderate, harsh, and go all the way up to the point of blood, but ours are profitable, beneficent, and unforgiving of anger used against wrongdoers. 7. Let's stand fast in these laws and adhere to them, so that, in granting small favors (for life here is trivial and worth nothing) we receive back great ones from God: his beneficence and hopes for over there.

Gr. Naz., Ep. 235
Date unknown

To Adamantius,

1. You ask me for books as if you were returning to your days studying rhetoric, a pursuit from which I retired as soon as, by the hand of God and because of God, I looked upward, once it became necessary for me then to stop playing around[285] and uttering the inarticulate sounds of adolescents and to raise my head to the true education and devote my eloquence, along with my other old possessions, to the Word. 2. It would have been nobler had you asked for divine books instead of these, since I'm certain that the former are more advantageous and appropriate for you. 3. Yet the worse impulses prevail and I cannot change your mind, so here, the books that you asked from me are yours, to the extent that they survived the moths and the smoke over which they were laid like sailors' oars at the end of a voyage and sailing season [Hes., *Op.* 45, 629]. 4. You paid me, though, in advance, with something proper to the sophist, not in a stingy or timid way but with real showmanship and valor, since the Cynegiruses and Callimachuses as well as their trophies Marathon and Salamis have great value to you;[286] you think that you're happy because of them and that they make young men happy. 5. Let's play with them for this exclusive purpose, even if they don't belong to our time of life or our purpose. Rather, they belong to our old relationship. 6. May you get them, and put what you've got to good use! Use them as much as you can with the divine fear, which everyone everywhere ought to honor, conquering your vanity, even if we cannot completely rid ourselves of it. 7. If you think that these words are spoken rightly but that it isn't philosophical to put a price on the books, send me some money and the poor will get rid of your objection.

Gr. Naz., *Ep.* 56
Date unknown

To Thecla,

1. I received the little addition to your letter as a great epistle. For you are mine and I am yours, because the Spirit has joined us together like this. 2. Given that you know this, pray for me and remain confident about everything, since you'll find no one more genuine than me, nor anyone who shares your interests more, even if neither substantial intimacy nor experience has taught this yet. 3. But as to the causes of your distress, what should I write except that I want those who regard it as an opportunity for the highest philosophy to endure suffering and thus fight against the agents of distress, since nothing else would be possible or holy?

Gr. Naz., *Ep.* 57[287]
372–75

To Thecla,

1. Last year a heavy frost came to our country and beat back the vines' lashes, already undone in the face of anguishes; the barren remains are what reached our parched and unwet wine cups. 2. What possible reason could I have for presenting you with a dramatization of the plants' fruitlessness? [I want] you to become for me, as Solomon has it, a blooming vine [cf. Song 2:13] and fruitful vine branch, not one that produces a cluster of grapes but one that, from the grape clusters, squeezes out dew for the thirsty. 3. Who are the thirsty? Those who are building the church's wall. Unable to give them any intoxicating beverage from the mountains to drink, I've come to your grape-filled right hand so that you might command the springs of your river to flow my way. 4. Indeed, your doing so soon will give relief to the dry mouths of many while, first and foremost, making me, an Attic beggar, happy.

Gr. Naz., *Ep.* 223
Date unknown

To Thecla,

1. You are understandably pained when I'm absent, but I am more so by the separation from Your Reverence. I would rather thank God for coming to you and not complain about my fatigue. 2. For I know

your steadfastness of faith in Christ, your praiseworthy isolation, and your philosophical solitude—that, having separated yourself from all the world's delights, you locked yourself up with God alone, as well as the holy martyrs with whom you dwell, and you drew near to God and are drawing near the living, pleasing sacrifice [Phil 4:18; cf. Rom 12:1] with your beloved children. 3. Let these words, then, be to you a consolation for your distresses, since even David the Great hid his agonies here in the good things over there,[288] where he would send his thoughts, when he said, "Because he hid me in his tent in the day of troubles" [Ps 26(27):5]. And not only does he bury the cause of his pain when he remembers God, but he also finds gladness. "For I remembered God," he says, "and I was gladdened" [Ps 76:4(77:5)]. 4. Those who cling to the world are in much greater pain than God's slaves: their pain is without profit, whereas our suffering pays dividends when we endure because of God.

5. Come, let us juxtapose present distresses to future pleasures, and we'll discover that the former aren't even a fraction [as bad as] the latter; that's how excellent the good things are. 6. We've got, then, a soothing drug: when we're in agony, we should then remember God, the objects of our hopes over there, David's experience, and the increase in tribulation [Ps 4:2(1)] but be neither confined by our thoughts nor concealed in our distress as though we were in a fog. But at that time especially, we should cling to our hope and look to the blessedness reserved over there for those who persevere. 7. We could definitely be persuaded to endure fearsome things like this and be above the masses when we're in pain, if we would reflect on what God promises us and what we hope for when we approach philosophy. 8. Should we expect wealth? Cheerfulness? Good luck in this life? Or affliction from our opponents? Ill plight? Confinement? Having to countenance everything, to persevere through everything [1 Cor 13:7], on account of our hope for future things? We should expect, I'm sure, the latter things, not the former. 9. I fear, then, that we're even cheating ourselves in our covenant with God when we seek the former and hope for the latter. Let's not end our work, but let's tolerate the latter in order to obtain the former. 10. The afflicters afflicted us, those who changed sides have caused us pain, but let's keep the soul from being enslaved to the passions. That's how we'll prevail over the agents of distress.

11. Examine also why we're afflicted: isn't it because of those who have departed?[289] Acting in their interest, what favor should we grant to them? Shouldn't it be our endurance? Let's give it to them, then. For I'm convinced that the souls of the saints perceive our efforts. 12. In light of everything and before everything else, let's draw this conclusion, that it's inappropriate to practice philosophy outside of necessity while appearing unphilosophical in the midst of sufferings and to fail to be as much an example of thanksgiving in good times as one of endurance in bad times. 13. I'm also writing these words not to teach you as if you were ignorant but to remind you as one who already knows. Would that the God of comfort [2 Cor 1:3] keep you unwounded in your sufferings, and grant me the favor of seeing Your Reverence again, and be persuaded through your actions that my exertion is not in vain [1 Thess 3:5] but that I am with you more than anyone else 14. because we share the affliction, inasmuch as we took a partner in philosophy, something perhaps owing to our gray hair and godly exertions.

Gr. Naz., *Ep.* 222
Date unknown

To Thecla,

1. Even though my body is weak, I rushed to visit Your Reverence in person and to simultaneously praise the endurance that you philosophically practice concerning your most blessed brother.[290] In fact, I had no doubt about it. 2. But since I was impeded by a certain incident, it's out of necessity that I've come to you in a letter, that I may offer you a philosophical treatment of your situation. 3. Where did the noble Sacerdos, God's authentic defender both now and in the past, come from? From God. And where is Sacerdos now? With God, having withdrawn—not unpleasantly, I know well—from the jealousy of and bouts with the Wicked One. 4. Where did we come from? Isn't it the same place? Where will we find our release? Isn't it with the same Master? May we too be there with equal license to speak freely! As his supplicants, we have carried on and we'll be transferred there once we've endured a few [more] plights—few especially in comparison to the object of our hope there—so that we may even perhaps come to know grace from our experience here. 5. Father, mother, brother, forebears—what are they? A number of

praiseworthy travelers. Thecla, the slave of God and first fruit of the virtues, will soon follow them too, remaining [here] a bit longer to honor them with endurance as much as to become an exemplar of philosophy in such situations for the masses. 6. Let us praise, then, the relationship of masters to slaves and accept the plan in a more elevated way than the masses do. Now, in place of me, hold on to these words and understand their underlying rationales, even if you come up with better ones on your own. 7. If I am deemed worthy to see you face-to-face with your entire entourage, thanks be even more to the benefactor!

Gr. Naz., *Ep.* 79
January–June 374

To Simplicia,

1. You praise our holy and common father as the prop of the faith, the standard of truth and defining characteristic of piety, the mature fullness of prudence, the one who has surpassed the boundaries of human life and virtue, the faithful caregiver and great high priest [Heb 4:14], the intermediary between God and humans [1 Tim 2:5], an abode for the Spirit.[291] You're right to do so, since every word falls short of that holy and blessed soul, unless a spell or a passion, intermingled with my yearning, deceives me. 2. But in this respect I'm also quite surprised at you, at how you praise him as a saint and, up to this point, honor him appropriately, yet you try to undo his work, as if he numbered among the unholy and those who especially deserve our outrage, who live and die in vain. 3. For if you were to lay claim to a fellow shepherd of mine as your own, as your captive, and chase after this small gain, I wouldn't know how to praise you (to put it mildly), and it would be terribly unworthy of Your Generosity. 4. For how would it not be incongruous to honor the divine with gold, silver, and the extravagances of creation (and in that case, wouldn't it be done perhaps more for ostentation than for piety?) while completely wanting to inflict harm upon the church and despoil her holiest votives?

5. But if you're upset because I've done this [ordained one of Simplicia's slaves] by fiat but not that I failed to consult with Your Nobility or to give you an opportunity for munificence, you'd be making a fair point and your suffering would be the result of your

human condition. Know, though, that you have the chance to make a greater endowment than you did before, in that yielding to recipients is an even more lavish act than the act of giving. 6. In his case, you only appeared to be giving something to God, and thus also to me, God's attendant and one thought worthy to bear his name. Therefore, don't get upset with him or me, for he was tyrannized, it's not wrong to say, and as for me, why is it surprising if I've gone ahead with [ordaining him], confident in your decency and at the same time trusting in the vote of approval from our whole region? 7. If some acted graciously or mischievously, they themselves would know, and they'll have to render an account to God. Knowing this or being privy to everyone's opinions isn't my business. But how would it be easier for me to push him away than to neglect those great tears of his or the long-standing destitution of the region, which is without caregiver, without shepherd, and has no spiritual authority?

8. But even this point before all others will be obvious to you, that those who previously supported us but now deny us conduct business befitting neither piety nor liberty. It would've been much better for them to oppose us back then than to flatter us now and destroy themselves, since they fear humans rather than God [cf. Acts 5:29]. 9. Back then you assumed that they spoke owing to their pliability, because they turned to you out of fear, and this, at any rate, was quite true. Since they must always make mistakes, they must always hunt down false excuses and contrive their defense like sophists. But if you think they're right in saying these things and you're asking me for an account of how I run things (for that's what I'm hearing, even if you're not demanding it in your letter), then ask with fairness and benevolence and I'll find no ground for fault. Indeed, it gives me no pleasure when the gentleness of masters is punished.

10. What still remains? Perhaps to censure the man as unworthy and therefore denounce his appointment? It would somehow be more fitting to level this charge. But to this I've got a simple and easy answer. Neither am I acquitting nor will I acquit anyone without investigating the causes; by no means does he number among my friends or those who have done right by me (for nothing deserves more respect than God and his rule). 11. But if you want someone to make an allegation, let him do so while you're there in person to

participate in the judgment. If not, and you're absent, were he to be found innocent after being investigated by me, even if he is a slave, let him go. Since God is the same father of slaves and masters alike [cf. Eph 6:5–9], justice is not determined by social rank. If he's convicted, he'll be condemned right then by his own sins. 12. That's how the rule and the departed[292] won't suffer dishonor (let's perhaps look past my own interests, since they're unimportant). For your part, you'll avoid the base suspicion that, because you treated me and the sound faith as strangers, you have contrived these things not nobly but sophistically—incited by one thing, you hurled your anger down upon another. 13. Here's my advice to you: don't become impassioned, since it's neither holy nor seemly; don't dishonor our laws by seeking recourse in outside laws;[293] and don't pick a fight with me but rather pardon me if I've done something in too simple a manner because of my freedom in grace, and, instead of wickedly conquering by going against the Spirit, welcome the chance to be nobly conquered.

Gr. Naz., *Ep.* 236
Date unknown

To Libanius the Sophist,

I, a mother by nature, have sent children to you, a father by eloquence. Well then, you'll take an interest [in them] just as I took an interest [in them].

Gr. Naz., *Ep.* 244
Date unknown

To Basilissa,

1. If it's not too much to rouse a toiling woman to [further] toils, for the sake of the community's stability I won't hesitate to strengthen your enthusiasm as much as I can, not by the addition of different or[294] strange precepts[295] but with reminders of what I've often said and what you continuously practice. 2. Here they are. Guide your soul over miseries with a lifestyle geared toward the most excellent things. Separate from your thought everything alien to virtue and unworthy of your judgment. Direct yourself toward piety and every form of orderly behavior. 3. Streamline your thinking so that it neither accepts any proposition nor forms its thoughts without scrutiny. Rule over your thought processes at all times and in every

way so that you're always in line with the advice of our devout predecessors. Prioritize righteousness with family members and strangers over enmity and friendship. 4. Have a cohabitator and conversation partner who will sincerely implant and firmly instill temperance in your soul. Don't change your ways to correspond with life's unpredictabilities and vicissitudes, 5. for it's not seemly to limit one's thoughts [only] when impoverished, nor is it safe to think great thoughts [only] when feeling well off, which is why it's best, in fact, to practice self-control among delightful things and endurance among distressing ones. 6. Pay no heed to your former wealth; ask for self-sufficiency, cherish what is given; hope for the best; tolerate bodily disease with meekness. Grumble at nothing. Don't complain [1 Cor 10:10], but be thankful for providence in whatever form it comes. 7. As to why things happen the way they do, keep it to yourself as often as you can, but don't ignore that [some things happen] because of merit. Should you attribute something to merit, think over what you'll say before blurting it out and what you'll do before doing it. Yes indeed, this is how you'll have no regrets about what you say and do. 8. Think it good to behave with decorum with respect to not only your outer covering but also the soul's greediness. Realize that the genuine and permanent wealth is being content with little, for permanent wealth comes not in the acquisition of many things but in the not needing of them. The latter perspective concerns you, the former concerns outsiders. 9. Bring your way of life into rhythm with forbearance, your routine into rhythm with calm detachment, your tongue into rhythm with taciturnity. With these, adorn your head by covering it, your brow by keeping it restrained, your eyes by bowing them down and glancing about with decency, your mouth by not speaking improperly, your ears by listening to only serious matters, and your whole face with the hue of shame. 10. In everything and by all means, keep yourself unmolested like an untouched relic. For gravity, constancy, temperance—these are the appropriate and proper adornment for a woman. 11. Realize that the best and most comfortable luxury at hand is needing food. Indeed, it's commendable in and of itself, desirable for a life lived in temperance, the best condition for health, and not unprofitable for moderation, further orderly behavior, and discipline.

NOTES

INTRODUCTION

1. For Prohaersius, see Gr. Naz., *Epit.* 5; for his education broadly, see Gr. Naz., *Ep.* 30.2; *Carm.* 2.1.11.211–20; *Or.* 43.15–23. At Athens, Gregory formed some of his most enduring friendships: see Gr. Naz., *Ep.* 30–36, 80, 87, 92, to Philagrius; 21–22, 29, 37, 39, 93, 135, to Sophronius; 189–91, to Eustochius; 67–69, to Julian; 1–2, 4–6, 8, 19, 40, 45–50, 58–60, 245–246, 248, to Basil. That Basil studied with Prohaeresius and Himerius, see Philip Rousseau, *Basil of Caesarea*, Transformation of the Classical Heritage 20 (Berkeley: University of California Press, 1994), 31–32.

2. On this event, see Gr. Naz., *Ep.* 8.1; *Or.* 1.1, 2.6, 3.2; *Carm.* 2.1.11.337–85.

3. The letter collection offers the names of several possible students—Evagrius, Sacerdos, Pronoius, Nicobulus—although it is possible that several other couriers were his students. See Neil McLynn, "Among the Hellenists: Gregory and the Sophists," in *Gregory of Nazianzus: Images and Reflections*, ed. Jostein Børtnes and Tomas Hägg (Copenhagen: Museum Tusculanum Press, 2006), 213–38. On Gregory's activities during the early years after his ordination, see the various episodes discussed by Marie-Ange Calvet-Sébasti, *Grégoire de Nazianze: Discours 6–12*, Sources chrétiennes 405 (Paris: Éditions du Cerf, 1995), 11–36; Susanna Elm, *Sons of Hellenism, Fathers of the Church: Emperor Julian, Gregory of Nazianzus, and the Vision of Rome*, Transformation of the Classical Heritage 49 (Berkeley: University of California Press, 2012); McLynn, "Gregory the Peacemaker: A Study of Oration Six," *Kyoyo-Ronso* 101 (1996): 183–216.

4. See Bradley K. Storin, *Self-Portrait in Three Colors: Gregory of Nazianzus's Epistolary Biography*, Christianity in Late Antiquity 6 (Oakland:

University of California Press, 2019), 150–56; Neil McLynn, "Gregory Nazianzen's Basil: The Literary Construction of a Christian Friendship," *Studia Patristica* 37 (2001): 178–93.

5. The nature of the dispute remains obscure: see Gr. Naz., *Ep.* 16–19; *Or.* 43.28.

6. See Gr. Naz., *Ep.* 40–46; *Or.* 43.37.

7. See Bas., *Ep.* 58, with Rousseau, *Basil of Caesarea*, 145, 148–49, which highlights the dismissiveness of Bas., *Ep.* 56, 289. See Gr. Naz., *Ep.* 45.2 for Basil's partisans; Bas., *Ep.* 99, 223 for evidence of antipathy toward his episcopacy.

8. On the division of Cappadocia, see Noel Lenski, *Failure of Empire: Valens and the Roman State in the Fourth Century a.d.*, Transformation of the Classical Heritage 34 (Berkeley: University of California Press, 2002), 285.

9. See Gr. Naz., *Ep.* 48–50; *Or.* 9, 11–13; *Carm.* 2.1.11.430–48, 460–75. On Gregory's reaction to Basil's fiat and their ultimate compromise, see Storin, *Self-Portrait in Three Colors*, 6–7.

10. For his father, see Gr. Naz., *Or.* 18 and *Epig.* 12–23; for his mother, Nonna, Gr. Naz., *Epig.* 24–74; for his brother Caesarius, Gr. Naz., *Or.* 7 and *Epig.* 85–86, 88–99; for his sister Gorgonia, Gr. Naz., *Or.* 8 and *Epig.* 101–3.

11. See Gr. Naz., *Carm.* 2.1.11.547–51; also Stephen Davis, *The Cult of Saint Thecla: A Tradition of Women's Piety in Late Antiquity* (Oxford: Oxford University Press, 2001), 3–80.

12. See Gustave Bardy, "Le concile d'Antioche (379)," *Revue Benedictine* 45 (1933): 196–213. Several of Gregory's acquaintances attended, including Gregory of Nyssa, Eusebius of Samosata, Diodore of Tarsus, and Meletius of Antioch: see the Verona Codex (PL 13:353D–354A) and Gr. Nyss., *V. Macr.* 386. On the fourth-century Trinitarian conflicts, see Lewis Ayres, *Nicaea and Its Legacy: An Approach to Fourth-Century Trinitarian Theology* (Oxford: Oxford University Press, 2004), 85–269; R. P. C. Hanson, *The Search for the Christian Doctrine of God: The Arian Controversy*, 318–381 a.d. (Edinburgh: T. & T. Clark, 1988).

13. See Gr. Naz., *Carm.* 2.1.11.596, 2.1.12.77–78.

14. For an excellent narrative of Gregory's time in Constantinople, see John McGuckin, *St Gregory of Nazianzus: An Intellectual Biography* (Crestwood, NY: St. Vladimir's Seminary Press, 2001), 350–69.

15. See Bas., *Ep.* 48.

16. See Gr. Naz., *Ep.* 77–78; *Or.* 33.3–13; *Carm.* 2.1.11.652–727.

17. See Gregory's praise for the entire Egyptian contingent at Gr. Naz., *Or.* 21, 34. For Maximus, see Gr. Naz., *Or.* 25–26 and *Carm.* 2.1.11.728–1112, 2.1.41; also Bradley K. Storin, "Autohagiobiography: Gregory of Nazianzus among His Biographers," *Studies in Late Antiquity* 1 (2017): 274–80.

18. See Ambr., *Ep.* 13–14; Dam., *Ep.* 5–6; Hier., *Vir. ill.* 117, 127; Soz., *H.e.* 7.9; Thdt., *H.e.* 5.8.

19. On Theodosius's ecclesiastical policies, see R. Malcolm Errington, "Church and State in the First Years of Theodosius I," *Chiron* 27 (1997): 21–72, esp. 36–37; Neil McLynn, "Moments of Truth: Gregory of Nazianzus and Theodosius I," in *From the Tetrarchs to the Theodosians: Later Roman History and Culture, 284–450 C.E.*, ed. Scott McGill, Cristiana Sogno, and Edward Watts, Yale Classical Studies 34 (Cambridge: Cambridge University Press, 2010), 215–39; Susanna Elm, "Waiting for Theodosius, or The Ascetic and the City: Gregory of Nazianzus on Maximus the Philosopher," in *Ascetic Culture: Essays in Honor of Philip Rousseau*, ed. Blake Leyerle and Robin Darling Young (Notre Dame, IN: University of Notre Dame Press, 2013), 182–97, esp. 185–86.

20. See Thomas R. Karmann, *Meletius von Antiochien: Studien zur Geschichte des trinitätstheologischen Streits in den Jahren 360-364 n. Chr.*, Regensburger Studien zur Theologie 68 (Frankfurt am Main: Peter Lang, 2009), 306–21; Hanson, *Search for the Christian Doctrine*, 509, 643–44, 809–10.

21. Dam., *Ep.* 5.

22. See Gr. Naz., *Carm.* 2.1.18, 52, 53, 68.

23. See Gr. Naz., *Or.* 42–43, with Susanna Elm, "A Programmatic Life: Gregory of Nazianzus' Orations 42 and 43 and the Constantinopolitan Elites," *Arethusa* 33 (2000): 411–27; Gr. Naz., *Carm.* 2.1.10–12 (along with most of his shorter autobiographical poems), with John McGuckin, "Autobiography as Apologia in St. Gregory of Nazianzus," *Studia Patristica* 37 (2001): 160–77.

24. See Bradley K. Storin, "In a Silent Way: Asceticism and Literature in the Rehabilitation of Gregory of Nazianzus," *Journal of Early Christian Studies* 19 (2011): 225–57.

25. Hier., *Vir. ill.* 117 mentions Gregory's death as occurring three years before Jerome composed this work, which Hier., *Ep.* 47.3 notes took place in the fourteenth year of Theodosius's reign—i.e., 392.

26. See Gr. Naz., *Carm.* 2.1.11.1506–918.

27. Several considerations help to determine the date. Nicobulus, for whom Gregory nominally compiled the collection, began his education while Gregory was still bishop—so between mid-382 and late 383 (see Gr. Naz., *Ep.* 167.3, 188.1)—and many of its important letters can securely be dated to the autumn of 383, therefore pushing the collection's publication to a date later than this. Perhaps a few months passed before Nicobulus embarked upon epistolographical training, a subject typically covered near the beginning of the curriculum; see Raffaella Cribiore, *Gymnastics of the Mind: Greek Education in Hellenistic and Roman Egypt* (Princeton: Princeton University Press, 2001), 215–19; Abraham Malherbe, *Ancient Epistolary Theorists* (Atlanta: Scholars, 1988), 6–7. Therefore, Gregory must have sent the collection to Nicobulus at the end of his episcopacy or shortly after retiring (i.e., in late 383 or early 384).

28. See Gr. Naz., *Ep.* 52.

29. See Gr. Naz., *Carm.* 2.1.11; *Epig.* 2–11, 79; *Or.* 10, 43. See also Storin, *Self-Portrait in Three Colors,* 150–56; McLynn, "Gregory Nazianzen's Basil."

30. My understanding of Gregory's involvement in Nicobulus's education is deeply influenced by the excellent reconstruction in McLynn, "Among the Hellenists," 214–19. Gregory asked Helladius to introduce Nicobulus to teachers in the city (*Ep.* 167.1), among whom may have been Stagirius, a newly minted sophist who had ties to Nicobulus's father (*Ep.* 190.3) and with whom Nicobulus initially enrolled (*Ep.* 188). Upon hearing that Nicobulus had signed up with Stagirius, Gregory's old classmate Eustochius protested. Gregory initially defended choosing Stagirius as Nicobulus's teacher (*Ep.* 190–91) but eventually acquiesced to his old friend and enlisted Nicobulus in Eustochius's school (*Ep.* 192), where he received regular instruction from the assistant Eudoxius, with whom Gregory had a long relationship (*Ep.* 37–38, 174–180, 187).

31. Writers both "published" their own works and disseminated the works of other writers (with or without authorial permission) by sending them to epistolary correspondents. See Harry Y. Gamble, *Books and Readers in the Early Church: A History of Early Christian Texts* (New Haven: Yale University Press, 1995), 140–43.

32. See Storin, *Self-Portrait in Three Colors,* chap. 2; Paul Gallay, ed., *Gregor von Nazianz: Briefe,* Die griechischen christlichen Schriftsteller der ersten Jahrhunderte 53 (Berlin: Akademie-Verlag, 1969); Gallay, ed. and trans., *Grégoire de Nazianze, Lettres,* Collection des Universités de France, publiée sous le patronage de l'Association Guillaume Budé, 2 vols. (Paris: Société d'Édition "Les Belles Lettres," 1964, 1967). The Maurist edition includes the so-called theological letters (Gr. Naz., *Ep.* 101–2, 202, which were transmitted not among Gregory's letters but rather with his orations) and is printed in Patrologia Graeca 37:21–388. To these, Gallay correctly added Gr. Naz., *Ep.* 245, published originally in Josiah Forschall, *Catalogue of the Manuscripts in the British Museum,* n.s., vol. 1 (London, 1840), 34, and again in Giovanni Mercati, *Studi e testi* 9 (Rome: Tipografia Vaticana, 1903); and Gr. Naz., *Ep.* 246–48, which had been included in Basil's collection (Bas., *Ep.* 169–71). However, his addition of Gr. Naz., *Ep.* 249 was incorrect, since it was authored by Gregory of Nyssa (Gr. Nyss., *Ep.* 1), as I discuss in the postscript.

33. Space simply does not permit a thorough discussion of these families. I encourage the reader to consult Storin, *Self-Portrait in Three Colors,* 37–82, for a comprehensive account, including tables, of the manuscripts and their respective arrangements of the collection.

34. See Storin, *Self-Portrait in Three Colors,* chaps. 3–5.

35. Gr. Naz., *Ep.* 77–78.

36. Bradley K. Storin, "The Letters of Gregory of Nazianzus: Discourse and Community in Late Antique Epistolary Culture" (PhD diss., Indiana University, 2012), 237–514.

37. The attribution was first challenged in Paul Gallay, *Les manuscrits des lettres de Saint Grégoire de Nazianze* (Paris: Les Belles Lettres, 1957), 128–30, then repeated with no substantial revision in Gallay, *Grégoire de Nazianze*, 1:xxxvi–xxxvii, and *Gregor von Naziranz*, lii–liii.

38. Gallay, *Les manuscrits*, 129.

39. Gallay, *Les manuscrits*, 130.

40. McGuckin, *St Gregory of Nazianzus*, 378.

41. Gallay, *Les manuscrits*, 131.

42. In Marcianus graecus 79 and Mutinensis Estensis graecus 229: αὕτη ἡ ἐπιστολὴ γρηγορίου ἐστὶ τοῦ νύσης, οὐχὶ τοῦ θεολόγου.

43. Giorgio Pasquali, *Gregorii Nysseni Epistulae*, Gregorii Nysseni Opera 8.2 (Leiden: Brill, 1959), x–xxx.

44. Ernst Honigmann, *Trois mémoires posthumes d'histoire et de géographie de l'Orient chrétien* (Brussels: Société des Bollandistes, 1961), 32–35; Paul Devos, "S. Grégoire de Nazianze et Hellade de Césarée en Cappadoce," *Analecta Bollandiana* 79 (1961): 91–101; Gallay, *Grégoire de Nazianze*, 2:139 n. 1, 171–72.

45. Jean Daniélou, "La chronologie des œuvres de Grégoire de Nysse," *Studia Patristica* 7 (1966): 159–69, esp. 164–65.

46. Gallay, *Gregor von Naziranz*, 41–44.

47. Reinhart Staats, "Gregor von Nyssa und das Bischofsamt," *Zeitschrift für Kirchengeschichte* 84 (1973): 153 n. 2.

48. Christoph Klock, "Überlegungen zur Authentizität des ersten Briefes Gregors von Nyssa," *Studia Patristica* 18 (1983): 15–19.

49. Pierre Maravel, "L'authenticité de la lettre 1 de Grégoire de Nysse," *Analecta Bollandiana* 102 (1984): 61–70, along with his critical edition, *Grégoire de Nysse: Lettres*, Sources chrétiennes 363 (Paris: Éditions du Cerf, 1990), 51–59, with notes on 82–105; Bernhard Wyss, "Gregor von Nazianz oder Gregor von Nyssa?," in *Mémorial André-Jean Festugière, Antiquité païenne et chrétienne*, ed. E. Lucchesi and H. D. Saffrey, Cahiers d'orientalisme 10 (Geneva: Patrick Cramer, 1984), 153–62.

50. Anna Silvas, *Gregory of Nyssa: The Letters—Introduction, Translation, and Commentary*, Supplements to Vigiliae Christianae 83 (Leiden: Brill, 2007), 105.

TRANSLATION

1. Eurystheus was the mythical king of Tiryns to whom Heracles was enslaved while performing his twelve labors.

2. I.e., the entire letter collection.

3. Referring to the Egyptian Nilometer, which represented cubits of inundation with pictures of infants playing around the river.

4. Here: τὴν σὴν συντυχίαν ἐφύγομεν, ἀλλ'. Paul Gallay, *Grégoire de Nazianze: Lettres,* Collection des Universités de France, publiée sous le patronage de l'Association Guillaume Budé, 2 vols. (Paris: Société d'Édition "Les Belles Lettres," 1964, 1967), 1:78: τὴν σὴν συντυχίαν ἐφύγομεν (τί μὲν οὖν;), ἀλλ'.

5. Perhaps a reference to patria potestas, the Roman legal structure granting fathers legal and economic authority over their dependents.

6. See also Gr. Naz., *Carm.* 2.1.11.310–20.

7. This letter and Gr. Naz., *Ep.* 4–6 pertain to Basil's ascetic community at Annesi, north of Cappadocia in Pontus.

8. A region near Nazianzus.

9. A mythical priest of Apollo who could, among other things, travel around the world on an arrow. See, e.g., Hdt., *Hist.* 4.36; Pl., *Chrm.* 158c; Iamb., *V.P.* 92–93, 215–21.

10. At the time of composition, Basil was in Pontus.

11. Referring to Bas., *Ep.* 14.

12. *Xouphērian.* This word vexed the Maurist editors, who rendered it *zophēphorian* ("gloom"), and Byzantine scribes, one of whom jotted down *muōxian* ("mousehole," used later in the sentence) in the margin of an eleventh-century manuscript (Paris Coisliniano 237), trying to clarify the meaning. The seventeenth-century philologist Charles du Fresne du Cange defined it as follows: "[Latin] MS. in the lexicon, [Greek] the mousehole, or the lair, or the extravagance, of the Pontics, from the letter of Gregory the Theologian, 'I'll admire your Pontus and Pontic *xoupheria.*' [Latin] The hole of a mouse, or animal den" (*Glossarium ad scriptores mediae et infimae graecitatis* [Lyon, 1688], vol. 1, col. 1022).

13. A river in modern Bulgaria and Greece that empties into the Aegean Sea at Kolpos Orphanou (the ancient Strymonic Gulf). Cf. Hes., *Th.* 7.75; A., *A.* 192; Hdt., *Hist.* 7.75.

14. The rapids and waterfalls of the Nile River.

15. An epistolary joke: Gregory exceeds the epistolary measure (*metron*) but asks Basil to be measured about his literary violation.

16. The opening clause here picks up on Gr. Naz., *Ep.* 4.13.

17. Gregory has substituted Homer's *hippou kosmon* ("decoration of the horse") with *ton esō kosmon* ("the decoration inside").

18. A Phaeacian king with a reputation for great hospitality. See, e.g., *Od.* 6.12ff, 13.70ff, 13.172ff.

19. *Geōphoron.* Paul Gallay, ed., *Gregor von Nazianz: Briefe,* Die griechischen christlichen Schriftsteller der ersten Jahrhunderte 53 (Berlin: Akademie-Verlag, 1969), 7 n. 6, has supplied this word in lieu of the variants in the manuscripts. Marcianus graecus 81 (Ξ) reads *geōlophos,* "earth-crested"

or substantively "a hill, hillock," while the u- and v- families attest *leōphoron*, "people-bearing" or substantively "a highway, thoroughfare."

20. A wordplay: "king" = *basileus*, "Basil" = *Basileios*.
21. Basil had already been elected bishop at the time of writing.
22. Π¹: "To Prohairesius."
23. A wordplay: "palace" = *basileion*; "Basil" = *Basileios*.
24. Likely a reference to Emperor Julian's release of all exiled Christians regardless of theological party.
25. While Gregory and Basil suspected Eusebius of obtaining the episcopacy uncanonically and perhaps holding heterodox views, the nature of Basil's conflict with Eusebius is unknown (cf. Gr. Naz., *Or.* 43.28).
26. Here: μέτριον; Gallay, *Grégoire de Nazianze*, 1:24: μετριώτερον.
27. Lit. "rubbing a man's head with one hand while striking his cheek with the other."
28. Likely quoting Eusebius's response to Gr. Naz., *Ep.* 16.
29. At this time, Gregory was a priest in a small city and Eusebius a metropolitan bishop.
30. Either a reference to the general theological conflicts of the time or, more likely, a specific reminder to Eusebius that the Homoian emperor Valens was coming to Caesarea.
31. The chief architect of the ancient Israelite tabernacle. Gregory aligns Basil with Bezalel by virtue of the similarity of both their names and their cunning compositional abilities. See Gr. Naz., *Or.* 43.43 for the same comparison.
32. Basil had already been elected bishop at the time of writing.
33. A monk.
34. A Caesarean nobleman who helped destroy a temple dedicated to Fortuna during the reign of Emperor Julian, for which he was sentenced to death and came to be regarded as a martyr. See Soz., *H.e.* 5.11.
35. The criticism being that Basil picks easy theological fights and avoids difficult ones.
36. Here: ὅ; Gallay, *Grégoire de Nazianze*, 1:75: ὁ.
37. Basil's cool reply in Bas., *Ep.* 71, which answered Gr. Naz., *Ep.* 58 and to which this letter now responds.
38. On the episode described in this and the two subsequent letters, see also Gr. Naz., *Carm.* 2.1.11.386–485; *Or.* 43.58.
39. During the provincial split of Cappadocia in early 372, Tyana became the metropolitanate of Cappadocia Secunda and Caesarea the metropolitanate of Cappadocia Prima. Many of the cities and bishops (and, therefore, prestige and revenue) previously under Basil's episcopal jurisdiction were transferred to Anthimus's. Seeing his authority greatly diminished, Basil fought to

regain some of his power, while Anthimus fought to defend his newly enhanced status by maintaining the provincial division.

40. Gr. Naz., *Ep.* 48.6–8 may be an extract from a previous letter that Gregory wrote to Basil.

41. As Gallay, *Grégoire de Nazianze*, 1:65 n. 1, notes, the Maurists rendered this word (*Limnōn*) as a proper noun, thereby suggesting that it was the name of a town. As a common noun, *limnē* means "a marsh." William M. Ramsay, *The Historical Geography of Asia Minor*, Royal Geographical Society's Supplementary Papers 4 (London: John Murray, 1890; reprint, [London:] Elibron Classics, Adamant Media, 2005), 294, describes it as a small town near Sasima, called Limna by Hellenophones and Göljik by Turkophones.

42. Anthimus accused Gregory of being merely a partisan for Basil.

43. Gregory sent this letter to Basil along with one that he received from Anthimus, which he here asks Basil to examine for himself.

44. Summoning a synod.

45. That is, Nazianzus is a small city (micropolitan), or not a real city (apolitan) in comparison to Caesarea.

46. This letter and Gr. Naz., *Ep.* 41–46 pertain to Basil's contentious episcopal election in 370. See also Gr. Naz., *Or.* 43.37.

47. Caesarea.

48. Written under the name of Gregory's father-bishop.

49. Written under the name of Gregory's father-bishop.

50. A town roughly eight miles northeast of Nazianzus.

51. The text reads ἐπόμενον (pass. part. of εἶπον, "to speak"), although it should say ἑπόμενον (dep. part. of ἕπομαι, "to follow"), as the critical apparatus says. The former must simply be a typographical error. Gallay, *Saint Grégoire de Nazianze*, 2:136, reads ἐχόμενον, based on h.

52. Here: ἐπαναγαγεῖν; Gallay, *Grégoire de Nazianze*, 2:137: ἀπαναγαγεῖν.

53. Gr. Naz., *Ep.* 246.

54. h: "Without addressee."

55. This letter and the next should be read in concert with Gr. Naz., *Ep.* 107–9, 111–14, 116–18 (the "silence dossier"). They all pertain to the ascetic silence that Gregory undertook in the spring of 382, after he returned to Cappadocia from Constantinople but before he resumed the Nazianzan episcopacy. See also Gr. Naz., *Carm.* 2.1.34–38, and perhaps *Carm.* 2.1.19–33, for poems written during the silence.

56. Locations unknown.

57. I.e., granting the properties tax exemptions.

58. Perhaps a reference to Gregory's ascetic silence during Lent of 382 (see also Gr. Naz., *Ep.* 107). The phrase is nearly the same as one attributed to the

philosopher Athenodorus (Plu., *Reg. et imp. apophth.* 207c), with the substitution of "verbal stillness" (*siōpē*) for its synonym "silence" (*sigē*). Cl. Alex., *Str.* 2.68.3 also quotes Athenodorus's phrase.

59. Perhaps Theodosia (the sister of Amphilochius of Iconium), on whose Constantinopolitan estate Gregory formed the Anastasia congregation.

60. The investigation of Bosporius is also discussed at Gr. Naz., *Ep.* 183.9–10.

61. Here: Ἐκεῖνο δὲ μὴ ἀνεκτὸν φανήτω τῇ σῇ εὐλαβείᾳ τὸ δημοσίοις δικαστηρίοις στηλιτεύεσθαι τὰ ἡμέτερα. Gallay, *Grégoire de Nazianze,* 2:76: Ἐκεῖνο δὲ μὴ ἀνεκτὸν φανήτω τῇ σῇ εὐλαβείᾳ στηλιτεύεσθαι τὰ ἡμέτερα.

62. In a nonextant letter.

63. In a nonextant letter, to which this one responds.

64. In a nonextant letter, to which this one responds.

65. In heaven.

66. v: "To Eidicius."

67. u, d, f, h: "To Eudicius."

68. u, d, g: "To Eudicius."

69. Probably Gr. Naz., *Ep.* 216.

70. I.e., those who introduced Sacerdos to the ascetic life.

71. Most manuscripts identify the addressee as Theodore of Tyana, but Λ adds a cautionary note: "rather to another, anonymous [person], as the letter makes clear."

72. Cf. Gr. Naz., *Ep.* 182.5, where Gregory embraces his appointment to Sasima.

73. Gregory's successor was his cousin Eulalius.

74. The investigation into Bosporius is also discussed in Gr. Naz., *Ep.* 185.

75. A town or region near Tyana.

76. Here: ᾐδέσθην; Gallay, *Grégoire de Nazianze,* 2:14: ἠδέσθην. Surely the latter is correct and the former a typographical error.

77. This letter, one of two (with Gr. Naz., *Ep.* 78) included in the collection that date to his time in Constantinople (379–81), came in the aftermath of the Paschal attack on the Anastasia, an event mentioned in several other places in his corpus: see Gr. Naz., *Carm.* 2.1.11.665, 2.1.12.103, 2.1.15.11, 2.1.30.125, 2.1.33.12; *Ep.* 77; *Or.* 23.5, 41.5, 42.27, perhaps 33.13.

78. Those on their way to baptism.

79. Here: ὁ δὲ ἀπαξιοῖ; Gallay, *Grégoire de Nazianze,* 1:96: ὃ δὲ ἀπαξιοῖ, surely a typographical error.

80. Gallay, *Grégoire de Nazianze,* 1:96: "seventy times" (*to hebdomēkontakis*), perhaps to correct Gregory's error: in the Matthean passage, Jesus's "seventy-seven times" does not supplement but rather replaces Peter's "seven times."

81. Here: ὑπεκκαόντων; Gallay, *Grégoire de Nazianze*, 1:97: ὑπεκκαιόντων. The omission of the iota is attested by u, v, d, and f and appears to be an atticism; the two words have the same meaning.

82. The missing antecedent for "this" (*touto*) suggests that this letter is only a fragment of a longer original, trimmed down through the manuscript transmission or by Gregory's editorial hand.

83. Following the suggestion of Gallay, *Grégoire de Nazianze*, 2:50 n. 4, to read ὀλίγα for ἐπ' ὀλίγοις.

84. Whether this refers to a letter in the collection or not is unknown.

85. The *Philocalia* is an anthology of Origenian texts on the subjects of scriptural interpretation, free will, and apologetics. Based on this letter, scholars have traditionally regarded Gregory and Basil as its editors.

86. A theological faction centered on the heterodox Christology of Apollinaris of Laodicaea (c. 315–92), a Homoousian ally of Athanasius of Alexandria. In 363, at the request of the emperor Jovian, Homoousian bishops delivered statements of Trinitarian faith; Apollinaris's included a detailed sketch of his unpopular Christology, which included statements on the preexistence of Christ's flesh, on Christ not possessing a human nous, or "mind," and on cosmic repetition. Gregory's critiques of Apollinaris are robust: see Gr. Naz., *Carm.* 1.1.10–11; *Ep.* 125 and 101–2, 202 (the "theological letters," not included in this translation); *Or.* 29–30.

87. v, IF: "To Photeinus"; Λ: "To Photinus."

88. A frequent epithet for Odysseus in the *Iliad* and the *Odyssey*.

89. Presumably Thecla, the sister of Sacerdos.

90. At the time, Gregory of Nyssa was perhaps on a tour of Arabia and Jerusalem, possibly after the Council of Constantinople in 381.

91. In a nonextant letter, to which this one responds.

92. Possibly a reference to Gregory's ascetic silence in 382. This letter, then, would be a post-Constantinople composition.

93. Again, Gregory of Nyssa was perhaps on a tour of Arabia and Jerusalem, possibly after the Council of Constantinople in 381.

94. This phrase seems to refer to the place where Basil's dead body would have rested before burial or the spot on which he died.

95. An estate near Nazianzus (in Ozizala?) that may have belonged to Amphilochius of Iconium's family.

96. Gregory's text reads *kata kairon*, although the scriptural text has *kath' hōran*.

97. A strange title for her, no doubt, but one that signals her embodiment of philosophy.

98. Cf. Gr. Naz., *Ep.* 183.6, where Gregory distances himself from his appointment to Sasima.

99. Manuscript family d pointedly distinguishes the addressee of this letter: "Not to [Gregory] of Nyssa, but to a Gregory of the same name." However, all other manuscript families identify the addressee as Gregory of Nyssa.

100. That is, with a sophistic paradox.

101. *Siōpēs*, often a synonym for, but not a precise equivalent of, *sigē*, "silence." See also Gr. Naz., *Ep.* 91.

102. Cf. Gr. Naz., *Carm.* 2.1.34.21–24.

103. Or "words."

104. u, v, h: "To Helladius."

105. u, v: "To Eulalius."

106. u, v: "To Eulalius."

107. Referring to the Paschal attack on the Anastasia in 380. See also Gr. Naz., *Carm.* 2.1.11.665, 2.1.12.103, 2.1.15.11, 2.1.30.125, 2.1.33.12; *Ep.* 77; *Or.* 23.5, 41.5, 42.27, perhaps 33.13.

108. The sagacious elder in the *Iliad* and the *Odyssey*. Gregory also likens himself to Nestor at Gr. Naz., *Ep.* 52.1.

109. Caesarius survived an earthquake that leveled Nicaea in 368: see Gr. Naz., *Or.* 7.15.

110. What Gregory has in mind here is uncertain. A tenth-century manuscript (Athous tēs ieras monēs Ibērōn 355 nunc 2413) notes in the margin, "It lies in the specious *Teaching of Peter*." This work does not survive.

111. Written while Caesarius was working in Emperor Julian's administration.

112. See Gr. Naz., *Or.* 4.5, 4.58, 4.83, 4.96, 7.11, where Gregory describes Julian's policies toward Christians as a bloodless persecution.

113. Lit. "a right hand."

114. Lit. "a left hand."

115. Written in the run-up to the council of Constantinople in 382.

116. Here: καὶ λόγους; absent from Gallay, *Grégoire de Nazianze*, 1:47.

117. Eustochius and Gregory were classmates in Athens under the tutelage of Prohaeresius and Himerius.

118. Referring to Stagirius, the addressee of Gr. Naz., *Ep.* 165–66, 188, 192.

119. In a nonextant letter, to which this one responds.

120. Individuals associated with sorcery and malingering (cf. Call., *Aet.*, frag. 75.65; Str., *Geogr.* 14.2.7).

121. Caucasian Iberia was located in what is now the Republic of Georgia, more than four hundred miles northeast of Nazianzus.

122. u: "To Theodosius or Theodore"; f: "To Theodosius or Bishop Theodore"; h: "To Theodore."

123. Here: σοὶ μὲν ἀκμὴ φιλοσοφεῖν; Gallay, *Grégoire de Nazianze*, 2:125: σὺ μὲν ἀκμὴν φιλοσοφεῖς.

124. Teachers of eloquence.

125. Eunomus was a musician whose cithara string broke during a contest. In its place, a cricket jumped onto the neck of the instrument and supplied the missing note. Cf. Str., *Geogr.* 6.1.9; Cl. Alex., *Prot.* 1.1.2.

126. I.e., Eudoxius will provide rhetorical services to Nicobulus, as he is paid to do, and act like a sophist by letting go of his grudge.

127. In a nonextant letter, to which this one responds.

128. This is an allusion to an epigram of Nestor of Nicaea (*Anth. Gr.* 9.537).

129. A reference to Eudoxius's profession as a teacher of rhetoric: he would have spent a portion of each day with students delivering prepared or extemporaneous speeches on fictional themes.

130. On earth.

131. Heaven.

132. Here the text reads πτεροῦ, the genitive of πτερόν. The string of imperatives around it, however, suggests that the accent is an error. That is, this word should be πτέρου, a second-person singular present active imperative of πτερόω.

133. See also Gr. Naz., *Ep.* 37.2, 38.3.

134. I.e., both Christian and pagan ideas.

135. The Sicilian king Phalaris (mid-sixth century BCE) was believed to have cooked his enemies alive within a bronze bull. See the version of the story that Gregory may have known best at Pi., *P.* 1.95.

136. Christian martyrs.

137. I.e., non-Christians.

138. That is, his body.

139. In the afterlife.

140. Referring to the church at Constantinople.

141. In a nonextant letter, to which this one responds.

142. A small town (perhaps modern Mazıköy) in Cappadocia not too far from ancient Nazianzus.

143. In the afterlife.

144. Christian and pagan ideas.

145. Presumably referring to any or all of the collection's letters to Philagrius.

146. Or "the Word [of God]."

147. I.e., the intellect.

148. *Hē trapedza*. To what precisely this refers is unclear. The sophist Libanius uses the term *trapedza* to refer to drinking parties (Lib., *Or.* 1.75) and as the location of shared friendship and eloquence (Lib., *Ep.* 1225.2).

149. The editio princeps identifies the recipient as Eudoxius. However, Gallay, *Grégoire de Nazianze*, 1:103 n. 1, notes that this is simply an error by the Maurist copyists, as u, v, d, f, g, and the Vienna Papyrus identify the addressee as Philagrius. The h-family identifies the recipient as "Gregory."

150. In a nonextant letter, to which this one responds.

151. h: "To Hellebechus."

152. In heaven.

153. The end of Asterius's office coincided with the end of office of Olympius, for whom he served as assessor. See Gr. Naz., *Ep.* 154.

154. Gregory does not want Nicobulus's affair to become a criminal prosecution.

155. Cf. Cl. Alex., *Str.* 1.14.61.1, which attributes this adage to Cleobulus.

156. A Cappadocian town of unknown location.

157. See 1 Sam 2:11–4:18.

158. A Cappadocian town of unknown location.

159. The scriptural text reads, "Do not give your wealth to women, and your mind and life to second thought."

160. Four Athenian generals, popular subjects of rhetorical speeches and exercises in Gregory's time (see also Gr. Naz., *Ep.* 235.4). Miltiades, Cynegirus, and Callimachus led troops at the battle of Marathon in 490 BCE (see Hdt., *Hist.* 6.94–140); Lamachus led troops in the Peloponnesian War in the late fifth century BCE (see Th., *Hist.* 4.75.1–2, 6.49–50, 6.101–3).

161. Written in the run-up to the council of Constantinople in 383.

162. The Strait of Gibraltar.

163. Written in the run-up to the council of Constantinople in 382.

164. That is, Gregory is sending a letter to Saturninus without having first received one from him.

165. Undoubtedly a reference to the council of Constantinople in 381.

166. f: "To the master Sophronius."

167. Written in the run-up to the council of Constantinople in 382.

168. Written in the run-up to the council of Constantinople in 382.

169. Zos. 4.25.2 notes that Modarius was a Scythian.

170. Likely a war against the Goths in Thrace in 380: see Zos. 4.25.2.

171. h: "To Domearius."

172. I.e., powerful and philosophical.

173. This letter and the next two to Celeusius should be read alongside Gr. Naz., *Ep.* 107–11, 116–19 as part of the "silence dossier," despite the fact that the u-family relocates them.

174. u, h: "To Basil"; Coisl.: "Basil to Gregory." However, an astute medieval reader was aware that the attribution to Basil was false, writing in the margin of the fourteenth- or fifteenth-century Codex Y, "One must read that

[Gregory] wrote not to the holy Basil, but rather to a certain Celeusius when he kept silent in Lamis."

175. The words that Gregory supplies to the swallows refer to a story concerning the Athenian king Pandion, who received military assistance from the Thracian king Tereus. In return, Pandion offered Tereus his daughter Procne in marriage, and the two had a son, named Itys. When Procne's sister, Philomela, came to Thrace to pay a visit, Tereus raped her and then cut out her tongue so that she couldn't say what he had done. Philomela informed Procne of the act by weaving words into a garment. The two sisters exacted revenge by killing, cooking, and serving Itys to an unknowing Tereus, who consumed his son, only to realize after the meal what had happened. He then tried to kill the sisters, but they escaped. All three characters ended up turning into birds: Procne became a swallow (or a nightingale), Philomela a nightingale (or a swallow), and Tereus a hoopoe. See Apollod., *Bib.* 3.14.8.

176. The date of the three letters to Bosporius hinges on whether Gregory refers to his refusal to take hold of the Nazianzan episcopacy upon his return from Constantinople in late 381 or to his upcoming retirement from it in late 383.

177. In a nonextant letter, to which this one responds. The "opponents" are likely Apollinarians.

178. h: "To Theodore."

179. A king of Tartessus in Spain who supposedly lived to 120 years old: see Hdt., *Hist.* 1.163.2, 1.165.2.

180. d, f, IFh: "To Vitalius"; Λ: "To Vitalius, who betrothed his daughter."

181. d, f, g, h: "To Vitalius."

182. d, f, g, h: "To Vitalius."

183. Here Simplicia's children are "orphaned" because their father, Alypius, has died.

184. I.e., exchanged letters.

185. I (secundo): "To governor Olympius."

186. I (secundo): "To governor Olympius."

187. Presumably referring to Alypius's involvement in the Palladius affair: see Gr. Naz., *Ep.* 82.

188. h: "To Olympius."

189. *Tous chlainophorous.* Marie-Madeleine Hauser-Meury, *Prosopographie zu den Schriften Gregors von Nazianz* (Bonn: Hanstein, 1960), 27 n. 14, speculates that the term refers to those who wear military garb, noting that in late antiquity, *chlaina* ("cloak," perhaps "poncho") was a synonym for *chlanis* ("shawl," "mantle"; cf. Gr. Naz., *Ep.* 86.3), which itself could stand for *chlamys* (military cloak). The context of the letter makes it clear that Gregory is applying the term to Alypius.

190. I (secundo): "To governor Olympius."

191. h: "To Eusebius."

192. Perhaps referring to the house in Alypius's jurisdiction mentioned at Gr. Naz., *Ep.* 82.1.

193. Gregory has substituted "stinginess" (*mikrologias*) for the original's "injustice" (*adikias*).

194. This parenthetical phrase justifies Gregory's change to the scriptural text (see previous note): to use it unaltered (i.e., to characterize as an injustice Aerius and Alypius's failure to bestow their inheritance on the church) would be slanderous, or "blasphemy" as the Greek literally has it.

195. I.e., in heaven.

196. An allusion to Nicobulus's upcoming marriage to Alypiane.

197. Provenance unknown.

198. Here: ὠφείλετο; Gallay, *Grégoire de Nazianze*, 2:18: ἀφείλετο.

199. Written in the run-up to the council of Constantinople in 382.

200. Emperor Theodosius, who knew Gregory from his tenure in Constantinople during the previous two years.

201. Here: λειτουργῶν; Gallay, *Grégoire de Nazianze*, 1:12: λειτουργούντων.

202. Julian revoked Constantius II's clerical tax exemptions (*C. Th.* 12.1.50), but Emperor Jovian seems to have restored them. Nevertheless, provincial tax collectors were slow to implement the policy.

203. Theognis of Megara, a seventh- or sixth-century BCE elegiac poet who often used drinking and parties as subjects.

204. Here: ἐχρῆν; Gallay, *Grégoire de Nazianze*, 1:20: χρῆν.

205. Gregory's father and Amphilochius's father were brothers.

206. Reading εἰ δ'οὐκ for εἰ δ'οὖν. Gallay nowhere shows this as an alternative, but the Maurist editors note that the sense requires the negative particle (Patrologia Graeca 37:45–46), with which I agree.

207. The junior Amphilochius had recently been consecrated bishop of Iconium.

208. Gregory's father died in the first half of 374: see Gr. Naz., *Or.* 18.

209. The younger Amphilochius's consecration.

210. Perhaps a reference to Basil's appointment of Gregory to Sasima.

211. An Egyptian town far east of the Nile with no direct water supply (see J., *B.J.* 4.661).

212. Ozizala was a Cappadocian village where Amphilochius lived at the time.

213. In a nonextant letter, to which this one responds.

214. Parnassus was a Cappadocian village approximately fifty miles northwest of Nazianzus.

215. Perhaps Bosporius of Colonia, whose orthodoxy was the subject of an investigatory council: see Gr. Naz., *Ep.* 185.

216. In Greek myth, a mortal fisherman who was transformed into a sea deity or a merman. Nothing is known about the man whom Gregory calls Glaucus here.

217. Something akin to a guitar pick.

218. v: "To Ulpian"; d, f, IH: "To Olympius"; F: "To governor Olympius."

219. Gr. Naz., *Ep.* 67–69 were written not long before Gr. Naz., *Or.* 19 (Christmas 374), which thanks their addressee, Julian, for arranging clerical tax exemptions.

220. Tyana was forty-five miles south of Nazianzus and served as the capital of Cappadocia Secunda during the provincial splits of 372 and 382.

221. The tax exemptions requested in Gr. Naz., *Ep.* 67.2.

222. This letter pertains to Basil's episcopal election in 370; see also Gr. Naz., *Ep.* 40–42, 45–46.

223. Perhaps a combination of Isa 61:3 ("oil of gladness") and 61:10 ("robe of righteousness").

224. Basil, Caesarea's new bishop.

225. Here: θαρροῦντας; Gallay, *Grégoire de Nazianze*, 1:57: θαρροῦντα.

226. Emperor Valens exiled Eusebius to Thrace in the 370s.

227. In a nonextant letter, to which this one responds.

228. v: "To Bishop Eusebius of Samosata."

229. Here: ηὔξατο; Gallay, *Grégoire de Nazianze*, 2:123: εὔξατο.

230. Written under the name of Gregory's father-bishop, this letter pertains to Basil's episcopal election in 370; see also Gr. Naz., *Ep.* 40–41, 44–46.

231. The deceased bishop of Caesarea, whom Basil would succeed.

232. This letter is not extant.

233. Basil.

234. This letter is not extant.

235. ΛF: "To Caesarius."

236. The administrative name for Nazianzus.

237. Referring to the Persian armies that conquered Cappadocian towns in 260 C.E.

238. I.e., the city.

239. I.e., the afterlife.

240. ΛF: "To Caesarius."

241. f: "To Alypius"; ΛF: "To Caesarius."

242. f: "To Alypius"; ΛF: "To Caesarius."

243. Here: φυχήν; Gallay, *Grégoire de Nazianze*, 2:2: ψυχήν. The latter is indubitably correct and the former a typographical error.

244. d, f: "To Alypius"; g: "To Governor Alypius."

245. Here: ἐπέτρεψας; Gallay, *Grégoire de Nazianze*, 2:35: διέτρεψας.

246. In the second half of the fourth century CE, Roman law did little to restrict the practice of divorce. However, Christian clergy generally opposed it, primarily on the basis of various New Testament passages forbidding it (e.g., Matt 5:31–32, 19:3–9; Mark 10:2–12; Luke 16:18; Rom 7:2–3; 1 Cor 7:10–11).

247. Referring to the provincial governor Olympius and the subject of Gr. Naz., *Ep.* 144.

248. ΛF: "To Caesarius."

249. u, v, d: "To Alypius"; f: "To Alypius the governor."

250. Approximately twenty miles southeast of Nazianzus.

251. d, f: "To Alypius"; g: "To Governor Alypius."

252. d, f: "To Alypius"; g: "To Governor Alypius."

253. Presumably tasks like housekeeping, stable cleaning, and tending to horses.

254. Gregory refers to the second division of Cappadocia, by Theodosius I in late 382. Nazianzus, thanks to Gregory's efforts (despite his rhetoric here), fell under the metropolitan jurisdiction of Tyana in Cappadocia Secunda, the more powerful of the two resulting provinces.

255. All of the manuscript families (u, v, d, f, g, h) supply ἀκινήτοις here, which Gallay, *Grégoire de Nazianze*, 2:46 n. 1, notes makes little sense, especially since the negative particle οὐκ appears before it in all the manuscripts. I thus maintain and translate Gallay's substitution of εὐκινήτοις.

256. Presumably tax officers trying to collect on the senior Nicobulus's estate.

257. Location unknown, but presumably in Cappadocia.

258. u, v: "To the Brotherhood at Sannabodae."

259. The occasion addressed here, and indeed for the letter as a whole, was the death of Leucadius himself.

260. A pre-Socratic philosopher (c. 570–495 C.E.) famous for his vegetarianism, among many other things.

261. The provenance of this quotation is unknown.

262. That is, Timothy's (nonextant) letter, to which this one responds.

263. As letter carrier.

264. u, v: "To Timothy."

265. On the afterlife.

266. u, v: "To Timothy."

267. This letter is not extant.

268. *Aleiphein*, literally "rubbing oil on": that is, being a part of the fighter's support team but not fighting oneself.

269. u, v: "To Timothy."

270. Constantinople.

271. Perhaps alluding to the myth about Triptolemus and Demeter. See Paus., *Gr. desc.* 7.18.2 for a reference to Triptolemus teaching humans agriculture.

272. I.e., poetry and rhetoric.

273. Likely a reference to his ordination in 362.

274. A reference to the emperor Julian's edict prohibiting Christians from teaching the classical texts of paideia.

275. Emperor Julian's government.

276. See Gr. Naz., *Or.* 4.5, 4.58, 4.83, 4.96, 7.11, which present Julian's anti-Christian policies as persecution.

277. d, f: "To Julian."

278. Modern Güzelyurt in Aksaray Province, Turkey.

279. The famous fourth-century BCE Cynic philosopher.

280. "Sojourner" is my translation of *paroikos*: Theotecnus was probably not a citizen of Nazianzus.

281. This letter, one of two (with Gr. Naz., *Ep.* 77) that Gregory wrote while living in Constantinople (379-81), came in the aftermath of the Paschal attack on the Anastasia, an event mentioned in several other places in his corpus: see Gr. Naz., *Carm.* 2.1.11.665, 2.1.12.103, 2.1.15.11, 2.1.30.125, 2.1.33.12; *Ep.* 77; *Or.* 23.5, 41.5, 42.27, perhaps 33.13.

282. That is, Theotecnus was recently baptized.

283. I.e., in the afterlife.

284. Perhaps the Paul mentioned at Gr. Naz., *Ep.* 77.16.

285. Here: παύσασθαι παίζοντας; Gallay, *Grégoire de Nazianze*, 2:126: παύσασθαι καὶ παίζοντας.

286. Cynegirus and Callimachus, Athenian generals who led troops at the battle of Marathon in 490 BCE (see Hdt., *Hist.* 6.94-140), were popular subjects for rhetorical speeches and exercises in Gregory's time (see also Gr. Naz., *Ep.* 233.1).

287. This epistle was transmitted among the manuscripts of Basil's letter collection, otherwise appearing only in the f-family of Gregory's collection and among four composite manuscripts (in all four of which it follows Bas., *Ep.* 174). Despite the manuscript evidence in favor of Basilian authorship, the scholarly consensus assigns it to Gregory, for primarily stylistic reasons: see Louis-Sébastien Le Nain de Tillemont, *Mémoires pour servir à l'histoire ecclésiastique des six premiers siècles: Volume 9, Les vies de Saint Basile, de Saint Grégoire de Nazianze, de Saint Grégoire de Nysse, et de Saint Amphiloque* (Paris: Charles Robustel, 1703), 660; M. Bessières, "La tradition manuscrite de la correspondance de Saint Basile: Chapitre 6," *Journal of Theological Studies* 23 (1922): 343; Paul Gallay, *Les manuscrits des lettres de Saint Grégoire de Nazianze* (Paris: Les Belles Lettres, 1957), 126-27.

288. "Here" refers to earthly existence, while "over there" refers to the heavenly one.

289. That is, Sacerdos. See Gr. Naz., *Ep.* 222.1-3.

290. Sacerdos.

291. This letter responds to a nonextant consoling letter that Simplicia sent after the death of Gregory's father-bishop in 374.

292. Presumably Gregory's father, mentioned at the beginning of the letter.

293. For a similar distinction between "our laws" and "outside laws," see Gr. Naz., *Ep.* 78.6.

294. Here: ἡ; Gallay, *Grégoire de Nazianze*, 2:132: ἥ. I read the latter, assuming the former is a typographical error.

295. Παραγγελμάτων. Missing from Gallay, *Grégoire de Nazianze*, 2:132.

WORKS CITED

PRIMARY SOURCES

Ambrose of Milan. *Epistulae*, edited by O. Faller and Michaela Zelzer, *Epistulae et acta*, Corpus Scriptorum Ecclesiasticorum Latinorum 82.1–3 (Vienna: Hoelder-Pichler-Tempsky, 1982, 1990).

Basil of Caesarea. *Epistulae*, edited by Yves Courtonne, *Basil de Cesarée: Lettres*, 3 vols. (Paris: Société d'Édition "Les Belles Lettres," 1957–66).

Damasus of Rome. *Epistulae*, Patrologia Latina 13:347–76.

Gregory of Nazianzus. *Carmina*, Patrologia Graeca 37:397–1600.

———. *Carmina* 1.1.1–1.1.5, 1.1.7–1.1.9, edited by Claudio Moreschini and translated by D.A. Sykes, *St. Gregory of Nazianzus: Poemata Arcana*, Oxford Theological Monographs (Oxford: Clarendon, 1997).

———. *Carmen* 2.1.11, edited by Christoph Jungck, *Gregory von Nazianz: De vita sua*, Wissenschaftliche Kommentare zu griechischen und lateinischen Schriftstellern (Heidelberg: Carl Winter Universitätsverlag, 1974).

———. *Epigrammata*, edited and translated by W.R. Paton, *Greek Anthology II, Book 7: Sepulchral Epigrams; Book 8: The Epigrams of St. Gregory the Theologian*, Loeb Classical Library 68 (Cambridge, MA: Harvard University Press, 1917).

———. *Epistulae* 1–100, 103–201, 203–49, edited by Paul Gallay, *Gregor von Nazianz: Briefe*, Die griechischen christlichen Schriftsteller der ersten Jahrhunderte 53 (Berlin: Akademie-Verlag, 1969); edited and translated by Paul Gallay, *Grégoire de Nazianze: Lettres*, Collection des Universités de France, publiée sous le patronage de l'Association Guillaume Budé, 2 vols. (Paris: Société d'Édition "Les Belles Lettres," 1964, 1967); Patrologia Graeca 37:21-387.

———. *Epitaphia,* Patrologia Graeca 38:11–80.

———. *Orationes* 1–3, edited by Jean Bernardi, *Grégoire de Nazianze: Discours 1–3,* Sources chrétiennes 247 (Paris: Éditions du Cerf, 1978).

———. *Orationes* 6–12, edited by Marie-Ange Calvet-Sébasti, *Grégoire de Nazianze: Discours 6–12,* Sources chrétiennes 405 (Paris: Éditions du Cerf, 1995).

———. *Oratio* 18, Patrologia Graeca 35:985–1044.

———. *Orationes* 20–23, edited by Guy Lafontaine and Justin Mossay, *Grégoire de Nazianze: Discours 20–23,* Sources chrétiennes 270 (Paris: Éditions du Cerf, 1980).

———. *Orationes* 24–26, edited by Guy Lafontaine and Justin Mossay, *Grégoire de Nazianze: Discours 24–26,* Sources chrétiennes 284 (Paris: Éditions du Cerf, 1981).

———. *Orationes* 27–31, edited by Paul Gallay and Maurice Jourjon, *Grégoire de Nazianze: Discours 27–31, Discours théologiques,* Sources chrétiennes 250 (Paris: Éditions du Cerf, 1978).

———. *Orationes* 32–37, edited by Claudio Moreschini, *Grégoire de Nazianze: Discours 32–37,* Sources chrétiennes 318 (Paris: Éditions du Cerf, 1985).

———. *Orationes* 42–43, edited by Jean Bernardi, *Grégoire de Nazianze: Discours 42–43,* Sources chrétiennes 384 (Paris: Éditions du Cerf, 1992).

Gregory of Nyssa. *Epistulae,* edited by Pierre Maravel, *Grégoire de Nysse: Lettres,* Sources chrétiennes 363 (Paris: Éditions du Cerf, 1990).

———. *Vita sanctae Macrinae,* edited by Pierre Maraval, *Grégoire de Nysse: Vie de sainte Macrine,* Sources chrétiennes 178 (Paris: Éditions du Cerf, 1971).

Jerome of Stridon. *De viris illustribus,* edited by E. C. Richardson, *Hieronymus, Liber de viris inlustribus Gennadius de viris inlustribus,* Texte und Untersuchungen zur Geschichte der altchristlichen Literatur (Leipzig, 1896).

———. *Epistulae,* edited by Isidorus Hilberg, *Sancti Eusebii Hieronymi epistulae,* Corpus Scriptorum Ecclesiasticorum Latinorum 54–56 (Vienna: F. Tempsky, 1890).

Sozomen. *Historia ecclesiastica,* edited by J. Bidez, *Sozomène: Histoire ecclésiastique,* Sources chrétiennes 306, 418, 495, 516 (Paris: Éditions du Cerf, 1983–2008).

Theodoret of Cyrrhus. *Historia ecclesiastica,* edited by L. Parmentier, *Théodoret de Cyr: Histoire ecclésiastique,* Sources chrétiennes 501, 530 (Paris: Éditions du Cerf, 2006, 2009).

SECONDARY SOURCES

Ayres, Lewis. *Nicaea and Its Legacy: An Approach to Fourth-Century Trinitarian Theology* (Oxford: Oxford University Press, 2004).

Bardy, Gustav. "Le concile d'Antioche (379)," *Revue Benedictine* 45 (1933): 196–213.

Bessières, M. "La tradition manuscrite de la correspondance de saint Basile: Chapitre 6," *Journal of Theological Studies* 23 (1922): 337–58.

Calvet-Sébasti, Marie-Ange, ed. *Grégoire de Nazianze: Discours 6–12*, Sources chrétiennes 405 (Paris: Éditions du Cerf, 1995).

Cornell, Tim, and John Matthews. *Atlas of the Roman World* (New York: Checkmark Books, 1982).

Cribiore, Raffaella. *Gymnastics of the Mind: Greek Education in Hellenistic and Roman Egypt* (Princeton: Princeton University Press, 2001).

Daniélou, Jean. "La chronologie des œuvres de Grégoire de Nysse," *Studia Patristica* 7 (1966): 159–69.

Davis, Stephen. *The Cult of Saint Thecla: A Tradition of Women's Piety in Late Antiquity* (Oxford: Oxford University Press, 2001).

Devos, Paul. "S. Grégoire de Nazianze et Hellade de Césarée en Cappadoce," *Analecta Bollandiana* 79 (1961): 91–101.

di Berardino, Angelo, and Gianluca Pilara, eds. *Historical Atlas of Ancient Christianity*, Institutum Patristicum Augustinianum (St. Davids, PA: ICCS Press, 2013).

du Cange, Charles. *Glossarium ad scriptores mediae et infimae graecitatis* (Paris, 1688).

Elm, Susanna. "A Programmatic Life: Gregory of Nazianzus' *Orations* 42 and 43 and the Constantinopolitan Elites," *Arethusa* 33 (2000): 411–27.

———. *Sons of Hellenism, Fathers of the Church: Emperor Julian, Gregory of Nazianzus, and the Vision of Rome*, Transformation of the Classical Heritage 49 (Berkeley: University of California Press, 2012).

———. "Waiting for Theodosius, or The Ascetic and the City: Gregory of Nazianzus on Maximus the Philosopher," in *Ascetic Culture: Essays in Honor of Philip Rousseau*, edited by Blake Leyerle and Robin Darling Young (Notre Dame, IN: University of Notre Dame Press, 2013), 182–97.

Errington, R. Malcolm. "Church and State in the First Years of Theodosius I," *Chiron* 27 (1997): 21–72.

Fedwick, Paul Jonathan, ed. *Basil of Caesarea: Christian, Humanist, Ascetic— A Sixteen-Hundredth Anniversary Symposium*, 2 vols. (Toronto: Pontifical Institute of Medieval Studies, 1981).

Forschall, Josiah. *Catalogue of the Manuscripts in the British Museum*, n.s., vol. 1 (London, 1840).

Gallay, Paul, ed. and trans. *Grégoire de Nazianze, Lettres*, Collection des Universités de France, publiée sous le patronage de l'Association Guillaume Budé, 2 vols. (Paris: Société d'Édition "Les Belles Lettres," 1964, 1967).

———, ed. *Gregor von Nazianz: Briefe*, Die griechischen christlichen Schriftsteller der ersten Jahrhunderte 53 (Berlin: Akademie-Verlag, 1969).

———. *Les manuscrits des lettres de Saint Grégoire de Nazianze* (Paris: Les Belles Lettres, 1957).

Gamble, Harry Y. *Books and Readers in the Early Church: A History of Early Christian Texts* (New Haven: Yale University Press, 1995).

Hanson, R. P. C. *The Search for the Christian Doctrine of God: The Arian Controversy,* 318–381 (Edinburgh: T. & T. Clark, 1988).

Hauser-Meury, Marie-Madeleine. *Prosopographie zu den Schriften Gregors von Nazianz* (Bonn: Hanstein, 1960).

Heather, Peter, and David Moncur, trans. *Politics, Philosophy, and Empire in the Fourth Century: Select Orations of Themistius,* Translated Texts for Historians 36 (Liverpool: Liverpool University Press, 2001).

Honigmann, Ernst. *Trois mémoires posthumes d'histoire et de géographie de l'Orient chrétien* (Brussels: Société des Bollandistes, 1961).

Jones, A. H. M., J. R. Martindale, and J. Morris, eds. *The Prosopography of the Later Roman Empire: Volume 1,* ad 260–395 (Cambridge: Cambridge University Press, 1971).

Karmann, Thomas R. *Meletius von Antiochien: Studien zur Geschichte des trinitätstheologischen Streits in den Jahren 360–364 n. Chr.,* Regensburger Studien zur Theologie 68 (Frankfurt am Main: Peter Lang, 2009).

Klock, Christoph. "Überlegungen zur Authentizität des ersten Briefes Gregors von Nyssa," *Studia Patristica* 18 (1983): 15–19.

Le Nain de Tillemont, Louis-Sébastien. *Mémoires pour servir à l'histoire ecclésiastique des six premiers siècles: Volume 9, Les vies de Saint Basile, de Saint Grégoire de Nazianze, de Saint Grégoire de Nysse, et de Saint Amphiloque* (Paris: Charles Robustel, 1703).

Lenski, Noel. *Failure of Empire: Valens and the Roman State in the Fourth Century* a.d., Transformation of the Classical Heritage 34 (Berkeley: University of California Press, 2002).

Malherbe, Abraham. *Ancient Epistolary Theorists* (Atlanta: Scholars, 1988).

Maravel, Pierre, ed. *Grégoire de Nysse: Lettres,* Sources chrétiennes 363 (Paris: Éditions du Cerf, 1990).

———. "L'authenticité de la lettre 1 de Grégoire de Nysse," *Analecta Bollandiana* 102 (1984): 61–70.

McGuckin, John. "Autobiography as Apologia in St. Gregory of Nazianzus," *Studia Patristica* 37 (2001): 160–77.

———. *St Gregory of Nazianzus: An Intellectual Biography* (Crestwood, NY: St. Vladimir's Seminary Press, 2001).

McLynn, Neil. "Among the Hellenists: Gregory and the Sophists," in *Gregory of Nazianzus: Images and Reflections,* edited by J. Børtnes and Tomas Hägg (Copenhagen: Museum Tusculanum Press, 2006), 213–38.

———. "Gregory Nazianzen's Basil: The Literary Construction of a Christian Friendship," *Studia Patristica* 37 (2001): 178–93.

———. "Gregory the Peacemaker: A Study of Oration Six," *Kyoyo-Ronso* 101 (1996): 183–216.

———. "Moments of Truth: Gregory of Nazianzus and Theodosius I," in *From the Tetrarchs to the Theodosians: Later Roman History and Culture, 284–450 ce*, edited by Scott McGill, Cristiana Sogno, and Edward Watts, Yale Classical Studies 34 (Cambridge: Cambridge University Press, 2010), 215–39.

———. "The Other Olympias: Gregory Nazianzen and the Family of Vitalianus," *Zeitschrift für antikes Christentum* 2 (1998): 227–46.

Mercati, Giovanni. *Studi e testi* 9 (Rome: Tipografia Vaticana, 1903).

Panella, Robert J., trans. *The Private Orations of Themistius*, Transformation of the Classical Heritage 29 (Berkeley: University of California Press, 2000).

Pasquali, Giorgio. *Gregorii Nysseni Epistulae*, Gregorii Nysseni Opera 8.2 (Leiden: Brill, 1959).

Ramsay, William M. *The Historical Geography of Asia Minor*, Royal Geographical Society's Supplementary Papers 4 (London: John Murray, 1890; reprint, [London:] Elibron Classics, Adamant Media, 2005).

Rousseau, Philip. *Basil of Caesarea*, Transformation of the Classical Heritage 20 (Berkeley: University of California Press, 1994).

Seeck, Otto. *Die Briefe des Libanius zeitlich geordnet* (Leipzig: J. C. Hinrich'sche Buchhandlung, 1906).

Silvas, Anna. *Gregory of Nyssa: The Letters—Introduction, Translation, and Commentary*, Supplements to Vigiliae Christianae 83 (Leiden: Brill, 2007).

Staats, Reinhart. "Gregor von Nyssa und das Bischofsamt," *Zeitschrift für Kirchengeschichte* 84 (1973): 149–73.

Storin, Bradley K. "Autohagiobiography: Gregory of Nazianzus among His Biographers," *Studies in Late Antiquity* 1 (2017): 254–81.

———. "In a Silent Way: Asceticism and Literature in the Rehabilitation of Gregory of Nazianzus," *Journal of Early Christian Studies* 19 (2011): 225–57.

———. "The Letters of Gregory of Nazianzus: Discourse and Community in Late Antique Epistolary Culture" (PhD diss., Indiana University, 2012).

———. *Self-Portrait in Three Colors: Gregory of Nazianzus's Epistolary Autobiography*, Christianity in Late Antiquity 6 (Oakland: University of California Press, 2019).

Van Dam, Raymond. "Governors of Cappadocia during the Fourth Century," *Medieval Prosopography* 17 (1996): 7–94.

van der Meer, F., and Mohrmann, Christine. *Atlas of the Early Christian World*, edited and translated by Mary F. Hedlund and H. H. Rowley (New York: Nelson, 1958).

Van Hoof, Lieve. "Libanius' *Life* and Life," in *Libanius: A Critical Introduction,* ed. Van Hoof (Cambridge: Cambridge University Press, 2014), 7–38.

Wyss, Bernhard. "Gregor von Nazianz oder Gregor von Nyssa?," in *Mémorial André-Jean Festugière, Antiquité païenne et chrétienne,* edited by E. Lucchesi and H. D. Saffrey, Cahiers d'orientalisme 10 (Geneva: Patrick Cramer, 1984), 153–62.

INDEX OF BIBLICAL, APOCRYPHAL, AND PSEUDEPIGRAPHICAL WRITINGS

Gen
- 2:10–14 — 59
- 8:21 — 149
- 19:24 — 94, 108
- 27:28 — 91
- 27:36 — 149

Exod
- 1:14 — 84
- 2:11–12 — 94
- 12:11 — 84
- 17:1–6 — 59
- 17:6–7 — 167
- 17:8–16 — 69
- 22:28–29 — 155
- 31:1–5 — 65
- 35:30–33 — 65

Num
- 12:1–16 — 94
- 16:1–40 — 66
- 17:8–10 — 61
- 25:6–11 — 94
- 34:1–15 — 84

Deut
- 8:7 — 191

1 Sam
- 2:11–4:18 — 215n157
- 2:24 — 139

2 Sam
- 2:17 — 87

1 Kgs
- 2:4 — 168

2 Kgs
- 5:6–7 — 72

1 Esd
- 4:35 — 107

Job
- 4:17 — 135
- 5:10 — 167
- 5:26 — 102
- 29:2 — 61
- 34:21 — 149

Ps
- 4:2(1) — 197
- 15(16):5 — 156
- 19:6(20:5) — 91, 163
- 22(23):4 — 59
- 26(27):5 — 197
- 26(27):10 — 132
- 30:25(31:24) — 186
- 31(32):3 — 108
- 34(35):19 — 87
- 38:2(39:1) — 108

39:10(40:9)	108
41:2(42:1)	168
44:5(45:6)	79, 126
49(50):21	108
54:7(55:6)	170
62:2(63:1)	119
65(66):12	169
72(73):3	127, 130
76:4(77:5)	197
76(77):25	167
77(78):25	163
77(78):70	92
86:7	84
93(94):19	169
102(103):5	170
105(106):30–31	94
112(113):9	87
119(120):5	103
127(128):5	169
127(128):6	169
140(141):4	91
140(141):9	140
143(144):12	91
146(147):8	167

Prov

5:11	139
6:25	140
10:6	156
15:17	164
16:8	156
31:3	139

Eccl

3:1	108

Song

2:13	196

Isa

27:13	62
42:14	108
61:3	218n223

Jer

2:6	119
10:19	86
15:18	86
40(33):6	85

Hos

6:4	94
11:8–9	94

Jonah

1:12–16	113
3:1–10	94

Hab

1:2	97

Sir

3:9	156
4:26	124
10:10	171
31:27	125

4 Macc

9:8	125

Matt

5:15	67, 71, 185
5:31–32	219n246
6:12	94
6:19	156
6:22	73
7:14	59
8:24	132
8:24–26	167
9:2–7	168
10:23	193
13:25	170
18:21–22	94
18:24–34	94
18:35	194
19:3–9	219n246
24:31	62
25:14–30	90
25:21–23	142
25:36	98
25:43	194

Mark

1:29–31	168
10:2–12	219n246

Luke		6:7	87
5:18–25	168	9:6	156
9:54–56	94	11:16	104
10:42	64	11:18	104
11:4	94		
13:6–9	95	Gal	
16:18	219n246	2:16	79
17:29	94, 108		
18:17	80	Eph	
22:36	186	3:16	127, 130
		5:27	73
John		6:1–4	108
2:9	189	6:5–9	201
4:10	167		
10:16	86	Phil	
16:15	99	2:15	167
16:25	107	4:18	197
18:10	94		
		Col	
Acts		1:24	74
5:29	200	2:17	187
14:15	63		
20:35	173	1 Thess	
28:7–8	168	2:19	167
		3:5	198
Rom			
3:20	79	1 Tim	
3:28	79	2:5	199
5:5	87	2:13–15	193
7:2–3	219n246	3:15	167
12:1	197	5:21	97
13:4	175		
14:3	147	2 Tim	
		4:7	156
1 Cor		4:7–8	181
1:13	98		
1:29	89	Titus	
3:6	61	3:7	161
3:13	108		
7:10–11	219n246	Heb	
10:10	202	4:14	199
13:7	197	8:5	187
13:12	187	11:13	84
		12:7–10	130
2 Cor			
1:3	198	Jas	
4:16	127, 130	1:27	174

INDEX OF CLASSICAL WRITINGS

Aeschylus
   A.   208n13
   Eu.   190

Aeschines
   Ctes.   61

Aesop
   Prov.   156

Apollodorus
   Bib.   60, 216n177

Aristophanes
   Ach.   191
   Eq.   124
   Nu.   59

Aristotle
   E.N.   127

Demosthenes
   Or.   61, 70, 117

Dionysius of Halicarnassus
   Lys.   126

Diogenianus
   Paroe.   125

Euripides
   Med.   116
   Or.   192
   Ph.   104, 105, 192

Herodotus
   Hist.   61, 150, 208n9, 208n13, 211n60, 216n179, 220n286

Hesiod
   Op.   104, 105, 195
   Th.   208n13
   Il.   55, 62, 117, 118, 121, 122, 126, 131, 132, 137, 138, 150, 158, 172, 188, 191

Isocrates
   Dem.   121
   Mantiss. prov.   187
   Od.   59, 60, 126, 145, 158, 208n18

Pausanias
   Gr. desc.   219n271

Philostratus the Younger
   Im.   56

Pindar
  Nem. 141, 191
  Olymp. 138, 153, 160, 190, 191
  P. 190, 214n35

Plato
  Chrm. 208n9
  Cra. 131
  Ep. 147
  Grg. 131
  Phd. 124, 127, 131
  Phdr. 125
  Resp. 118, 120, 124, 147, 187
  Tht. 110, 187

Polybius
  Hist. 150

Plutarch
  Alex. 117
  Reg. et imp. apophth. 211n58

Pythagoras
  Ep. 105

Sophocles
  Aj. 190

Sextus Empiricus
  M. 125

Simonides
  Epig. 169

Solon 176

Sophron 118

Strabo
  Geogr. 213n120, 214n125

Thucydides
  Hist. 215n160

Theocritus
  Id. 163, 191

Theognis
  El. 161

Xenophon
  H.G. 132

Founded in 1893,
UNIVERSITY OF CALIFORNIA PRESS
publishes bold, progressive books and journals
on topics in the arts, humanities, social sciences,
and natural sciences—with a focus on social
justice issues—that inspire thought and action
among readers worldwide.

The UC PRESS FOUNDATION
raises funds to uphold the press's vital role
as an independent, nonprofit publisher, and
receives philanthropic support from a wide
range of individuals and institutions—and from
committed readers like you. To learn more, visit
ucpress.edu/supportus.

www.ingramcontent.com/pod-product-compliance
Lightning Source LLC
Chambersburg PA
CBHW030539230426
43665CB00010B/950